PLANTS

of the

Lewis and Clark Expedition

H. WAYNE PHILLIPS

2003
Mountain Press Publishing Company • Missoula, Montana

First Printing, May 2003

Lewis and Clark quotations are from the University of Nebraska Press edition of the JOURNALS OF THE LEWIS AND CLARK EXPEDITION, edited by Gary E. Moulton. Used by permission of the University of Nebraska Press.

All photographs by H. Wayne Phillips unless otherwise noted.

Front cover images:
beargrass *(Xerophyllum tenax)*
elkhorns *(Clarkia pulchella)*
beargrass and elkhorns illustrations from
Frederick Pursh's *Flora Americae Septentrionalis* (1814)

Library of Congress Cataloging-in-Publication Data

Phillips, Wayne, 1941-
Plants of the Lewis and Clark Expedition / H. Wayne Phillips.
p. cm.
Includes bibliographical references and index.
ISBN 0-87842-477-6 (pbk. : alk. paper)
1. Lewis and Clark Expedition (1804-1806) 2. Botany—West (U.S.)—History. 3. Plant collecting—West (U.S.)—History. 4. West (U.S.)—Discovery and exploration. I. Title.
QK5.P46 2003
581.978—dc21

2002156730

PRINTED IN HONG KONG BY MANTEC PRODUCTION COMPANY

Mountain Press Publishing Company
P.O. Box 2399 • Missoula, Montana 59806
(406) 728-1900

This book is dedicated to Meriwether Lewis and Frederick Pursh for introducing us to the amazing plant diversity found west of the Mississippi River.

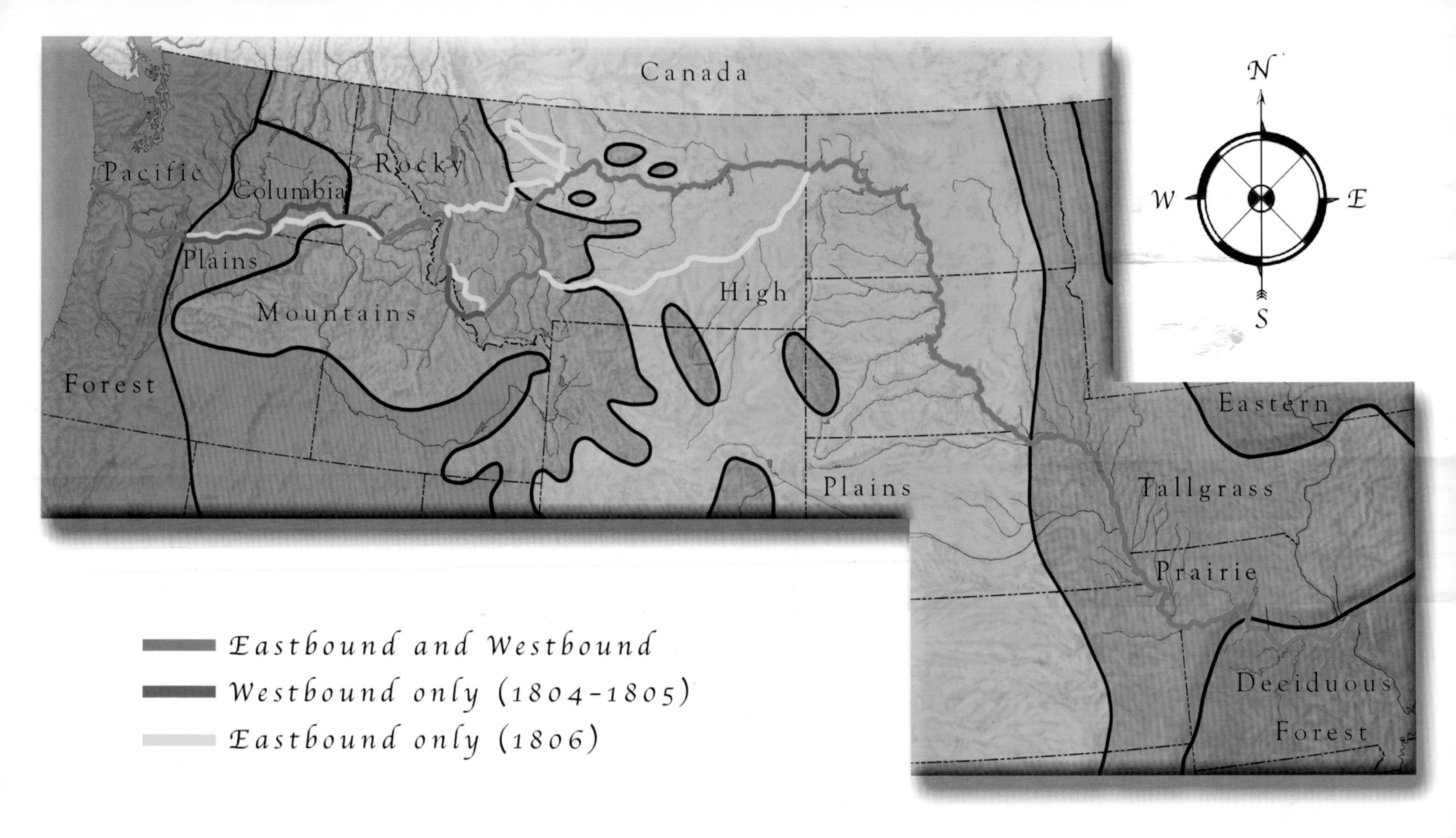

The geographic regions Lewis and Clark passed through

CONTENTS

ACKNOWLEDGMENTS

It is exciting to find Lewis and Clark plants in bloom, especially when they are in the area where the explorers collected specimens almost two hundred years ago! It would not have been possible for me to find the plants to photograph or gather the information in this book without the support of many people to whom I owe a great deal of gratitude. Many of you are close friends, others I met only briefly along the Lewis and Clark Trail. All of you were kind and generous to offer me your time, assistance, and advice. Thank you all so very much.

The following people helped me photograph plants, either by assisting me in the field or by giving me information that helped me find the plants. For this I am very grateful.

IDAHO: Sue McKenna, Island Park; Lillian Pethtel, Kamiah; Rob Phillips and Monika Mahal, Boise. **MONTANA:** Joann Bernard and Jane Schmoyer-Weber, Great Falls; Katie R. Bump, Dillon; Craig Ferris, Fort Benton; Jack Hann and John Pavlovick, Big Sandy; David Hanna, Choteau; Peter Lesica, Sheila Morrison, John Pierce, Susan Rinehart, Peter Stickney, and Virginia Vincent, Missoula; Terra Luna, East Glacier; Maria Mantas, Whitefish; Mike and Anita McNeil, Florence. **NEBRASKA:** Larry Haight and Kelly Kindscher. **NORTH DAKOTA:** Keith Frankki, Lisbon; Cindy Haakenson and John Moeykens, Knife River Indian Villages, Stanton; Rob Self, McLeod; Joe Washington, Dickinson; Tod Winter, Medora. **OREGON:** Ken Gervais and Jack Poff, Portland; Gayle Hansen, Newport; Nancy Eid and Lynne Johnson, Fort Clatsop; Mike Igo, Mosier. **TEXAS:** Wayne Murphy, Whitt; Lejeune and Burlie Northington, Mineral Wells. **WASHINGTON:** Art Krukeburg, Kelly Phillips, and Laura Martin, Seattle. **WISCONSIN:** Bryan and Alice Johannes, Eldorado; Mark Schneider, New Holstein.

Thanks to Harry and Ann Lubrecht of Port Jervis, New York, for helping me acquire Frederick Pursh's *Flora Americae Septentrionalis,* and Bob Doerk of Fort Benton, Montana, for loaning me *Lewis and Clark: Linguistic Pioneers,* by Elijah Harry Criswell.

Thanks to William Maxwell of Great Falls, Montana, for his advice on Indian tobacco and Osage orange; to Ken Woody of Crow Agency, Montana, for sharing the tobacco seed; and to Hal Colburn of Great Falls, Montana, for allowing me to photograph his relic bows and arrows. Thanks to Joan Hockaday of Bainbridge Island, Washington, Bert Lindler, Dorothy Patent, and Monica Rekiel of Missoula, Montana, and Tom Kotynski, Jane Schmoyer-Weber, Mike Enk, Andrew Kling, Don Peterson, and Sue Buchel of Great Falls, Montana, for their advice and support.

I am grateful for the encouragement and support of Gary E. Moulton of Lincoln, Nebraska. Dr. Moulton's editorial narratives, extensive footnotes, and thorough indexes in his twelve-volume set *The Journals of the Lewis and Clark Expedition* have been a pleasure to read and use for research.

I wish to thank the following people for helping me with herbarium searches and with plant identification and verification: Richard Olmstead, Art Krukeburg,

David Giblin, and Robert Waaland of Seattle; Gayle Hansen of Newport, Oregon; Matt Lavin and Cathy Seibert of Bozeman, Montana; Ronald L. Shimek of Wilsall, Montana; Peter Stickney and Virginia Vincent of Missoula, Montana; Won S. Hong of Great Falls, Montana. I am especially grateful to Dr. Hong and Andrea Pipp, who provided me with liverwort herbarium specimens to photograph.

Thanks to Drake Barton of Clancy, Montana, Stephen Foster of Fayetteville, Arkansas, and Kathleen Sayce of Ilwaco, Washington, for providing me with needed plant photographs, and Katie R. Bump of the United States Forest Service in Dillon, Montana, for the photograph of Lemhi Pass.

I am especially thankful for the support of Kathy Lloyd and Drake Barton of Clancy, Montana, who read and edited the entire text, helped me with plant searches, evaluated the accuracy of my plant slides, and listened to and evaluated my ideas; to Katie Meyers of Great Falls, Montana, who also edited part of the text; and to Susan Wilcox of Portland, Oregon, who introduced me to local botanists, helped me locate plants, and shared her expertise and interest in Lewis and Clark botany while I visited Oregon and Washington.

I want to thank Publisher John Rimel at Mountain Press Publishing for agreeing to publish this book and my editor, James Lainsbury, for working closely with me through the editing process.

Thanks to my wife, Marilyn, who has been patient with my obsessive behavior and supportive throughout this project.

Thanks to all of you for your openness and kindness along the Lewis and Clark Trail. Without you I could not have created this book.

A Brief History of the Plant Collections

Botany I rank with the most valuable sciences, whether we consider its subjects as furnishing the principal subsistence of life to man and beast, delicious varieties for our tables, refreshments from our orchards, the adornments of our flower borders, shade and perfume of our groves, materials for our buildings, or medicaments for our bodies.

JEFFERSON[1]

Thomas Jefferson spent years planning an expedition and promoting the idea of exploring the West via the Missouri River because of his interest in scientific discovery and westward expansion. He tried, and failed, several times to initiate an expedition, the first in 1783. Then, in March 1803, President Jefferson secured congressional approval to launch an expedition to the Pacific Ocean. On April 30, 1803, the United States acquired western territories from France through the Louisiana Purchase, placing an even greater national interest in western exploration. The time was right to send explorers into the wilderness of the West.

To lead the expedition President Jefferson wanted "a person who to courage, prudence, habits & health adapted to the woods, & some familiarity with the Indian character, joins a perfect knoledge of botany, natural history, mineralogy & astronomy" (Moulton, vol. 2). He selected Meriwether Lewis based on Lewis's diverse qualifications. For example, Jefferson knew that Lewis's mother was a practicing herbalist and that Lewis grew up fascinated with natural history and plants and their medicinal value. He was also knowledgeable of the West and the Native American people, was a proven military officer, and was a practiced woodsman who would be able to handle the rigors of living in the wilds for an extended period of time. Perhaps equally important to Jefferson was that Lewis had volunteered to lead an expedition to the Pacific that Jefferson had convinced the American Philosophical Society to finance in 1793. Although Jefferson selected André Michaux as the leader, and the expedition ultimately failed, Lewis had established himself as an interested party in leading such an undertaking.

During the final preparations in July of 1803, Lewis received instructions from President Jefferson detailing the trip's objectives. Botanical exploration was one of the objectives. The leaders were directed to notice "the face of the country, it's growth & vegetable productions; especially those not of the U.S. . . . the dates at which particular plants put forth or lose their flowers, or leaf" (Cutright, 1969). President Jefferson felt that the plants the explorers discovered would be of great interest to him and the citizens of the United States.

---

1 Epigraph taken from the Thomas Jefferson Papers at the Library of Congress, Manuscript Division, Series 1, General Correspondence. 1651–1827. Thomas Jefferson to Thomas Cooper, October 7, 1814.

Leaving nothing to chance, Jefferson sent Lewis to Philadelphia in the spring of 1803 for last minute training with distinguished authorities in various fields, including botany. Dr. Benjamin S. Barton of the University of Pennsylvania was Lewis's botany instructor. Barton was a colleague of Jefferson's, being a member of the American Philosophical Society. He authored the first American textbook on botany. His book, *Elements of Botany, or Outlines of the Natural History of Vegetables,* had been published that year in Philadelphia. Lewis purchased a copy, which became a valuable reference to him, and carried it on the expedition.

The Plant Collections
St. Louis to Fort Mandan

From May 1803 to May 1804 Lewis and his handpicked coleader, William Clark, gathered the necessary equipment and supplies and selected and trained their men. The party spent the winter at Camp Dubois on the Illinois side of the Mississippi River opposite the mouth of the Missouri River and St. Louis, Missouri. They left Camp Dubois on May 14, 1804, and worked up the Missouri River, eventually reaching Mandan and Hidatsa Indian villages near the Knife River on October 26. Here they established their winter quarters—Fort Mandan—in what is now North Dakota.

Inspired by his new botanical training and motivated by Jefferson's instructions, Lewis collected plants and described them in his journals from the start of the journey. He collected two plants while still in St. Louis in May of 1804 and continued collecting as they ascended the Missouri River. He preserved the plants as botanical specimens by placing them on sheets of paper and pressing them tightly between layers of blotting paper. Most likely he changed the blotting paper often until the plant specimens were completely dry. Once fully dried, the plant specimens remained the approximate shape and color they were when Lewis collected them. Many of Lewis's plant specimens remain well preserved today in the Lewis and Clark Herbarium at the Academy of Natural Sciences of Philadelphia.

Lewis usually attached a tag or label to the sheet that the plant specimens were mounted on, denoting the date and place where they were collected, and often a brief comment on the habitat or the use of the plant by animals or Native Americans. Unfortunately, today Lewis's original labels occur with only 34 of the 239 specimens that still exist (Moulton, vol. 12). Most of the remaining specimens have labels with information that we believe a botanist later copied from Lewis's original labels.

Lewis assigned a number to each of the plants collected from St. Louis to the expedition's winter quarters at Fort Mandan. He numbered the first fourteen plants in the order they were collected. The remaining plants were not chronologically numbered, which suggests that Lewis assigned them numbers while at the winter quarters rather than when he collected them.

On April 7, 1805, the Captains sent a keelboat downriver loaded with precious cargo for President Jefferson. William Clark's journal of April 3 stated that the party had been busy "packing up Sundery articles to be Sent to the President of the U.S."

According to Clark's April 3 list, they included the following plant materials: "some Ricara's [Arikara] tobacco seed . . . a ear of Mandan Corn . . . a Carrote of Ricaras *Tobacco* . . . Specimens of Plants numbered frome 1 to 60 . . . a Specimon of a plant, and a parcel of its roots highly prized by the natives as an efficatious remidy in Cases of the bite of the rattle Snake or Mad Dog." The last plant mentioned was probably narrow-leaved purple coneflower *(Echinacea angustifolia)*.

Lewis organized a plant list that he described as "a List of specimines of plants collected by me on the Mississippi and Missouri rivers—contain such observations on the vegitable kingdom spread to our view in this rich country as they have occurred to my mind.—or as the several subjects have presented themselves to my view." Although this list is undated, it was likely prepared at Fort Mandan in the winter of 1804–5. I have referred to this list throughout the book as Lewis's "transmittal" list because the plants listed are among those the explorers sent to President Jefferson in April 1805 and were then received in Philadelphia in November 1805.

What follows is an example of the information that Lewis included on this list: "No. 1 a species of Cress, taken at St. Louis May 10th 1804. it is common in the open growns on the Mississippi bottoms, appears in the uncultivated parts of the lots gardens and orchards, the seed come to maturity by the 10th of May in most instances." Unfortunately the specimen that went with this entry was lost. Botanists today speculate that it might have been field pennycress *(Thlaspi arvense)*, a weedy plant introduced from Europe.

This cargo was delivered safely to President Jefferson, who sent it to the American Philosophical Society in Philadelphia. He wanted his colleagues, many of whom were the distinguished scientists of the day, to have access to the plant, animal, and mineral specimens. An official at the American Philosophical Society, John Vaughn, listed the plants the organization received in the society's Donation Book. Vaughn's entry began: "Donations November 16, 1805 from Meriwether Lewis Dried Plants &c [etc.] put into Dr. B. S Bartons hands for examination." Vaughn listed the plants by number, sometimes paraphrasing the plant information from Lewis's transmittal list.

From these records we know that the explorers sent more than sixty numbered plant specimens to President Jefferson from Fort Mandan. Only thirty of these numbered specimens are known to exist today, the others were somehow lost after they were turned over to Dr. Barton. Mysteriously, there are an additional ten dated specimens that exist today that Lewis collected in 1804 below Fort Mandan. Although collected on the same dates that numbered specimens were, Lewis did not assign a number to these specimens nor did he mention them in his Fort Mandan transmittal list. We don't know why these specimens were not catalogued with the other plants collected during this time or if they were shipped with the same cargo. There are also several undated specimens that Lewis likely collected at or below Fort Mandan in 1804 as well.

The Plant Collections: Fort Mandan to the Pacific Ocean and Back to St. Louis

On April 7, 1805, as the keelboat headed downriver, the expedition left Fort Mandan and resumed its voyage up the Missouri River. When the explorers reached the falls of the Missouri (near present-day Great Falls, Montana) in June, they faced their first major physical obstacle. In order to get beyond the series of falls, they portaged about 18 miles and abandoned their largest boat. They cached cargo, including plant specimens, for later retrieval. On June 26, 1805, Lewis wrote, "Capt. C. also scelected the articles to be deposited in the cash . . . [including] my specimens of plants minerals &c. [etc.] collected from fort Mandan to that place."

A year later, on July 13, 1806, Lewis described his return visit to the "Great Falls" of the Missouri River: "removed above to my old station opposite the upper point of the white bear island . . . had the cash opened found my bearskins entirly destroyed by the water, the river having risen so high that the water had penetrated. all my specimens of plants also lost." The loss must have been devastating. Water had destroyed the plants that he had discovered, collected, and so meticulously dried and cared for.

The plants they collected from present-day Great Falls, Montana, to Camp Fortunate (now inundated by Clark Canyon Reservoir in Montana) apparently met a similar fate. Lewis had his men prepare a cache near Camp Fortunate on August 20, 1805, and then wrote in his journal: "I made up a small assortment of medicines, together with the specemines of plants, minerals, seeds &c. which, I have collected betwen this place and the falls of the Missouri which I shall deposit here." A single specimen of golden currant *(Ribes aureum)* from this period of collection is found in the Lewis and Clark Herbarium.

The explorers continued collecting specimens from August 22, 1805, when Lewis's party closed the cache and left Camp Fortunate, to September 23, 1806, when the expedition members arrived, at last, in St. Louis. Lewis carried these last plant specimens with him as he traveled on to Washington D.C. and Philadelphia.

The Study and Preservation of the Plant Specimens

Accounting for the specimens that made the trip back to the East Coast is a science in itself. Over the years, Lewis and Clark scholars have reunited most of the specimens at the Academy of Natural Sciences of Philadelphia. At the academy, many of the Lewis and Clark plant specimens were initially scattered throughout the large herbarium. In 1966 Paul Russell Cutright and Academy curator Alfred E. Schuyler brought all of these specimens together as the Lewis and Clark Herbarium and arranged them alphabetically by scientific name. Today, 239 plant specimens collected by Lewis and Clark exist in three locatons: 227 at the Academy of Natural Sciences of Philadelphia, 11 at the Royal Botanic Gardens at Kew near London, and 1 at the Charleston Museum in South Carolina (Moulton, vol. 12). According to my calculations, these specimens represent 175 species of plants. The total number of *specimens* differs from the total number of *species* because Lewis and Clark occasionally collected several specimens of the same plant species. What follows is a brief account of what happened to the specimens before they ended up in the Lewis and Clark Herbarium.

Frederick Pursh

Frederick Pursh was one of the botanists who looked at Lewis and Clark's specimens. Born in 1774 in Grossenhain, Germany, he was educated in Dresden and worked at the Royal Botanic Gardens there. In 1799 he traveled to the United States, and from 1803 to 1805 he managed Woodlands, a botanical garden near Baltimore, Maryland.

In 1805 Pursh began to work for Dr. Benjamin Barton, the same Dr. Barton who had given Meriwether Lewis a crash course in the science of botany. From 1806 to 1807 Pursh did fieldwork for Dr. Barton, who was planning to write a flora of North America. Pursh claimed he traveled 3,000 miles on foot each of these two seasons collecting plants and observing the geography, soil, and vegetation of the Atlantic states. In 1806 he collected 895 plant specimens while traveling through the southern states from Maryland to North Carolina. In 1807 his botanical explorations took him north to New Hampshire and the Great Lakes area.

In April 1807 Lewis arrived in Philadelphia with the plant specimens he and the explorers collected on the second half of their trip. A local florist, Bernard McMahon, introduced Lewis to Pursh. Lewis was impressed with Pursh and left these specimens with the botanist. He paid Pursh seventy dollars to organize the collection, write botanical descriptions of the plants, and prepare some drawings. Lewis intended to publish the botanical information with his journals. Pursh described the collection as "a small but highly interesting collection of dried plants.... consisting of about one hundred and fifty specimens, contained not above a dozen plants well known to me." These were the plants that the explorers collected, according to Pursh, "during the rapid return of the expedition from the Pacific Ocean . . . A much more extensive one, made on their slow ascent towards the Rocky mountains . . . had unfortunately been lost, by being deposited [in caches] . . . at the foot of those mountains" (Pursh, 1814).

Lewis never saw the expedition's journals published. He died tragically in 1809. Pursh—apparently without Clark's permission—took plant specimens from Lewis's collection with him to New York and eventually London. It appears that he took duplicate specimens of some of the species and snipped segments off others.

In 1810, after Lewis's death, Clark turned over what he thought was Lewis's entire plant collection (minus the specimens Pursh had) to Dr. Barton, reminding Barton of his promise to help the explorers with the scientific work on their plant discoveries. Barton failed to honor his promise, and the planned publication documenting the scientific discoveries of the expedition never materialized.

In London in 1811, Pursh became acquainted with Sir Joseph Banks, who was willing to share his extensive American botanical collections with Pursh, and with

A. B. Lambert, a benefactor willing to finance a publication. Pursh completed *Flora Americae Septentrionalis,* Latin for "Flora of North America," and presented it to the Linnaean Society at its meeting in December of 1813. Officially published in 1814, the manual includes 3,076 American plant species and was the first botanical manual to span North America. That same year, the journals of Lewis and Clark were published in Philadelphia in *History of the Expedition Under the Command of Captains Lewis and Clark.* It was a literary paraphrase of the journals edited by Nicholas Biddle—a travelogue that contained none of the expedition's scientific discoveries.

To prepare his *flora,* Pursh used plant specimens from fifty-five sources to supplement his own extensive collection. He used specimens from the collections of famous botanists such as John and William Bartram, John Bradbury, Aloysius Enslen, Archibald Menzies, André Michaux, Henry E. Muhlenberg, Thomas Nuttall, and Meriwether Lewis. In the preface of his book, Pursh wrote: "I had the pleasure to form an acquaintance with Meriwether Lewis, Esq. . . . who had lately returned from an expedition across the Continent of America to the Pacific Ocean, by the way of the Missouri and the great Columbia rivers . . . A small but highly interesting collection of dried plants was put into my hands by this gentleman [Lewis], in order to describe and figure those I thought new, for the purpose of inserting them in the account of his Travels. . . . This valuable work, by the unfortunate and untimely end of its author, has been interrupted in its publication." In his book, Pursh credited the plant descriptions he made using Lewis and Clark's specimens with "M. Lewis v.s. in Herb. Lewis," meaning, "I have seen the plant in a dried state in the Herbarium of Meriwether Lewis."

Pursh used Lewis and Clark's specimens to identify 132 species. He assigned a new species status to 94 of them, and the names of 40 of these have been retained as accepted scientific names (Reveal, 1999). Pursh also named three new genera, which are still recognized. He named two in honor of Lewis and Clark: *Lewisia* and *Clarkia.* The third new genus was *Calochortus,* which is Greek for "beautiful grass." Pursh also named several species in Lewis's honor: *Linum lewisii,* Lewis's blue flax; *Philadelphus lewisii,* mockorange or syringa (state flower of Idaho); and *Mimulus lewisii,* Lewis's red monkey-flower. Thirteen of the twenty-four illustrations in Pursh's book were species new to science that Lewis and Clark had collected.

However, Pursh failed to recognize the opportunity to name several additional new genera from the Lewis and Clark collection, including *Balsamorhiza, Camassia, Lomatium,* and *Purshia* (in 1816 P. A. Poiret named *Purshia* in Frederick Pursh's honor).

Pursh later collected plants in Canada and was working on a Canadian flora when a fire destroyed his collection in Montreal. He died there in 1820, penniless, at the age of forty-six.

The Role of Edward Tuckerman

When Pursh died in 1820, the Lewis and Clark specimens that he took to London remained there with his benefactor, A. B. Lambert. Following Lambert's death in 1842 the specimens were sold on the auction block. Fortunately, the auction attracted the attention of a visiting American, Edward Tuckerman, a recent Harvard graduate. Tuckerman successfully acquired the Lewis and Clark plant collection at the auction and brought it back to the United States. In 1856 he contributed this historically significant collection to the Academy of Natural Sciences of Philadelphia where it remains today. The forty-seven specimens contributed by Tuckerman are still referred to as "Lambert specimens," with "Ex Herb. A. B. Lambert" stamped or written on most of the herbarium sheets.

Thomas Meehan and the American Philosophical Society

In 1896, Thomas Meehan was employed as a botanist at the Academy of Natural Sciences of Philadelphia. A colleague of his, Professor Charles S. Sargent, suggested to Meehan that a search of the American Philosophical Society's collections might yield additional Lewis and Clark plant specimens. The search was fruitful. Meehan found several packages of Lewis and Clark plant specimens that had been packed away and forgotten about. Meehan initially identified the plants and then sent them to the Gray Herbarium at Harvard in Boston where Dr. B. L. Robinson and Dr. J. M. Greenman carefully identified the specimens. In 1898 Meehan wrote a paper that appeared in the academy's proceedings describing the results. His paper listed the scientific names of the specimens he found, data from the plant labels, and information about the species from Pursh's *Flora Americae Septentrionalis.* The plant specimens that Meehan rediscovered can be found in the Lewis and Clark Herbarium, on permanent loan from the American Philosophical Society. These specimens are distinguished with a label that states: "American Philosophical Society, Lewis and Clark Herbarium, from the Atlantic to the Pacific" (Moulton, vol. 12).

Recent Updates

During his research at the University of Nebraska, Gary E. Moulton found eleven more Lewis and Clark plant specimens at the Royal Botanic Gardens at Kew near London. He also located a Lewis and Clark specimen at the Charleston Museum in South Carolina. Most of these specimens were duplicates of species already held at the Academy of Natural Sciences of Philadelphia, but there were two new species that were not: rusty lupine *(Lupinus pusillus)* at Kew, and common snowberry *(Symphoricarpos albus)* at Charleston. In 1999 Moulton published the results of his research in *Herbarium of the Lewis and Clark Expedition, the Journals of the Lewis and Clark Expedition,* volume 12.

In 1999 James L. Reveal, a distinguished botanist from the University of Maryland, examined the Lewis and Clark Herbarium and Pursh's 1814 floral manual in collaboration with Moulton and Alfred E. Schuyler. The results of this important work were published in the Proceedings of the Academy of Natural Sciences of Philadelphia in 1999. Although not treated in their work, they acknowledged that Lewis collected three nonvascular plants: a marine algae *(Egregia menziesia),* a moss *(Eurhynchium oreganum),* and a liverwort (currently identified as *Bazzania trilobata*). I included these three plants in this volume.

Introduction to Field Guide

From the information available, I believe that Lewis and Clark collected specimens of 211 plant species during the expedition. This includes the specimens of 175 species that still exist in three locations, and 36 species whose specimens were lost. I used Gary E. Moulton's *The Journals of the Lewis and Clark Expedition,* volume 3 (chapter 10, part 3), to identify half of these lost specimens. The other half I identified using Pursh's 1814 *Flora Americae Septentrionalis.* Besides the specimens we know Lewis and Clark collected, they also mentioned other plants in their journals. According to Elijah H. Criswell in *Lewis and Clark: Linguistic Pioneers,* they mentioned about 260 plants in 64 plant families. I included 19 species that they discussed in their journals but, as far as we know, they didn't actually collect.

In all, I chose to feature photographs and descriptions of 225 plant species in this book and photographs of 6 others: 15 trees, 61 shrubs, 131 herbaceous wildflowers, 12 grasses, 3 vines, 2 ferns, 2 algae, 2 liverworts, and 1 horsetail, moss, and cactus. This includes all of the plant species we know Lewis and Clark collected based on existing specimens, and all but 5 of the species botanists have determined the explorers collected even though the specimens no longer exist. I included species names only, not varieties or subspecies.

Geographic Regions

I divided the expedition route into six distinctive geographic regions: the Eastern Deciduous Forest, the Tallgrass Prairie, the High Plains, the Rocky Mountains, the Columbia Plains, and the Pacific Forest. On the outbound, westward portion of their journey, they collected most of their specimens in the Eastern Deciduous Forest, Tallgrass Prairie, and High Plains regions. Overall, the bulk of the specimens the explorers collected on their entire trip they gathered in the Rocky Mountains, Columbia Plains, and Pacific Forest regions on the homeward portion of their journey in 1806. The unlabeled specimens, in which the date and place of collection are unknown, I placed in the geographic area of the species' natural range where suitable habitat would have occurred along the expedition route. I included a color-coded map and plant list for each region so you could see where the explorers were when they collected particular species.

I described each geographic region in terms of its topography, climate, and general vegetation characteristics. I also summarized the dates that the Lewis and Clark expedition traveled through the region and the number of plants they collected in the region. I further divided the larger regions into smaller areas. For example, I divided the Pacific Forest into two areas: *Fort Clatsop* and the *Columbia River Gorge.*

Lewis and Clark collected more than one specimen for several species. I described these species in the geographic region where the explorers first described or collected the species. However, the plant lists with the maps and the list in the appendix include all the species collected in each region.

Plant Names and Descriptions

I listed the common name of each plant first. While common names for plants are not universally accepted, I made an effort to use the names most often used in the geographic areas where the plants were collected or were noted in the journals. In some cases it was necessary to list more than one common name.

On the other hand, scientific names are supposed to be universally accepted. Unfortunately, plant classification and plant nomenclature are constantly being reviewed and revised. For this reason I sometimes listed more than one scientific name: the most recently assigned one, and a more recognizable, previously applied name.

Scientific names include the genus, the specific epithet, and the authority. For example, the scientific name of bitterroot is *Lewisia rediviva* Pursh. The genus *Lewisia* is applied to several related plant species, while the specific epithet, *rediviva,* narrows the classification down to a single species. The authority, "Pursh," is the botanist who first described the species in a published source. In this case Frederick Pursh described *Lewisia rediviva* in his book *Flora Americae Septentrionalis* in 1814. Sometimes two authorities are given. If one of the authorities appears in parentheses, for example *Atriplex canescens* (Pursh) Nuttall, it means that Pursh was the first authority to publish a name for the species (as *Calligon canescens* Pursh) and Nuttall later determined that a new and different genus *(Atriplex)* described the species more accurately, but he retained Pursh's epithet *canescens.* If the first authority is followed by "ex," for example *Erysimum capitatum* Douglas ex Hooker, it means that Douglas first proposed the name but Hooker was the first authority to publish it.

The plant family name follows the common and scientific names. In the hierarchical classification of plants, the family is the next level up from the genus, with all closely related genera and species included in the same family. Family names are derived from the name of a genus in the family, followed by *aceae.* For example, bitterroot is in the Portulacaceae (purslane) family, which is named for the genus *Portulaca.*

Descriptive information follows the family name. I arranged this information with five subcategories: Plants, Flowers, Fruits, Flowering Season, and Habitat/Range. Because of limited space these descriptions are brief. I emphasized key characteristics to help readers separate the discussed species from related ones. I also listed regional floras in the reference section for those who desire more information.

Elijah H. Criswell, in *Lewis and Clark: Linguistic Pioneers,* lists nearly two hundred descriptive scientific words found in Meriwether Lewis's journals. Most are technical botanical terms like "quinquepetallous" and "decursively pinnate." I tried to minimize my use of technical terms in this book but found it impossible to avoid them completely. A glossary is in the back to help readers with unfamiliar terms.

From the Journals

In this section I included the date and place that Lewis and Clark collected a plant specimen if that information is known. If pertinent quotations about the subject plant—from Lewis's plant label and/or from the journals—are available, I have included them. In the journals Lewis and Clark often mentioned a plant found on a date, or in a place, that doesn't match the information on the plant label. The journal quotations may also include the explorers' activities on the day the subject plant was collected and general descriptions of the landscape or vegetation. Both Lewis and Clark wrote poetic descriptions of "the face of the country" as directed by Jefferson. The journal quotations come from Gary E. Moulton's twelve-volume set, *The Journals of the Lewis and Clark Expedition.* I have used brackets [ ] for my editorial insertions within the quotes, but the phrases enclosed in parentheses are those of the person quoted. A different style bracket { } encloses Moulton's editorial insertions.

To retain the flavor of Lewis and Clark's journals, I used the place names the explorers used and their spelling when possible. These place names appear in quotation marks—for example, "quawmash flatts"—or they are followed by the current name in parentheses—for example, Kooskooske (Clearwater) River. For those terms that appear in quotation marks, their present-day equivalents can be found in the chapter introductions.

PREFACE

In April of 2002 I was near The Dalles, Oregon, photographing plants that Lewis and Clark had collected there almost two hundred years earlier. Although the area was new to me, I successfully found many species I had been searching for. Others were more elusive and my time was running out. With about an hour of daylight left, and an appointment on the Oregon coast in the morning, I ended my plant search and drove west toward Portland on I-84. As I passed the Mosier exit I remembered reading in *Jolley's Field Guide* that Poet's shooting star could be found along the Dry Creek Road. Impulsively I exited the interstate, drove into Mosier, and stopped at the grocery store for information, not realizing how fortuitous the stop would be.

Besides the clerk there was another man at the counter. He looked like a local, so I asked the clerk my question with a loud voice in order that the other man might hear. "Could you tell me how to get to the Dry Creek Road?"

The man who looked like a local turned to me and said, "I'm going up Dry Creek. You can follow me there if you wish."

As I followed him out the door I added, "The reason I am going to Dry Creek is to find shooting stars. Have you seen any?"

The man replied, "Yes, I'll be glad to show them to you." I followed his truck up the hilly road. He soon pulled to the roadside, pointed, and parked. I was pleased to see a couple of Poet's shooting stars in bloom. I thanked the man and told him that this plant was one that I needed to photograph for a book I was writing about the plants of the Lewis and Clark Expedition. He nodded and motioned for me to wait while he went to his truck. He soon returned with a 2002 video, *Lewis and Clark Scientific Collections,* produced by his father, Jerry Igo. Realizing that I had, by some quirk of fate, contacted the best local source of information on the subject, I quickly introduced myself to Mike Igo, and asked him where I could find checker lily. Without hesitating, he gave me easy directions to find that plant in bloom. I was soon back on I-84 headed for Portland with a big smile on my face.

At 3:00 A.M. the next morning I was in the van of my newfound Portland friends, Ken and Susan, headed for Seal Rock, Oregon, and an appointment with marine biologist Gayle Hanson. According to Gayle we could find feather boa kelp at low tide at Seal Rock. I had already spent two futile days searching for this elusive marine algae near the mouth of the Columbia River where Meriwether Lewis had collected it in November of 1805. Nancy Eid, the biologist at Fort Clatsop, had recommended that I seek out Gayle for help. So, on a rainy dawn at low tide I found myself totally out of my element clamoring over the intertidal rocks with a huge sea lion watching just offshore and harlequin ducks diving in the foaming surf. And yes, feather boa kelp was at last visible in my camera lens!

As I drove back home to Great Falls, Montana, a few days later, I reflected on what I had accomplished on my photo trip. Just like Lewis and Clark, the kindness and help offered by native residents had been crucial to my expedition's success.

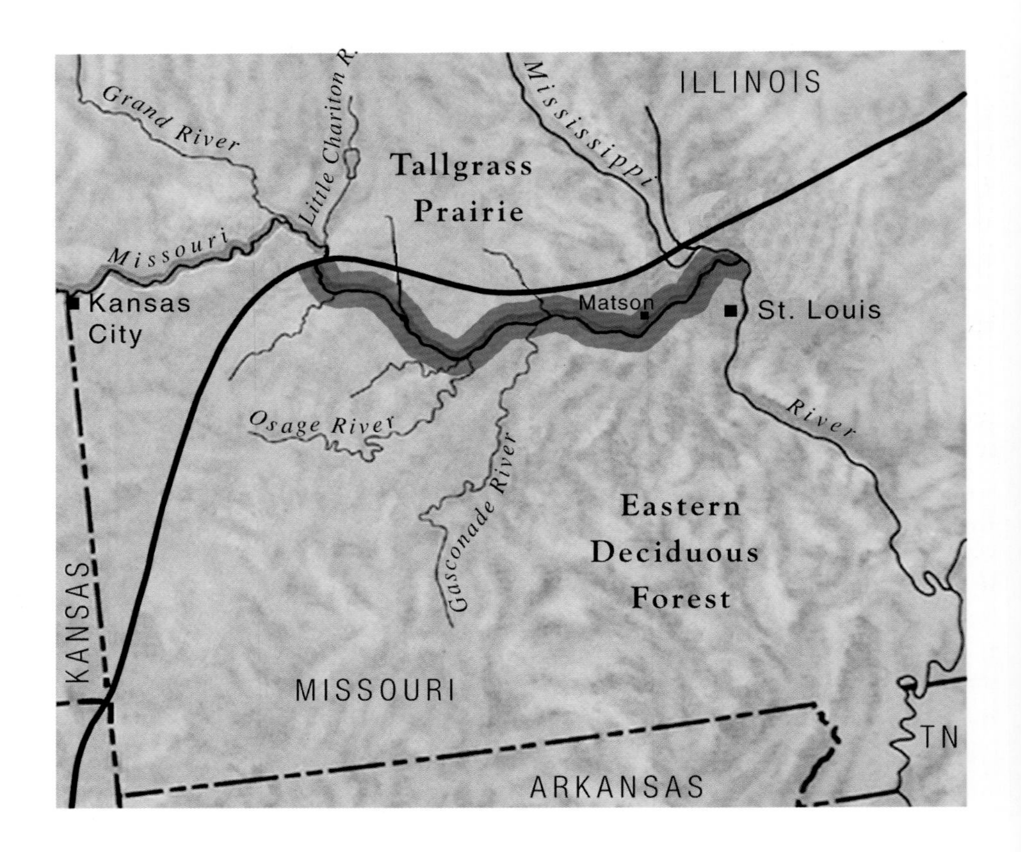

Thlaspi arvense[1]
Anemone caroliniana[2]
Maclura pomifera
Asimina triloba
Amorpha fruticosa
Populus deltoides
Hydrastis canadensis
Asarum canadense
Astragalus crassicarpus

1. *See* Introduction.

2. *Not included in this book.*

The Eastern Deciduous Forest

The Eastern Deciduous Forest, also known as the inland oak-hickory forest, includes northeastern Oklahoma, northern Arkansas, southeastern Missouri, and Tennessee north to west-central Minnesota, southern Wisconsin, southern Michigan, Ohio, and western Pennsylvania. Elevations range from 80 to 1,700 feet above sea level.

The climate is humid and temperate. Summers are hot with frequent thunderstorms. Precipitation varies from 20 to 50 inches a year, occurring mostly during the growing season. Under natural conditions, oak and hickory tree species dominate the forest cover with flowering dogwood, sassafras, and hophornbeam common in the understory. American elm, tulip tree, and sweet gum are common on wetter sites along streams.

Meriwether Lewis entered the Eastern Deciduous Forest when he crossed the Appalachian Mountains in July 1803 on his way to St. Louis. After supervising the construction of his keelboat and gathering supplies at Pittsburgh, Lewis started down the Ohio River on August 31, 1803. On September 2, Lewis noted in his journal, "observed today the leaves of the *buckeye*, Gum, and sausafras begin to fade, or become red," and on September 11, "the walnuts and Hickory nuts the usual food of the squirrell appears in great abundance on either side of the river." This broadleaf forest was familiar to Lewis, not unlike that found in his homeland of Virginia.

William Clark and his Kentucky recruits came on board at Clarksville, Indiana. The Captains Lewis and Clark continued to gather volunteers from frontiersmen as they made their way down the Ohio River and up the Mississippi to St. Louis. Eighteen miles up the Mississippi River from St. Louis and directly across from the mouth of the Missouri River, the newly recruited expedition members cleared an opening in the deciduous forest and constructed Camp Dubois. Here they remained for five months from December 13, 1803, to May 14, 1804, training and preparing for the trip ahead.

In May the explorers started up the Missouri River, traveling in the Eastern Deciduous Forest to the confluence with the Chariton River in Missouri, which they reached on June 10, 1804. Here they found the oak-hickory forest become savannah-like, intermingling with the Tallgrass Prairie. Two years and three months later the weary travelers reentered this region at the Chariton River on September 18, 1806, reaching their final destination in St. Louis five days later on September 23, 1806.

While traveling on the Missouri River through the Eastern Deciduous Forest Lewis collected at least thirteen plant specimens, which represented eight plant species. Only one specimen, osage orange, still exists. The other twelve specimens were lost. Fortunately Lewis's transmittal list included adequate descriptions for botanists to identify six of these lost species. We know of another lost species, Carolina anemone *(Anemone caroliniana),* which I don't discuss in this book, from Pursh's 1814 floral manual.

In all, I included eight plant species from the Eastern Deciduous Forest. This includes seven species that we know Lewis collected, and pawpaw, which we gleaned from the journals. Field pennycress *(Thlaspi arvense)* is discussed in the *Introduction*. I arranged the plants geographically (rather than alphabetically) from east to west for readers who might be following the Lewis and Clark Trail.

The Eastern Deciduous Forest

Osage Orange

Maclura pomifera (Raf.) Schneid.
MULBERRY FAMILY (Moraceae)

Plants: Small- or medium-sized trees, up to about 40 feet or more tall, with thorny branches and milky sap. Leaves entire and not lobed, arranged alternately or clustered on the spurs of the branches. **Flowers:** Numerous small male and female flowers found on separate round clusters about ½ to 1 inch in diameter. Male flowers with four stamens opposite the sepals; female flowers without petals, consist of four sepals and a simple pistil. **Fruits:** Resembling green oranges, they are large (3 to 6 inches in diameter) and round, consist of a hard, wrinkled, corky rind with many single-seeded achenes deeply embedded in the dense pulp. **Flowering Season:** May, with fruit ripening in August and September. **Habitat/Range:** Woods, ravines, field margins. Native to Texas, Oklahoma, Arkansas.

FROM THE JOURNALS: On April 10, 1804, while the expedition was at Camp Dubois waiting to start up the Missouri, Clark noted, "no appearance of the buds of the Osage Apple." Previous to this, on March 16, Lewis sent some cuttings of Osage orange with a letter to President Jefferson in which he described the plant in detail. A specimen of this species exists in the Lewis and Clark Herbarium, but there is no label indicating when or where it was collected. Lewis is known to have discussed this unusual species with Jean Pierre Chouteau, who first introduced the Osage orange to St. Louis. Perhaps Chouteau's garden was the source of this specimen. Named for the Osage Indians, the strong wood of the Osage orange was highly prized by these and other Indian tribes for making bows. It was sometimes (perhaps erroneously) called "arrowwood." Clark wrote in an undated list that "Papaws[,] arrow wood and elder are found as high as the little Nemahaw [River]."

Frederick Pursh was so taken with this species that he featured it in the preface of his 1814 *Flora Americae Septentrionalis.* Pursh wrote: "Here I cannot refrain from drawing the attention of future botanists . . . to two highly interesting plants . . . The first is what Mr. Lewis in his journals calls 'the Osage Apple,' or 'Arrowwood of the Missouris.' This is a tree . . . with leaves resembling those of a pear-tree, but broader in proportion; they are alternate, and have a recurved thorn near their base; the flowers are of separate sexes, and appear in axillary, peduncled, globular catkins, which produce a depressed globular fruit, in size and colour resembling an orange, in interior structure approaching near to the genus Morinda . . . on account of its fruit and handsome foliage, must be highly ornamental : the wood, being excessively hard, is preferred by the natives to any other for making their arrows; and as it does not spontaneously grow in their neighbourhood, they travel annually to a considerable distance South-west, to procure it. About the village of the Osage Indians a few trees have been planted, from which one has been introduced into one of the gardens at St. Louis on the Mississippi. Perfect seeds from the last-mentioned tree were given by Mr. Lewis to Mr. M'Mahon, nursery and seedsman, at Philadelphia, who raised several fine plants from them."

Osage Orange fruit *Maclura pomifera*

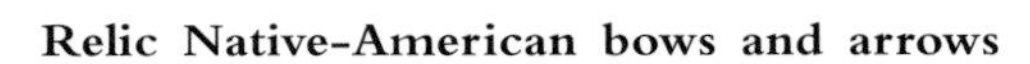

Relic Native-American bows and arrows

Pawpaw

Asimina triloba (L.) Dunn
CUSTARD APPLE FAMILY (Annonaceae)

Plants: Shrubs or small trees, often growing in clumps. Leaves alternate, simple, entire, tapering to a prolonged point. Buds dark brown with golden hair. **Flowers:** Include purple petals in two series; the three inner petals form a cup with three points and the three outer petals are larger and flattened out. There are three sepals that fall off soon after flowering, numerous stamens, and three to fifteen pistils. **Fruits:** Fleshy, 6 inches long and almost 2 inches thick, they hang down from the stems like a banana. Color from green to brown or purplish black. Edible; said to have the flavor of bananas and pears and the texture of sweet potatoes. **Flowering Season:** April to May. Fruits ripen August to September. **Habitat/Range:** Deciduous forests along streams, usually in shade; New York to Minnesota, southwest to Nebraska, and south to Texas and Florida.

FROM THE JOURNALS: Although no known plant specimen was collected, pawpaws were an important food source on the final days of the expedition. On September 11, 1806, while the party camped below the Nodaway River in Missouri, Clark observed, "The pawpaws nearly ripe." Four days later, below the the Kansas River, Clark said, "we landed one time only to let the men geather Pappaws or the Custard apple of which this Country abounds, and the men are very fond of." On September 18 Clark wrote: "our party entirely out of provisions Subsisting on poppaws. we divide the buiskit which amounted to nearly one buisket per man, this in addition to the poppaws is to last is down to the Settlement's which is 150 miles the party appear perfectly contented and tell us that they can live very well on the pappaws." The next day Clark wrote, "men ply their oares & we decended with great velocity, only Came too once for the purpose of gathering pappows." On September 20 they came in sight of civilization at the little French village of La Charette, which was near present-day Marthasville, Missouri, and arrived in St. Louis at noon on September 23, 1806, two years, four months, and nine days after the voyage began.

Indigo Bush

Amorpha fruticosa L.
BEAN FAMILY (Fabaceae)

Plants: Erect shrubs 3 to 12 inches tall, branching from the base and bushy at the top. Leaves pinnately compound with nine to thirty-one leaflets, each ¾ to 2 inches long and up to 1 inch wide. **Flowers:** Arranged in densely flowered, spikelike racemes on the end of the branches. Each flower has a single purple petal about ¼ inch long and ten stamens. **Fruits:** Curved, beanlike pods 2 to 3 inches long. **Flowering Season:** May to June. **Habitat/Range:** Moist soil in woods and along streams. Found in the eastern half of the United States and west to Wyoming, Colorado, New Mexico, Arizona, and southern California.

FROM THE JOURNALS: The expedition left Camp Dubois on May 14, 1804. Indigo bush was number 3 in Lewis's plant collection. On the transmittal list he wrote: "No. 3. Was taken on the 23rd of May 1804, near the mouth of the Osage

Upper Left: Indigo Bush ***Amorpha fruticosa***
—Steven Foster photo

Upper Right: Lead Plant ***Amorpha canescens***
A similar species in flower

Lower Right: Pawpaw flower ***Asimina triloba***
—Steven Foster photo

Woman's creek [near present-day Matson, Missouri], it is a srub and resembles much in growth the *bladder scenna*, it rises to hight of eight or ten feet and is an inhabitant of a moist rich soil.— usually the verge of the river bank.— it is a handsome Shrub." Although this specimen is among those mysteriously lost, Lewis collected another specimen of indigo bush on the return trip on August 27, 1806, in the High Plains at the lower end of the Big Bend of the Missouri (now under Lake Sharpe in South Dakota). Lewis was recovering from a gunshot wound at the time and Clark wrote, "My friend Capt Lewis hurt himself very much by takeing a longer walk . . . than he had Strength to undergo, which Caused him to remain very unwell all night." Lewis may have collected the specimen on this walk. Two sheets of this specimen exist today.

Plains Cottonwood

Populus deltoides Marsh
WILLOW FAMILY (Salicaceae)

Plants: Large trees, 65 to 100 feet tall, with broad, rounded crowns. Leaves triangular in shape, about 2½ inches long and equally wide. **Flowers:** Male and female flowers occur on separate trees (dioecious) and the numerous unisexual flowers are arranged in catkins 2 to 5 inches long, which hang loosely from the branches. **Fruits:** Capsules with three or four valves, which release the tiny seeds carried in the wind by tufts of cottonlike hairs. **Flowering Season:** March to June. **Habitat/Range:** Streamsides from Quebec to Alberta and south to Pennsylvania, Missouri, and New Mexico.

FROM THE JOURNALS: Lewis collected plains cottonwood on May 25, 1804, at La Charette, Missouri, which he portrayed as "the last settlement on the Missouri; and consists of ten or twelve families mostly hunters." He described plains cottonwood in detail on the transmittal list: "No. 4 . . . this specimine is the seed of the Cottonwood which is so abundant in this country, it has now arrived at maturity and the wind when blowing strong drives it through the air to a great distance being supported by a parrishoot of this cottonlike substance which give the name to the tree . . . the wood is of a white color, soft spungey and light, perogues [open boats] are most usually made of these trees, the wood is not durable nor do I know any othe valuable purpose which it can answer except that just mentioned." In fact, the expedition made much use of this tree for shelter, for canoes, and for the wheels and axles used for hauling cargo on the long portage around the "great falls" of the Missouri. The explorers built Fort Mandan out of cottonwood trees and used it for fuel during the bitter winter they spent there. They also noted that the Indians fed the bark to their horses in winter. Lewis referred to this species as "the wide leafed cottonwood."

Golden Seal

Hydrastis canadensis L.
BUTTERCUP FAMILY (Ranunculaceae)

Plants: Perennial herbs 6 to 20 inches tall. Plants have a large basal leaf and two stem leaves. All leaves deeply lobed with serrated margins. **Flowers:** Solitary, ½ inch wide, consisting of three sepals, no petals, numerous greenish white stamens, and five to fifteen pistils. **Fruits:** Aggregate of dark red berries. **Flowering Season:** Spring. **Habitat/Range:** Moist deciduous forests; Iowa to Massachusetts and south to Virginia and Mississippi. Declining today from loss of habitat and commercial harvesting for the herb market.

FROM THE JOURNALS: According to Lewis's notes, included with his transmittal list, "No. 8 Was taken the 29th of May 1804 below the mouth of the Osage Rivr. this plant is known . . . by the name of yellow root—it is a sovereighn remidy for a disorder common in this quarter called the Soar eyes . . . it is a violent inflamation of the eyes attended with high fevers and headach, and is extreemly distressing, and frequently attended with the loss of sight—this root affords a speady and efficasious remidy for this disorder." The notes continued by describing how to prepare the

Plains Cottonwood
Populus deltoides

Middle right: Golden Seal flower
***Hydrastis canadensis* —Steven Foster photo**

Bottom right: Golden Seal fruit
—Steven Foster photo

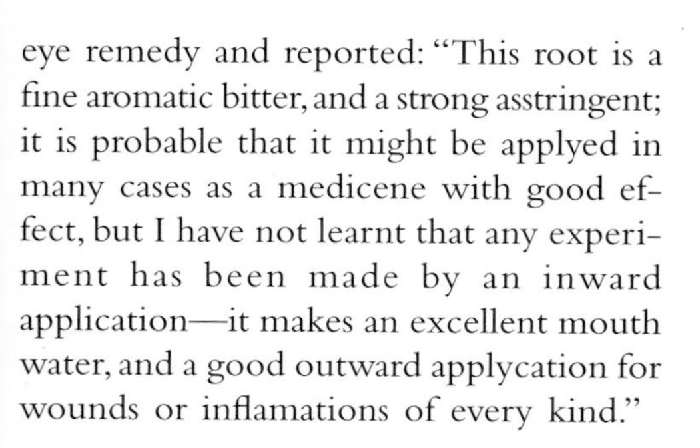

eye remedy and reported: "This root is a fine aromatic bitter, and a strong asstringent; it is probable that it might be applyed in many cases as a medicene with good effect, but I have not learnt that any experiment has been made by an inward application—it makes an excellent mouth water, and a good outward applycation for wounds or inflamations of every kind."

Eastern Wild Ginger

Asarum canadense L.
BIRTHWORT FAMILY (Aristolochiaceae)

Plants: Perennial herbs without aerial stems, have a single pair of heart-shaped leaves. **Flowers:** Single, upright flowers with three showy purplish or tan sepals, no true petals, twelve distinct stamens, and an ovary with the styles joined into a column. **Fruits:** Fleshy capsules. **Flowering Season:** Spring to early summer. **Habitat/Range:** Deciduous forests from Minnesota to Oklahoma and east to Maine and Georgia.

FROM THE JOURNALS: Listed as specimen number 10, Lewis recorded that it "was taken the 1st of June at the mouth of the Osage river; it is known in this country by the name of the *wild ginger,* it resembles that plant somewhat in both taste and effect; it is a strong stomatic stimelent, and frequently used in sperits with bitter herbs—it is common throughout the rich lands in the Western country."

Ground Plum

Astragalus crassicarpus Nutt.
BEAN FAMILY (Fabaceae)

Plants: Perennial herbs that trail on the ground. Leaves alternate with distinct stipules and fifteen to twenty-seven leaflets per each pinnately compound leaf. **Flowers:** In small clusters (racemes) of five to twenty-five beanlike flowers. Sepals form a tube with sharp teeth and black appressed hairs. Petals vary in color from purple to light blue, yellowish, or creamy white. **Fruits:** Round pods about 1 inch in diameter; tinged green or red to purplish and fleshy when young; edible. **Flowering Season:** April to July. **Habitat/Range:** Open forests, prairies, and high plains from New Mexico to Tennessee and north to Alberta and Manitoba.

FROM THE JOURNALS: Lewis described this specimen on the transmittal list: "No. 11. Was taken the 3rd of June above the mouth of the Osage river; it is the groath of high dry open praries . . . the Indians frequently use the fruit of this plant to alay their thirst . . . bears from {two?} to four podds, which in their succulent and unripe state as at this season of the year are about the sise of a pullet's egg . . . the pulp is crisp & clear and tasts very much like the hull of a gardin pee.—when ripe the fruit is of a fine red coulour and sweet flavor."

Eastern Wild Ginger
Asarum canadense
—Steven Foster photo

Ground Plum flower *Astragalus crassicarpus* **Ground Plum fruit**

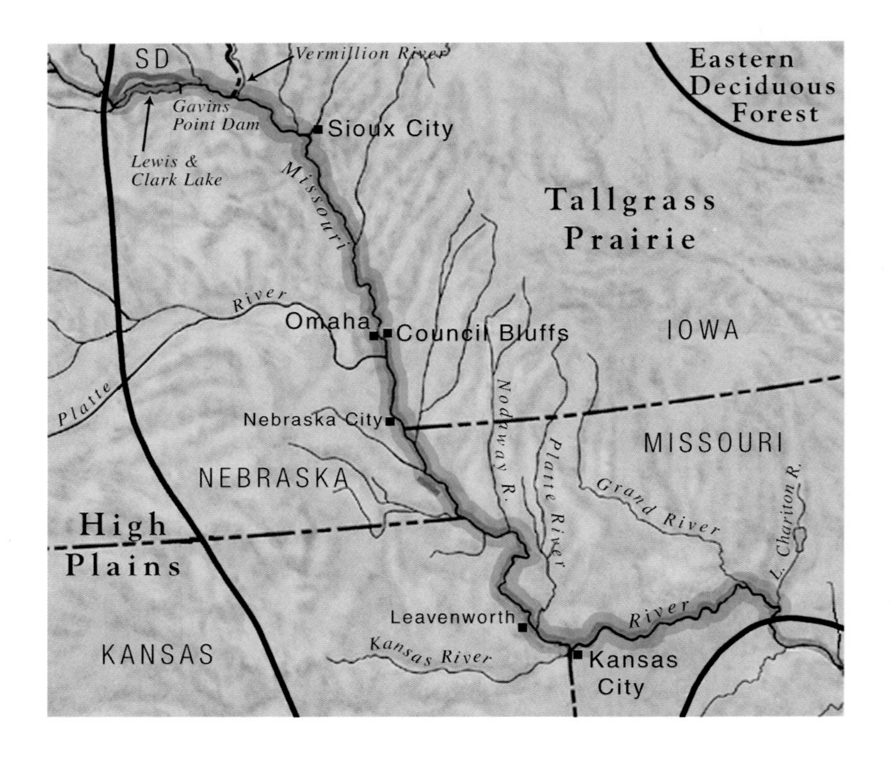

Salix exigua
Salix amygdaloides
Phalaris arundinacea
Ampelopsis cordata
Artemisia ludoviciana
Calystegia sepium
Chamaecrista fasciculata
Dalea purpurea
Dalea candida
Andropogon gerardi
Elymus virginicus[1]
Elymus canadensis[2]

1. Not included this book.
2. See Andropogon gerardi.

Desmanthus illinoensis
Ribes americanum
Symphoricarpos occidentalis
Euphorbia marginata
Equisetum arvense
Grindelia squarrosa
Anemone canadensis
Cleome serrulata
Polanisia dodecandra
Psoralidium lanceolatum
Mentzelia decapetala
Mirabilis nyctaginea
Artemisia frigida

The Tallgrass Prairie

The Tallgrass Prairie forms a transition between the Eastern Deciduous Forest and the treeless High Plains. Gently rolling plains are interspersed with draws, bluffs, hills, and ridges. Prairies of tall grasses are intermingled with groves and strips of oak-hickory forest, especially along streams and north-facing slopes. In some places there are savannahs of prairie grasses and scattered trees. The prairies are dominated by tall grasses including big bluestem, little bluestem, switchgrass, and Indian grass. Many species of wildflowers grow with the tall grasses, like prairie blazing star, purple prairie clover, showy goldenrod, purple coneflower, black-eyed Susan, and blue aster. The oak-hickory forest groves in the prairie are similar in composition to those in the Eastern Deciduous Forest.

The climate is temperate and subhumid with hot summers and cold winters. Annual precipitation ranges from 20 to 40 inches, which falls mainly during the growing season, but is largely offset by high evaporation and transpiration rates. High winds, violent thunderstorms, and tornados are common.

In 1804 the tallgrass prairie stretched from present-day Manitoba to Texas, and in the center of its range it bulged eastward from eastern Nebraska and Kansas to western Indiana. Today the rich, black soils of this ecosystem are largely cultivated in the agricultural corn-belt.

The Tallgrass Prairie

The expedition entered the Tallgrass Prairie at the confluence of the Missouri and Chariton Rivers in present-day Missouri on June 10, 1804. They labored up the Missouri River through this region for almost four months until they reached the Niobrara River of present-day Nebraska on September 4, 1804, where they entered the High Plains. On the return trip they reentered the Tallgrass Prairie on September 1, 1806, passing swiftly downriver to the Chariton River where they exited the region on September 18, 1806.

We know Lewis collected thirty-three specimens while in this region, most of them in 1804. Unfortunately, only ten of these plants exist today in the Lewis and Clark Herbarium. Most of the others were among the specimens lost when they were sent down the Missouri River from Fort Mandan in the spring of 1805. Botanists have been able to tentatively identify fourteen more species by studying the descriptions of the lost specimens in Lewis's transmittal list. We know of one other lost species, *Mentzelia decapetala,* from Frederick Pursh's *Flora America Septentrionalis.*

Below I have included all but one—Virginia wildrye, *Elymus virginicus*—of the twenty-five plant species that we know Lewis and Clark collected in the Tallgrass Prairie. I arranged them geographically from southeast to northwest, according to where they were collected, along the Missouri River from its confluence with the Chariton River to the Niobrara River.

The Tallgrass Prairie

Sandbar Willow

Salix exigua Nutt.
WILLOW FAMILY (Salicaceae)

Plants: Shrubs up to 12 feet tall that form dense thickets and spread by underground stems. Leaves 2 to 6 inches long and less than ½ inch wide; slowly taper to a sharp tip; green on both sides, often hairy (at least when young). **Flowers:** Unisexual with sexes on separate shrubs; arranged in catkins that emerge after the leaves. Male flowers each have two stamens. **Fruits:** Capsules hairy to smooth, about ¼ inch long, have numerous seeds with long silky hair for wind distribution. **Flowering season:** May to June. **Habitat/Range:** Sandbars and streambanks, very common throughout the Great Plains and foothills to moderate elevation in mountains; New Brunswick to Alaska and south to Virginia, Tennessee, Louisiana, Texas, Arizona, and northern Mexico.

FROM THE JOURNALS: Although this specimen was lost, Lewis described sandbar willow at length in his transmittal list: "No. 13. The *narrow leaf willow* taken on the 14th of June [1804] . . . This tree is invariably the first which makes it's appearance on the newly made Lands on the borders of the Mississippi and Missouri, and seems to contribute much towards facilitating the operation of raisin this ground still higher; they grow remarkably close and some instances so much so that they form a thicket almost impenetrable[;] the points of land [sandbars] which are forming allways become eddies when overflown in high water these willows obstruct the force of the water and makes it more still which causes the mud and sand to be deposited in greater quantities; the willow is not attal imbarrassed or injured by this inundation, but puts forth an innumerable quantity of small fibrous roots . . . which further serve to collect the mud . . . this willow never rises to any considerable sise, it is seldom seen larger than a mans arm, and scarcely every rises higher than 25 feet . . . and is generally used by the watermen for *setting poles* [used to propel the boats] in preference to anything else . . . these willow [sand]bars form a pleasant beacon to the navigator."

Peach-Leaved Willow

Salix amygdaloides Anderss.
WILLOW FAMILY (Salicaceae)

Plants: Small trees up to 40 feet tall, often with several large trunks and drooping branches. Leaves 1½ to 3½ inches long and about 1 inch wide with fine teeth on the margin, taper to a long, tail-like tip; green on the upper surface, whitish underneath. **Flowers:** Male and female flowers found on separate trees; small, nonshowy, unisexual flowers arranged in loose catkins emerge with the leaves. Male flowers have three to seven stamens. **Fruits:** Smooth capsules, oval in outline, about ¼ inch long, have numerous seeds with long, silky hair. **Flowering Season:** May. **Habitat/Range:** Common along streams of the plains and foothills from Quebec and New York to British Columbia and south to Pennsylvania, Texas, and Arizona.

Sandbar Willow
female flowers ***Salix exigua***
Inset: Sandbar Willow male flowers

Peach-Leaved Willow
female flowers ***Salix amygdaloides***
Inset: Peach-Leaved Willow male flowers

FROM THE JOURNALS: Although among the lost specimens, Lewis described this plant that he collected June 14, 1804: "No. 14 The *wide leaf willow* or that species which I believe to be common to most parts of the Atlantic States. it grows in similar situations to that described with rispect to the narrow leaf willow, but is never found in such abundance, it arrives to a greater size sometimes to forty feet in hight and eighteen inches in diameter, the leave is smoth ovate, pointed, finely indented, a pale green on the upper side and of a whiteis green or silver coulour underneath—like the narrow leaf willow the leaf is widest in the middle where it is from one inch to ¾ wide.—it bears its seed in the manner described of the other and the plants ar likewise male and female."

Reed Canarygrass

Phalaris arundinacea L.
GRASS FAMILY (Poaceae)

Plants: Large perennial grasses about 3 to 7 feet tall. Leaf blades flat, 4 to 16 inches long, and about ½ inch wide. Leaf sheaths divided into cross partitions with obvious air chambers. Plants spread aggressively by rhizomes. **Flowers:** Numerous grass florets (one fertile floret per spikelet) arranged in dense panicles, 3 to 7 inches long, often reddish during flowering. **Fruits:** Grains; the grain-filled florets fall from the glumes, which remain on the stems. **Flowering Season:** May to July. **Habitat/Range:** Wetlands in swales, marshes, and streamsides throughout the Northern Hemisphere.

FROM THE JOURNALS: Lewis collected a specimen that botanists believe is reed canarygrass around June 16, 1804. It was lost with the Fort Mandan shipment. Lewis described specimen number 19: "Taken at the old village of the little Osages; the seed were now ripe; it grew in great abundance in the prarie from five to six feet high . . . the small birds feed on the seed which are very abundant . . . when ripe they fall very easily from the stem. the leaf of this grass does not decline or wither as many others do at the time the seed ripens but still continues succulant and green . . . the horses were very fond of this grass and I am disposed to believe that it would make a valuable grass for culture.—this grass is common in the prairies or bottom lands as high as the river Platte and perhaps further—it is a fine sweet grass and I am confident would make good hay."

Raccoon Grape

Ampelopsis cordata Michx.
GRAPE FAMILY (Vitaceae)

Plants: Vines that climb high into trees and have tight-barked stems covered with dots (lenticels) and tendrils with slender tips for climbing and holding. Leaves simple, oval in shape with a heart-shaped base. Leaf margins coarsely and sharply toothed. **Flowers:** Unisexual. Male flowers with five greenish petals and five functional stamens. Female flowers with five greenish petals, five vestigial stamens, and an ovary half-buried in a cup-shaped disk. **Fruits:** Round berries; at first green, then orangish pink, and finally turquoise. Not edible, often called "false grape." **Flowering Season:** May to July. **Habitat/Range:** Rocky, wooded hillsides and streams from Ohio to Nebraska and south to South Carolina and Texas.

FROM THE JOURNALS: A specimen of raccoon grape in the Lewis and Clark Herbarium is the last plant we know the expedition collected. The plant label, in Frederick Pursh's handwriting, states: "near Counsel Bluffs Missouri. Septb. 14th 1806." This label is confusing, since the expedition passed the "Council bluffs" near present-day Fort Calhoun, Nebraska, on September 8, 1806. On September 14 they were near present-day Leavenworth, Kansas. In either case they were in the Tallgrass Prairie when they collected the specimen.

In his journal for September 8 Clark described the expedition's stop at the "Council bluffs": "Capt Lewis and myself walked up on the bluffs and around to examine the Country . . . the Situation appeared to us eaqually as eligable as when

Reed Canarygrass ***Phalaris arundinacea***

Raccoon Grape ***Ampelopsis cordata***
—Steven Foster photo

we passed up for an establishment, the hill high and Commanding with a high rich bottom of great extent below. we proceeded on . . . they ply'd their orers very well, and we arrived at our old encampment at White Catfish Camp 12 miles above the river platt . . . haveing made 78 Miles to day." On September 14, 1806, Clark described their meeting with three large boats coming up the river: "those young men received us with great friendship and pressed on us Some whisky for our men, Bisquet, Pork and Onions, & part of their Stores, we continued near 2 hours with those boats, makeing every enquirey into the state of our friends and Cournty &c [etc.] . . . we proceeded on to an Island . . . and encamped haveing decended only 53 miles to day. Our party received a dram and Sung Songs until 11 oClock at night in the greatest harmoney."

Prairie Sagewort or White Sagewort

Artemisia ludoviciana Nutt.
ASTER FAMILY (Asteraceae)

Plants: Aromatic herbs, 1 to 3 feet tall, covered with white, dense, woolly hair (at least when young). Leaves variable in shape from entire and lance shaped to deeply divided into narrow lobes. Spreads by rhizomes forming communities. **Flowers:** Many small, brownish flower heads that have disk flowers arranged panicle-like on stem ends. **Fruits:** One-seeded achenes, smooth and without pappus. **Flowering Season:** June to October. **Habitat/Range:** Dry, open places. Widespread in North America from central Canada to Mexico.

FROM THE JOURNALS: In his transmittal list, Lewis described this specimen, which he collected near or below the Tarkio River in Missouri or adjacent Nebraska on July 13, 1804: "No. 30. was taken at the bald praries and is common to both low and high praries it usually grows in a single stem and appears to be an annual groath the leaves are white and like the stem appear to be covered with a white down—this is common to all the praries above the Kancez [Kansas] river; from it's resemblence in taste smell &c [etc.] to the *common* Sage I have called it the wild Sage."

In the journals Lewis often mentioned aromatic herbs when describing the vegetation. On April 14, 1805, at the entrance of the Little Missouri River in present-day North Dakota, Lewis wrote, "on these hills many aromatic herbs are seen; resembling in taste, smel and appearance, the sage, hysop, wormwood, southern-wood." Although this specimen was lost, Lewis collected two additional white-sage specimens that still exist. One he collected on the High Plains on October 1, 1804, and the other on the Columbia Plains in April 1806.

Hedge Bindweed

Calystegia sepium (L.) R. Br.
Also *Convolvulus sepium* L.
MORNING GLORY FAMILY (Convolvulaceae)

Plants: Perennial vines up to 10 feet long. Leaves heart shaped with sharply angled lateral lobes at the base. **Flowers:** Funnel-shaped, white to pinkish flowers are arranged singly on stalks from the leaf axils. Two leaflike bracts conceal the sepals. **Fruits:** Capsules partly concealed by the persistent bracts. **Flowering Season:** June to August. **Habitat/Range:** Moist soil, often along rivers from Massachusetts to Washington and south to North Carolina and New Mexico.

FROM THE JOURNALS: Lewis collected this 1804 specimen near the present-day Iowa-Missouri state line. He commented on his transmittal list that specimen number 28 was "taken on the 17th July at the at the bald prarie—is a large convolvalist [genus *Convolvulus*] a fine white colour; the vines are very extensive and run in every direction intwining themselves about the larger weeds and bending them down is {in} such manner as to make the open grownds or praries where they grow almost impassable; the root is about the size and shape of the vine and enters it so deep that I could not find it's brances tho' I dug as much as 2 feet in surch of it. –the leaf is of a tonge like form pale green even on the edges." This specimen was among those lost.

Prairie Sagewort
or White Sagewort
Artemisia ludoviciana

Hedge Bindweed
Calystegia sepium

Showy Partridge Pea

Chamaecrista fasciculata (Michx.) Greene
Also *Cassia fasciculata* Michx.
Cassia chamaecrista L.
CAESALPINIA FAMILY (Caesalpiniaceae)

Plants: Annual herbs, ½ to 4 feet tall, with hairy stems and compound leaves that have eight to twenty pairs of leaflets arranged pinnately or featherlike. Leafstalk has gland below lowest pair of leaflets. **Flowers:** Found singly or in two- to seven-flowered racemes from the leaf axils; have five narrow sepals, five rounded bright yellow petals, and ten yellow to dark red stamens. **Fruits:** Small, flat pods up to 2½ inches long. **Flowering Season:** June to October. **Habitat/Range:** Sandy or rocky soils of open woodlands and prairies; eastern half of the United States to the edge of the Great Plains.

FROM THE JOURNALS: Specimen number 29, according to Lewis's transmittal list, was "Taken on the 18th of July.—an annuel plant putting up many branches from the root has a leaf like the pateridge bea [partridge bean], is jointed bears a number of yllow *pea-like* flowers which grow on the seed stems which project from the main branches and which are unattended with leaves; these flowers grow all arround this stem and give it the appearance of a tausell. The {l}eaf stems ar long and have 24 par of leaves." This specimen was lost.

The expedition was traveling near present-day Nebraska City on this date when Clark described a landslide, "this Hill . . . about ¾ of a mile in length & about 200 feet in Depth has Sliped into the river." He then saw a starved dog on the bank and, in an act of compassion, "gave him Som meet [meat]."

Purple Prairie Clover

Dalea purpurea Vent.
Also *Petalostemon purpureus* (Vent.) Rydb.
BEAN FAMILY (Fabaceae)

Plants: Perennial herbs with slender, erect stems about ½ to 3 feet tall. Leaves alternate and compound, having three to nine shiny, narrow leaflets less than 1 inch long and ⅛ inch wide. **Flowers:** Tiny, bright purple flowers with five protruding orange stamens; arranged on the stem ends in dense cylindrical spikes; blooming from the bottom first and progressing upward. **Fruits:** Small, round pods dotted with glands, containing a single seed. **Flowering Season:** May to August. **Habitat/Range:** Sandy and rocky soils of dry prairie, plains, and open woods from Manitoba to Alberta and south to Alabama and New Mexico.

FROM THE JOURNALS: Lewis collected three specimens of this species. The first one he collected on July 20, 1804, above present-day Nebraska City, Nebraska, was lost. Lewis wrote about this specimen on his transmittal list: "No. 15 . . . a pieniel [perennial] plant, an inhabitant of the open praries or plains, high situations, where the grass is low. The flower is a pale purple colour[,] small[,] form a kind of button of a long conic like form which terminate it's branches which are numerous—it grows abot 2 1/2 or three feet high—it is a stranger to me.—the leaves are small and narrow, and divided into three on a stem." Lewis's comment, "it is a stranger to me," denotes that this species was foreign to him. It was among the first of many new and strange species that he would soon encounter as the party ventured deeper into the uncharted American wilderness.

While Lewis's specimen number 15 was lost, two additional specimens of purple prairie clover still exist. Lewis collected specimen number 53(A) in the Tallgrass Prairie above "Bonhomme Island" in Nebraska (now inundated by Lewis and Clark Lake) on September 2, 1804. Lewis's original label for this specimen stated that "the Indians use it as an application to fresh wounds. they bruise the leaves adding a little water and apply it." He collected the third specimen in the High Plains west of present-day Cut Bank, Montana, on July 22, 1806.

wy Partridge Pea ***Chamaecrista fasciculata***
—Steven Foster photo

Purple Prairie Clover ***Dalea purpurea***

White Prairie Clover

Dalea candida Michx. ex Willd.
Also *Petalostemon candidus* (Willd.) Michx
BEAN FAMILY (Fabaceae)

Plants: Perennial herbs with slender erect stems about ½ to 2½ feet tall. Leaves alternate and compound, having five to nine narrow leaflets less than 1½ inches long and less than ¼ inch wide. **Flowers:** White with five protruding stamens; arranged on the stem ends in dense, cylindrical spikes; bloom from the bottom first and progress upward. **Fruits:** Small, round pods dotted with glands. **Flowering Season:** May to August. **Habitat/Range:** Rocky soils of dry prairie and plains from the east slope of the Rocky Mountains throughout the western Great Plains and southwest to Utah and Arizona.

FROM THE JOURNALS: Lewis's specimen number 16 is undated, but we presume—because of its similarity to purple prairie clover *(Dalea purpurea)* and a reference to that specimen (number 15)—that it was collected on July 20, 1804, near the Cass-Otoe County line in Nebraska, the same date Lewis collected purple prairie clover and the same location. On his transmittal list, Lewis simply stated, "this is much the same as No. 15 with this difference that the blume of the conic tausel are white in stead of purple and it's leaves single fewer and longer." On that day Clark wrote that they "passed the mouth of *l'Eau que pleure* the English of which is *the water which Cry's* [present-day Weeping Water Creek] . . . at this Creek I went on Shore . . . and went up this Creek Several miles & Crossed thro: the plains to the river above with the view of finding Elk . . . I killed an emence large yellow Wolf—The Countrey throu which we walked after leaveing the Creek was good land covered with Grass interspersed with Groves & Scattering timber near and about the heads of Branches." This is a fairly accurate description of the Tallgrass Prairie landscape.

Big Bluestem

Andropogon gerardii Vitman
GRASS FAMILY (Poaceae)

Plants: Perennial grasses usually growing in bunches but sometimes spreading by short rhizomes forming turf. Flower stalks mostly 3 to 6 feet, but up to 9 feet, tall. Leaves up to 2 feet long and less than ½ inch wide. **Flowers:** Arranged at the tops of tall stems, usually in three dense clusters 2 to 4 inches long that originate from a common point. Spikelets in pairs, the fertile one without a stalk. **Fruits:** Grains enclosed in lemma and palea; hairy, with long, twisted, bristlelike awns. **Flowering Season:** July to October. **Habitat/Range:** Lowland prairies and swales in southern Canada, and in the United States from Maine to Montana and south to Florida, New Mexico, and Mexico.

FROM THE JOURNALS: Big bluestem is one of the most abundant grasses in the Tallgrass Prairie. Lewis collected it on July 27, 1804, when the explorers were traveling beyond their "White Catfish Camp," ten miles above the Platte River near present-day Bellevue, Nebraska. Lewis collected six grass species on this date. He described them on the transmittal list: "No 22. 23. 24 & 25. Are various species of grasses which appear in the praries, No. 23 [big bluestem] is the most common of any other grass, it rises to the hight of 4 to 8 feet & never bears any flower or seed that I ever observed and suppose therefore that it must propegate by means of the root: *common* to all praries in this country." On the same date Lewis collected specimen number 20, Canada wildrye *(Elymus canadensis)*. Lewis described it as "A specemine of wild Rye . . . this grass is common to all the low praries above the Canez [Kansas] river . . . it resembles the rye extreemly . . . the geese and ducks feed on it."

p Right: White Prairie Clover ***Dalea candida***

tom Left: Canada wildrye ***Elymus canadensis***

om Right: Big Bluestem ***Andropogon gerardii***

Illinois Bundleflower

Desmanthus illinoensis (Michx.) MacM.
MIMOSA FAMILY (Mimosaceae)
Also BEAN FAMILY (Fabaceae)

Plants: Perennial herbs with turnip-shaped roots and tough, slender, grooved stems 1 to 5 feet tall. Leaves pinnately divided in branches that are again divided pinnately (like a feather) into many tiny leaflets less than ¼ inch long. **Flowers:** Tiny, white flowers arranged in round heads at the ends of stalks that sprout from the leaf axils. Each flower has five white petals and five longer, yellow-tipped stamens. **Fruits:** A round cluster of curved brown pods; each pod flat and waferlike. **Flowering Season:** June to August. **Habitat/Range:** Prairies, streambanks, and open wooded slopes from Pennsylvania to North Dakota, south to Florida and New Mexico.

FROM THE JOURNALS: Lewis stated on his transmittal list: "No. 18. was taken 30th July grows in the praries in high situations . . . it's colateral brances are short and furnished with many leaf stems which are garnished by a great number of small leaves which are attatch by pairs on either side and resemble some of the sensative bryers, tho I could not discover that this plant partook of that quality.—its flower is of a gloubelar form composed of a number of fibers of a yellowish white, and produces as a fruit a bunch of little pees which are all bent edgeways into the form of a semicircle and so closely connected and compressed as to form a globular figure of a curious appearance." The bundleflower specimen was lost. On July 30 the party traveled only 3¼ miles and camped near the present-day town of Fort Calhoun, Nebraska, north of Omaha. Lewis and Clark took a walk and Clark described the country as "one Continual Plain as fur as Can be Seen . . . the most butifull prospect . . . which I ever beheld; The River meandering the open and butifull Plains, interspursed with Groves of timber, and each point Covered with Tall timber, Such as willow Cotton Sun Mulberry, Elm, Sucamore, Lynn [linden] & ash . . . Groves contain Hickory, Walnut, Coffeenut & Oake."

Wild Black Currant

Ribes americanum P. Mill.
CURRANT FAMILY (Grossulariaceae)

Plants: Shrubs 3 to 5 feet tall; stems smooth. Leaves simple with three main lobes and two smaller ones near the base. Leaf margins have coarse teeth and lower leaf-surfaces have yellow, resinous dots. **Flowers:** six to fifteen arranged in a drooping raceme. Five greenish white to yellowish sepal lobes; five creamy white to yellowish petals; five stamens. **Fruits:** Round, black berries crowned with the floral remains. **Flowering Season:** May to June. **Habitat/Range:** Along streams and in thickets from New Brunswick to Alberta and south to Pennsylvania and New Mexico.

Illinois Bundleflower
Desmanthus illinoensis
—Steven Foster photo

Wild Black Currant flower
Ribes americanum
Inset: Wild Black Currant fruit

FROM THE JOURNALS: Lewis collected specimen number 12 on August 1, 1804, and wrote: "one of our hunters brought us a bough of the purple courant, which is frequently cultivated in the Atlantic states; the fruit was ripe; I presume it is a native of North America—here it grows generally in the praries but is not very abundant.—No. 12 is a specimine of it's leaves." This specimen was lost.

August 1 was Clark's birthday. In his journal for the day he described the prairie below their camp: "rich Covered with Grass from 5 to 8 feet high intersperced with Copse of Hazel, Plumbs, Currents (like those of the U.S.) Rasberries & Grapes of Dift. Kinds . . . and a great Variety of Plants & flours not Common to the U S. What a field for a Botents {botanist} and a natirless {naturalist}."

Western Snowberry or Wolfberry *Symphoricarpos occidentalis* Hook.

HONEYSUCKLE FAMILY (Caprifoliaceae)

Plants: Shrubs, usually 2 to 4 feet tall, that spread by underground runners and often form large colonies. Leaves simple and arranged in opposite pairs on the stems; usually oval, egg shaped, or almost round in outline, but sometimes irregularly lobed. **Flowers:** Arranged in clusters of up to twelve; each pink to white flower has spreading lobes revealing the dense hair, style, and stamens that protrude from the throat. **Fruits:** Greenish white, round berries, which turn purple to black in the fall or winter. **Flowering Season:** June to July. **Habitat/Range:** Swales, streamsides, and moist prairies from Manitoba to British Columbia and south to Missouri, Oklahoma, New Mexico, Utah, and Washington.

FROM THE JOURNALS: Lewis described this species in his transmittal list: "No. 26.—Taken on the 2ed of August in the parie [prairie] at the Cuncil bluff [near present-day Fort Calhoun, Nebraska, and the namesake for Council Bluffs, Iowa]. it is a species of honeysuccle; the flower is small and the tube of the flour is very small and short they smell precisely like the English Honeysuccle so much admired in our gardens; this is a shrub and does not run or vine . . . This species of shrub Honeysuccle has some of it's leaves much indented; the fruit nearly ripe when the plant is still in blume; it makes a pretty groath and is a pleasant looking pla{n}t rises to three or four feet high and limbs are much branchd." Clark further described this species in his journal on August 1, 1804: "two Kind of *honey Suckle* one [coralberry, *Symphoricarpos orbiculatus*] which grows to a kind of a Srub. Common about Harrods burgh in Kentucky the other [western snowberry] are not So large or tall and bears a flow{er} in Clusters Short and of a light Pink Colour, the leaves differ from any of the othe Kind in as much as the Lieves are Distinkd & does not Surround the Stalk as all the other Kind does."

Snow-on-the-Mountain *Euphorbia marginata* Pursh

SPURGE FAMILY (Euphorbiaceae)

Plants: Annual herbs with milky juice, about 3 feet tall, with fine hair on the stems. Lower leaves alternate, opposite or whorled at the base of the umbel branches, up to 4 inches long and 2½ inches wide with pointed tips and rounded bases; upper leaves have white margins. **Flowers:** Numerous small (and strange) flower heads with five white petal-like structures around the tiny unisexual (one female and several male) flowers. **Fruits:** Three-celled capsules with one seed per cell. **Flowering Season:** June to October. **Habitat/Range:** Dry, calcareous soil of grasslands of the Great Plains from Minnesota to Montana and south to Texas and New Mexico.

FROM THE JOURNALS: Lewis described specimen number 27 in his transmittal list: "taken 4th of August [near present-day Blair, Nebraska], and furst observed at the bald prarie—it is a beatifull plant with a variagated leaf—these leaves incompass the flowers which are small and in the center of them; at a small distance they resemble somewhat a white rose the leaf near the large stem is green and is edged with white; they grow smaller and more numerous as they approach the flower or the extremity of the limb. the plant is much branched; the leaf is smoth on both sides and edge, of an ovate form and pale green colour, rises to five or six feet, is annual[,] at every point that it branches it has a pair of opposite leaves and from th[r]ee to four branches." While specimen number 27 was lost, a second specimen—that still exists—was collected. We believe Clark collected it because the plant label states: "On the Yellowstone River. July 28 1806." On this date Clark's party was descending the Yellowstone River in present-day Rosebud County, Montana, while Lewis's party was traveling to the mouth of the Marias River in Montana fleeing the scene of their bloody fight of the previous day. This is one of many plants in this book that Frederick Pursh first named and described for botanical science in his 1814 *Flora Americae Septentrionalis.* Pursh credited Lewis's plant collection as the source of the specimen he used for his description.

Western Snowberry or Wolfberry
Symphoricarpos occidentalis

Snow-on-the-Mountain
Euphorbia marginata

Field Horsetail

Equisetum arvense L.
HORSETAIL FAMILY (Equisetaceae)

Plants: Perennial herbs with rushlike stems. The fertile stems are not branched, pale brownish in color, develop in early spring; the infertile ones develop later and have many green branches arranged in whorls that look like a horse's tail. **Flowers:** No true flowers; these primitive plants reproduce in cones on the ends of the unbranched fertile stems. **Fruits:** No true fruits; instead, numerous spores are produced in the cones. **Flowering Season:** April to June. **Habitat/Range:** Along streams, ponds, and seeps. Cosmopolitan, found throughout the world.

FROM THE JOURNALS: Lewis may have had another idea for the origin of horsetail's name when he wrote in his transmittal list that specimen number 31 was "a species of sand rush, joined [jointed] and so much branched as to form a perfect broom; it is common to every part of this river at least as far as Latitude 42 N. it grows near the water's edge in moist sand; the horses are remarkably fond of it." He collected this specimen on August 10, 1804, in either present-day Burt County, Nebraska, or Monona County, Iowa. The specimen still exists.

Clark calculated that the men had traveled up the Missouri 22¼ miles that day before camping on a willow island about 4 miles east of Blackbird Hill. Clark described the hill in his August 10, 1804, field notes: "*Black bird* the late King of the *Mahars* [Omaha Indians] Toom [tomb] or inclosed grave on the top of a high round Hill of about 300 feet in the Prarie." The next day Lewis, Clark, and ten men visited the site. Clark wrote in his journal for August 11: "we landed at the foot of the hill on which Black Bird The late King of the mahar who Died 4 years ago & 400 of his nation with the Small pox was buried . . . and went up and fixed a white flag bound with Blue white & read on the Grave which was about 12 foot Base & circueller . . . passed a Creek Called *Wau-Con di peche* C or *Bad God* Creek of bad Spirits."

Curly-Cup Gumweed

Grindelia squarrosa (Pursh) Dunal
ASTER FAMILY (ASTERACEAE)

Plants: Biennial or perennial herbs with glands (especially on the leaves and flower bracts) that exude aromatic resin. Stems 4 to 40 inches tall. Leaves simple, often tapering toward the base, with teeth on the margin. **Flowers:** In heads with numerous small, yellow, ray flowers around the yellow disks. Heads surrounded by sticky, aromatic, green, leafy bracts that curl back and downward. **Fruits:** Single-seeded achenes with pappus of two to eight stiff awns as long as the disk flowers. **Flowering Season:** July to October. **Habitat/Range:** Dry, open, disturbed places in the plains and mountains from British Columbia to Minnesota and south to California and Texas.

FROM THE JOURNALS: Lewis's succinct description of gumweed on his transmittal list demonstrates his skill as a naturalist: "No. 40.—Taken at our camp at the Maha [Omaha Indian] vilage August 17th 1804. it is a handsome plant about

Curly-Cup Gumweed *Grindelia squarrosa*

Field Horsetail *Equisetum arvense*

3 feet high much branched bears a yellow circular flower carnished with meany small narrow ovate petals of the same colour, the leaf about an inch and a quarter in length[,] thick[,] smoth[,] indent finely, incompassing the stalk about ⅔'s and of a tongue-like form; ynnual plant is covered with a gumlike substance which adheres to the fingers and yealds a pleasant smell." This specimen, collected near present-day Homer, Nebraska, still exists. There are three sheets of it, all in good shape, including one with Lewis's original label.

Meadow Anemone

Anemone canadensis L.
BUTTERCUP FAMILY (Ranunculaceae)

Plants: Perennial herbs 8 to 24 inches tall with dense hair on leaves and stems. Leaves three to five lobed and sharply toothed. **Flowers:** White, solitary, or arranged in few-flowered cymes on the ends of long stalks. **Fruits:** Achenes arranged in tight, spiny heads that are often broader than they are long. **Flowering Season:** May to July. **Habitat/Range:** Wet prairies or woodlands from eastern Quebec to British Columbia and south to Maryland and New Mexico.

FROM THE JOURNALS: The expedition collected meadow anemone in the prairies near the Omaha-Indian village Tonwontonga between present-day Homer and Dakota City, Nebraska, on August 17, 1804. Lewis didn't mention this specimen in his transmittal list, but it still exists in the Lewis and Clark Herbarium.

Clark's journal for August 17 says, "Set the Praries on fire to bring the Mahars [Omaha] & Soues [Sioux] if any were near, this being the usial Signal." The explorers apprehended a deserter, Private Moses B. Reed, on this day. The following day was his trial and punishment, "run the Ganelet [gauntlet] four times thro." August 18, 1804, was also Lewis's thirtieth birthday.

Rocky Mountain Bee Plant

Cleome serrulata Pursh
CAPER FAMILY (Capparaceae)

Plants: Annual herbs 1 to 5 feet tall, have compound leaves with three narrow lance-shaped leaflets. **Flowers:** Clusters of pink (purple to white) flowers arranged in racemes on the ends of the stems, expanding upward as the long flowering-season progresses. Each flower has four sepals, four petals, and six stamens; filaments twice the length of the petals. **Fruits:** Beanlike capsules that arch downward from the stems. **Flowering Season:** June to August. **Habitat/Range:** Disturbed areas of prairies, open woodlands, and washes from Manitoba to Oklahoma and south to Washington and Arizona.

FROM THE JOURNALS: Three sheets of this species still exist. One sheet has an original label in Lewis's hand that simply states, "No. 43. August 25th growth of the open Praries." This, and a second sheet, is plant material they collected on August 25, 1804, above the mouth of the Vermillion River in present-day South Dakota. The third sheet includes a slip of paper with the following remarkable writing in Clark's hand: "Received of Captain Meriwether Lewis four hundred and Eight Dollars Thirty three and 1/3 cents in full of my monthly pay as an Indian enterpreter from the Seventh of April 180 five [1805] until the Sixteenth of August 180 six [1806] inclusive at 25$ pr month having Signed duplicate receipts of the same Rec. & for one horse Par pd. by him of me on Dec. 1805 for Public sum R. Lodge on." This slip of paper is evidently a copy of the receipt-of-payment to Toussaint

Meadow Anemone *Anemone canadensis*
—Steven Foster photo

Rocky Mountain Bee Plant *Cleome serrulata*

Rocky Mountain Bee Plant flower

Charbonneau, who was discharged from the expedition on August 17, 1806, when they returned to the vicinity of their 1804–5 winter quarters at Fort Mandan in North Dakota. A note on the back side of this slip of paper, in an unidentified hand, indicates that this third sheet of Rocky Mountain bee plant was collected on the White River of South Dakota, which the expedition passed on its return journey on August 29, 1806.

Clammy-Weed

Polanisia dodecandra (L.) DC.
Also *Polanisia trachysperma* T. and G.
CAPER FAMILY (Capparaceae)

Plants: Annual herbs covered with sticky, glandular hairs that give the plant a unique odor when brushed. Leaves compound, having three leaflets that taper toward the base. **Flowers:** Arranged in racemes, four sepals, four white or purplish petals, and ten to twenty, pink to purple stamens. **Fruits:** Capsules ¾ to 2¾ inches long that stand erect on the stems. **Flowering Season:** May to October **Habitat/Range:** Disturbed places and gravelly soils of the prairies and plains from southern Saskatchewan to Arkansas and northern Mexico, and west to the Rocky Mountains.

FROM THE JOURNALS: This specimen does not have a label, so we don't know for sure where or when it was collected. However, this specimen was mounted on the same herbarium sheet as Rocky Mountain bee plant *(Cleome serrulata)* until Thomas Meehan moved it to a separate sheet in 1898. The expedition may have collected the clammy-weed specimen at the same time and place, August 25, 1804, above the mouth of the Vermillion River in present-day South Dakota. Clark's notes for this date describe an overland foot-trip that he and Lewis made with a large party of the men to the "Spirit Mound," or "mound which the Indians Call Mountain of *little people*," above "White Stone Creek" (Vermillion River). After observing the mound Clark wrote, "we Concluded it was most probably the production of nature." Clark also described seeing vast numbers of martins and other birds, and tells of the party refreshing itself on "delisious froot Such as Grapes Plumbs, & Blue Currents." Lewis noted that "on our return from the mound of sperits saw the first *bats* that we had observed since we began to ascend the Missouri."

Lemon Scurfpea

Psoralidium lanceolatum (Pursh) Rydb.
Also *Psoralea lanceolata* Pursh
BEAN FAMILY (Fabaceae)

Plants: Perennial herbs covered with distinctive, dark, glandular dots; often grow in colonies. Stems erect, usually less than a foot tall, and with many branches. Leaves compound with three narrow leaflets. **Flowers:** Arranged in loose, slender racemes from the leaf axils. Petals are white with a purple-tipped keel. **Fruits:** Round pods less than ¼ inch in diameter, with dark, glandular dots like the leaves and sepals. **Flowering Season:** May to August. **Habitat/Range:** Sandy prairies, sand dunes, and stream valleys from southern Saskatchewan to southern Alberta and south to Iowa, Oklahoma, and New Mexico.

FROM THE JOURNALS: Botanists question whether Lewis and Clark actually collected the lemon-scurfpea specimen that exists in the Lewis and Clark Herbarium. It doesn't have a label to establish the date or place of its collection. According to Moulton, Lewis's specimen number 42 (now lost) was also lemon scurfpea. From

Clammy-Weed ***Polanisia dodecandra***

Lemon Scurfpea ***Psoralidium lanceolatum***

Lewis's transmittal list we know that specimen number 42 was collected on August 27, 1804, at the "Chalk Bluffs" near present-day Yankton, South Dakota. On this date Clark described these white bluffs: "Several mile in extent of white Clay Marl or Chalk, under this bank we discovered Large Stone resembling lime incrusted with a Substanc like Glass which I take to be Cabolt, also ore, three mes [miles] above this Bluff we Set the Prarie on fire, to let the Soues [Sioux] Know we wished to see them at two oClock an Indian Swam to the Perogue, we landed & two other Came they were boys, They informed us that the *Souex* were Camped near, on the R Jacke [James River] one Maha [Omaha Indian] boy informed us his nation was gorn to make a peace with the Pania's {Pawnee} we Send Sjt. Pryor . . . to the camp to See & invite their Great Chiefs to Come and Counsel with us at the Callemet Bluffs."

Evening Star or Blazing Star

Mentzelia decapetala (Pursh) Urban and Gilg.
STICKLEAF FAMILY (Loasaceae)

Plants: Biennial or perennial herbs covered with short, bristly hairs that are rough to the touch; thistlelike in appearance. Stems up to 2 feet tall, bearing leaves with a deep, wavy margin and/or coarse teeth. **Flowers:** Showy white to cream colored flowers 3 to 6 inches across with ten overlapping petals and numerous yellow stamens. **Fruits:** Cylindrical capsules 1¼ to 2 inches long that open and release seeds at valves on the top. **Flowering Season:** July to September. Flowers open in late afternoon and close around midnight, attracting night-flying pollinators. **Habitat/Range:** Exposed, disturbed places, often on substrate with high salt concentration.

FROM THE JOURNALS: Frederick Pursh provides our knowledge of Lewis's evening-star specimen. In his 1814 book, Pursh wrote a colorful narrative about evening star, which he named *Bartonia ornata* in honor of Dr. Benjamin Barton. "This beautiful plant, whose large white flowers open during the night and spread a most agreeable odour, was discovered in the year 1804, on the white bluffs near the Maha [Omaha] village, by the late M.Lewis, Esquire. In 1807 I made a drawing and description of it, for the publication of that gentleman's Tour across the Continent of America to the Pacific Ocean. . . . [The specimen was found] On Chalky soil and arid volcanic grounds, on the borders of the Missouri." Both the specimen and Pursh's drawing were lost. Pursh credited Lewis's collection as the source of the specimen that he described, and his comments on the year and location of its discovery lead us to believe that Lewis collected it in July or August, 1804, possibly near the Omaha Indian village of Tonwontonga, near present-day Homer, Nebraska, but more likely near the white chalk bluffs below the mouth of the James River near present-day Yankton, South Dakota.

Wild Four-O'Clock

Mirabilis nyctaginea (Michx.) MacM.
FOUR-O'CLOCK FAMILY (Nyctaginaceae)

Plants: Perennial herbs with erect stems 2 to 4 feet tall and widely spaced, opposite leaves. Leaves up to 4 inches long and have heart-shaped bases and pointed tips. **Flowers:** Arranged in umbels on the top of forked stems. Each cluster of three to five, pink to red or purple flowers is seated in a cuplike base of leafy bracts. **Fruits:** Yellowish or brown achenes about ⅛ inch long. **Flowering Season:** May to October. Flowers open in late afternoon. **Habitat/Range:** Disturbed places, especially on sandy soil, from Wisconsin to Montana and south to Tennessee and New Mexico.

FROM THE JOURNALS: The Lewis and Clark Herbarium includes two sheets of wild four-o'clock, both from material collected on September 1, 1804. The expedition had spent three days camped at Calumet Bluffs near present-day Yankton, South Dakota, where they counseled with the Yankton Sioux Indians. Clark described the trip of September 1: "pass Calumet Bluff of a yellowish read [red] & a

Top left: Evening Star or Blazing Star *Mentzelia decapetala*

Top right: Wild Four-O'Clock *Mirabilis nyctaginea*

Bottom right: White Four-O'Clock *Mirabilis albida* **A flower similar to Wild Four-O'Clock**

brownish white Hard clay, this Bluff is about 170 or 180 foot high . . . opposit the Bluffs is Situated a large Island Covered with timber close under the L. S. [larboard side] . . . this Clift is Called White Bear Clift one of those animals haveing been killed in a whole in it . . . Drewyer Killed a Buck Elk, it is not necessary to mention fish as we catch them at any place on the river, Camped at the lower point of Bonhomme Island." This island has since been inundated by Lewis and Clark Lake, which is above the Gavins Point Dam.

Fringed Sagewort

Artemisia frigida Willd.
ASTER FAMILY (Asteraceae)

Plants: Aromatic herbs or shrublets less than 2 feet tall, covered with white or grayish, soft, feltlike hair. Leaves are numerous and finely divided into many small, thin, narrow segments. **Flowers:** The tiny, yellow flowers are arranged in small, rayless heads in open or contracted panicles. **Fruits:** Small achenes without pappus. **Flowering Season:** August to September. **Habitat/Range:** Dry, open, often sandy plains from Wisconsin to Alaska and south to Kansas and Arizona.

FROM THE JOURNALS: There are two specimens of fringed sagewort in the Lewis and Clark Herbarium. Lewis collected the first one on September 2, 1804, while the party camped above "Bonhomme Island," now inundated by Lewis and Clark Lake; the second one he collected on October 3, 1804, on the High Plains. In his journals for September 2, Clark described in detail what he believed were ancient military fortifications, which today we believe are natural sand-ridges. Clark noted that their hunters "Killed four fat Elk on the Isld. We had them Jurked [jerked for drying] & the Skins Stretched to Cover the Perogues [open boats] water riseing, I observe *Bear grass* & Rhue in the Sides of the hills at Sunset the {wind} luled and cleared up cool—Aired the meet [meat] all in high Spirits." Clark's "Bear grass" was a common name for yucca *(Yucca glauca),* and by "rhue" Clark was referring to sumac (a *Rhus* species). These plants are common today around Lewis and Clark Lake.

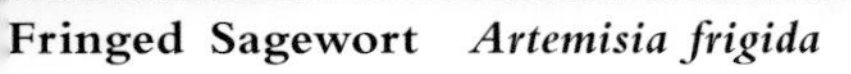

Fringed Sagewort *Artemisia frigida*

Yucca *Yucca glauca*

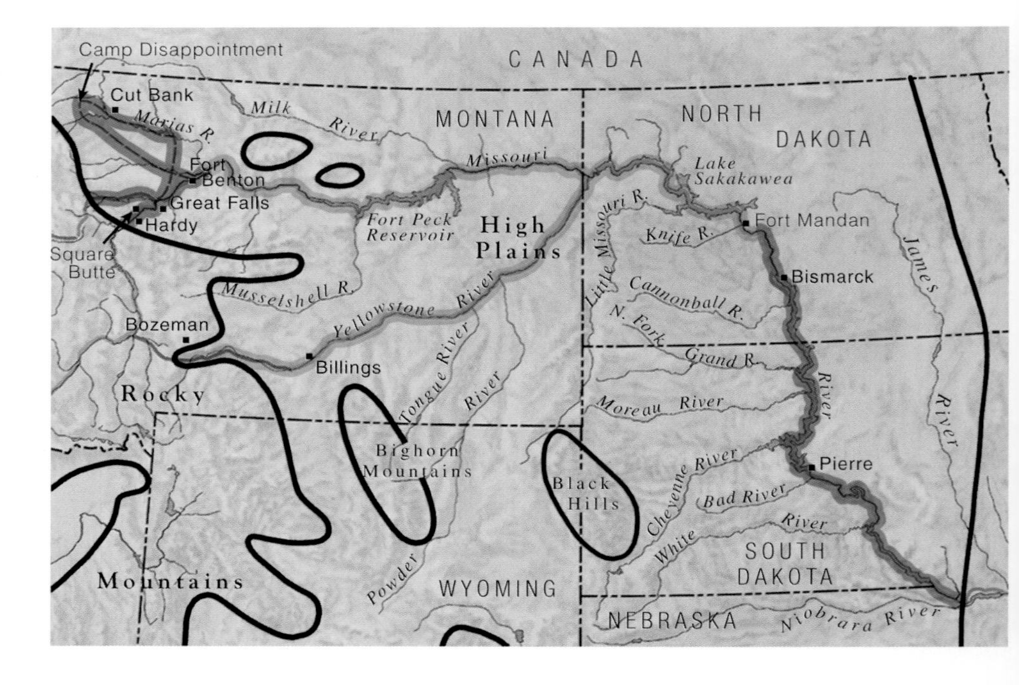

Amorpha nana[1]
Corispermum hyssopifolium[2]
Shepherdia argentea
Quercus macrocarpa
Rosa arkansana
Zizania aquatica
Liatris aspera
Solidago rigida
Astragalus canadensis
Artemisia dracunculus
Machaeranthera pinnatifida
Astragalus missouriensis
Liatris pycnostachya
Gutierrezia sarothrae
Psoralidium tenuiflorum
Atriplex canescens
Chrysothamnus nauseosus
Salvia reflexa
Amorpha fruticosa[3]
Aster oblongifolius
Rhus aromatica
Artemisia ludoviciana[4]
Artemisia cana
Juniperus scopulorum
Artemisia longifolia
Artemisia frigida[4]
Euphorbia cyathophora
Nicotiana quadrivalvis
Nicotiana rustica[5]
Juniperus horizontalis
Juniperus communis
Pediomelum argophyllum

Aquilegia canadensis
Echinacea angustifolia
Artemisia campestris
Arctostaphylos uva-ursi
Lilium philadelphicum
Zea mays

Polygala alba
Populus deltoides[3]
Euphorbia marginata[4]
Prunus virginiana
Pediomelum esculentum
Glycyrrhiza lepidota
Lupinus pusillus

Populus angustifolia
Potentilla pensylvanica
Ribes cereum
Opuntia polyacantha
Helianthus annuus
Stipa comata
Linum lewisii
Hordeum jubatum
Oenothera caespitosa
Sarcobatus vermiculatus
Atriplex gardneri
Dalea purpurea[4]
Symphoricarpos occidentalis[4]
Sphaeralcea coccinea
Krascheninnikovia lanata
Senecio canus
Astragalus tenellus
Allium textile

1. *Not included in this book.*
2. *Not included in this book. Date and place of collection unknown.*
3. See Eastern Deciduous Forest.
4. See Tallgrass Prairie.
5. See Nicotiana quadrivalvis.

THE HIGH PLAINS

The High Plains is a vast, dry region that stretches from Canada to Texas. Lewis and Clark passed through this region as they traversed the present-day states of Nebraska, South Dakota, North Dakota, and Montana. In these states the High Plains consist of flat or gently sloping benchlands interspersed with rolling hills, canyons, and buttes. Elevation ranges from 2,500 to 5,500 feet above sea level. This area has a temperate, semiarid climate where evaporation exceeds the annual precipitation of 10 to 25 inches. Winters are cold, and the summers are warm to hot. High winds, hail, blizzards, tornadoes, dust storms, and drought are common.

The vegetation is short-grass prairie consisting of sodgrasses like buffalo grass and blue grama, and also bunchgrasses like bluebunch wheatgrass and needle-and-thread grass. Low shrubs, especially sagebrush, are often scattered among the grasses, and in some places they dominate the landscape. Numerous wildflowers like purple coneflower, sunflower, and dotted gayfeather color the plains in their blooming season. Trees are scarce, usually restricted to the riparian zone along the margins of streams and ponds. Plains cottonwood is the most common tree.

Lewis and Clark first entered the High Plains on September 4, 1804, as they traveled up the Missouri River past the mouth of the Niobrara River in present-day South Dakota and Nebraska. They endured the bitter winter of 1804-5 in the High Plains at Fort Mandan in present-day North Dakota, and they left the region above the "great falls of the Missouri" River as they entered the Rocky Mountains at "pine island rapids" near present-day Hardy, Montana, on July 17, 1805.

Lewis reentered the High Plains on July 8, 1806, when he dropped out of the Rocky Mountains below Lewis and Clark Pass between present-day Lincoln and Simms, Montana. Here he crossed the Dearborn River and followed the Sun River to Great Falls, Montana. Clark and his separate party returned to the High Plains on July 15, 1806, when they left the Rocky Mountains between present-day Bozeman and Livingston, Montana, and began to follow the Yellowstone River for a rendezvous with Lewis at its confluence with the Missouri. The parties rejoined below the mouth of the Yellowstone River on August 12, 1806, and exited the High Plains below the mouth of the Niobrara River on September 1, 1806.

They encountered many new plant species on the High Plains. Thirty-four of them were listed on Lewis's transmittal list and were shipped from Fort Mandan on April 7 and arrived in Philadelphia on November 16, 1805. Specimens for all but three of these species are still intact in the Lewis and Clark Herbarium. Inexplicably, the explorers collected additional plants in 1804 in the High Plains that Lewis did not mention in his transmittal list. These dated specimens, also in the Herbarium and discussed below, were collected in September and October 1804 but lack specimen numbers to link them to the Fort Mandan shipment.

We are not so fortunate concerning the plant collections they made above Fort Mandan in the spring and summer of 1805. When the explorers reached the "great falls of the Missouri," they placed the plants they had collected to that point in storage caches meant to be retrieved on the homeward journey. When they opened the caches in July 1806 they discovered that moisture had destroyed the plant specimens that Captain Lewis had so meticulously preserved. How many plant specimens were lost? We will never know the answer. However, Frederick Pursh, in the preface to his 1814 *Flora Americae Septentrionalis,* said that he had received about 150 specimens from Lewis that had been collected "during the rapid return of the expedition from the Pacific Ocean . . . [whereas] A much more extensive one, made on their slow ascent towards the Rocky mountains . . . had unfortunately been lost, by being deposited . . . at the foot of those mountains." From Pursh's statement, we can infer that the "extensive" High Plains collection numbered more than 150 specimens.

From the information available we know the expedition collected at least fifty-eight plant species on the High Plains. Forty-four of these specimens still exist in the Lewis and Clark Herbarium. Botanists have also identified fourteen of the lost specimens—three by studying Lewis's Fort Mandan transmittal list and eleven from references in Pursh's 1814 book (see the *High Plains Table* in the *Appendix*).

I included all but three of the species the explorers collected in the High Plains—hyssop-leaved tickseed *(Corispermum hyssopifolium),* dwarf wild Indigo *(Amorpha nana),* and small Arikara tobacco *(Nicotiana rustica).* Seven of the species they collected were duplicates of species I discussed in other regions: *indigo bush* and *plains cottonwood* in the *Eastern Deciduous Forest; prairie sagewort, fringed sagewort, purple prairie clover, snow-on-the-mountain,* and *western snowberry* in the *Tallgrass Prairie.*

I discuss the remaining forty-eight species collected on the High Plains below. To these I have added five species that are mentioned in the journals but we aren't sure the explorers ever collected. I arranged these plants geographically from east to west, according to where they were first collected or discussed in the journals, starting along the Missouri River at its confluence with the Niobrara River.

The High Plains

White Cliffs of the Missouri River in Montana

Silver Buffaloberry

Shepherdia argentea (Pursh) Nutt.
OLEASTER FAMILY (Elaeagnaceae)

Plants: Silvery, erect shrubs with stiff branches ending in sharp spines. Leaves have a grayish green color, arranged in pairs opposite each other on the stems. Leaves oblong with rounded ends and entire margins. **Flowers:** Small, yellowish, appearing just as the leaf buds burst. **Fruits:** Reddish orange, tart, juicy berries. **Flowering Season:** May to June. **Habitat/Range:** Ravines and dry hillsides from Minnesota to British Columbia and south to Nebraska, New Mexico, and California.

FROM THE JOURNALS: Two sheets of silver buffaloberry, collected at the mouth of the Niobrara River in present-day Nebraska on September 4, 1804, still exist. One has an original label in Lewis's hand. He wrote that specimen number 39 was "obtained at the mouth of the River Quiccourre [Niobrara] from which place upwards it is abundant in the Missouri bottoms it is a pleasant burry to eat—it has much the flavor of the cranbury, and continues on the brush through the winter—this is an evergreen shrub." Clark noted this about buffaloberry on October 1, 1804: "The Mandans Call a red berry common to the upper part of the Missouri *As-say* the engages [French boatmen] call the Same berry grease de Buff—grows in great abundance a makes a Delightfull Tart."

The mouth of the "River Quiccourre" marks the boundary between the Tallgrass Prairie and the drier High Plains. As they entered the High Plains the explorers recorded their first sighting of a mule deer on September 5, 1804. They anticipated many new plant and animal discoveries ahead.

Bur Oak

Quercus macrocarpa Michx.
OAK FAMILY (Fagaceae)

Plants: Trees with large, glossy leaves that have lobes with deep sinuses, which often extend more than halfway to the midrib, and a large terminal lobe. **Flowers:** Inconspicuous, unisexual flowers appearing with the leaves in spring. Male flowers in catkins that hang downward. Female flowers singly or in small clusters in leaf axils. **Fruits:** One-seeded nuts embedded in, and one-half to two-thirds covered by, a fringed cup. Mature the year of flowering. **Flowering Season:** April to May. **Habitat/Range:** Woods and valley floors, often forming savannahs in grasslands, from New Brunswick to Saskatchewan and south to southeastern Montana, Nebraska, Texas, and east to Maryland.

FROM THE JOURNALS: Of the two specimens of bur oak that still exist, one has an original Lewis label: "No. 34. The leaf of oak which is common to the Praries 5th September 1804." Lewis collected the other specimen at the same time and place, but it has a Pursh label. Lewis described bur oak in his journal for September 16, 1804: "a considerable quanty of a small species of white oak which is loaded with acorns of an excellent flavor very little of the bitter roughness of the nuts of most species of oak, the leaf of this oak is small pale green and deeply indented, it seldom

Silver Buffaloberry *Shepherdia argentea*

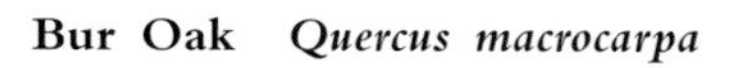

Bur Oak *Quercus macrocarpa*

rises higher than thirty feet is much branched, the bark is rough and thick and of a light colour; the cup which contains the acorn is fringed on it's edges and imbraces the nut about one half; the acorns were now falling, and we concluded that the number of deer which we saw here had been induced thither by the acorns of which they are remarkably fond. almost every species of wild game is fond of the acorn, the Buffaloe Elk, deer, bear, turkies, ducks, pigegians and even the wolves feed on them."

Prairie Wild Rose

Rosa arkansana Porter
ROSE FAMILY (Rosaceae)

Plants: Low shrubs 4 to 20 inches tall. Stems lined with slender, unequal prickles. Alternate, pinnately compound leaves that have nine to eleven leaflets. **Flowers:** Clustered three or more at the ends of branches; pink to white or deep rose color. **Fruits:** Red, fleshy hips containing fifteen to thirty achenes. **Flowering Season:** May to August. **Habitat/Range:** Prairies, open woodlands, and thickets from New York to Alberta and south to Indiana and New Mexico.

FROM THE JOURNALS: A specimen of prairie wild rose with two labels, indicating that there were originally two specimens, still exists. The earliest dated-label (in Pursh's hand) places the collection above the mouth of the Niobrara River in present-day Nebraska or South Dakota on September 5, 1804. The second is an original label on which Lewis stated: "No. 50 Octobr 18th The small Rose of the prairies it rises from 12 to 14 Inches high does not vine." This latter collection was made near the Cannon Ball River in Sioux County, North Dakota. Prairie wild rose is today the floral emblem of North Dakota.

On September 5, 1804, Lewis described seeing pronghorn antelope: "Saw some wild goats or antelopes on the hill above the Glauber Salts Springs they ran off we could not discover them sufficiently distinctly to discribe even their colour their track is as large as a deer reather broader & more blont at the point—This day one of our hunters brought us a Serpent beautifully variagated with small black spots of a romboydal form on a light yellow white ground." The "Serpent" was a bull or gopher snake that Lewis measured at 4 feet 6 inches long.

Wild Rice

Zizania aquatica L.
GRASS FAMILY (Poaceae)

Plants: Annual aquatic grasses with solitary, stout, hollow stems 2 to 7 feet tall. Leaf blades up to 3 feet long, sheaths with conspicuous cross nerves. **Flowers:** Arranged in large panicles of unisexual spikelets; the drooping, reddish male spikelets arranged below the more upright, lighter female ones. **Fruits:** A dark grain. **Flowering Season:** August to September. **Habitat/Range:** Wetlands from southern Canada into the United States east of the Rocky Mountains.

FROM THE JOURNALS: A wild rice specimen still exists with an original label, on which Lewis wrote, "No. 59. 8th Sept. the growth of moist and very wet prairies." On September 8, 1804, the expedition camped on Boat Island (now Chicot, or Strehlow Island) on the present-day Gregory-Charles Mix County line in South Dakota. No mention is made of the collection. Clark walked on shore that day to observe the prairie dogs and pronghorn antelope. He saw a great number of buffalo and white wolves. Lewis stayed near the boats that day and killed a buffalo.

Prairie Wild Rose *Rosa arkansana*

Wild Rice *Zizania aquatica*

Rough Blazing Star

Liatris aspera Michx.
ASTER FAMILY (Asteraceae)

Plants: Perennial herbs with a single, erect stem 1 to 4 feet tall. Leaves narrow, up to 16 inches long, but progressively smaller towards the top of the stem. **Flowers:** Heads have only disk flowers (no rays) arranged in cylindrical, spikelike clusters of sixteen to thirty-five pinkish purple florets. **Fruits:** Achenes with finely barbed pappus. **Flowering Season:** August to October. **Habitat/Range:** Dry, sandy soils of prairies and open woods of the eastern Great Plains, east to South Carolina and north to eastern Canada.

FROM THE JOURNALS: A specimen of rough blazing star still exists with a label on which Lewis wrote, "No. 58 12th September. growth of high & dry prarie." On September 12, 1804, the expedition passed "Troublesom Island," now known as Durex or Hiram Wood Island and inundated by Lake Francis Case, in present-day Brule County, South Dakota, below the mouth of the White River. Clark wrote that "at the upper pt of this Island the river was so crouded with Sand bars that we found great dificulty in getting the boat over, she turned on the Sand 4 times and was verry near turning over. We camped on the L. S. [larboard side] near a village of Prarie Dogs."

Rigid Goldenrod

Solidago rigida L.
ASTER FAMILY (Asteraceae)

Plants: Perennial herbs, 1 to 5 feet tall, densely covered with short hairs. Leaves stiff and leathery, oval in shape with pointed tips. **Flowers:** Dense clusters of orangish yellow heads, arranged in flat-topped clusters on top of the stems. **Fruits:** Achenes, prominently ribbed and smooth. **Flowering Season:** August to October. **Habitat/Range:** Dry, rocky, or sandy, open places from New York to Georgia and west to Alberta and New Mexico.

FROM THE JOURNALS: A fine specimen of rigid goldenrod exists with a label that says, "High dry prairies Septb: 12, 1804." This label places its location in Brule County, South Dakota, below the mouth of the White River, which the explorers reached on September 15, 1804. On September 12 Clark wrote: "we Camped on the L. S. opsd. [larboard side, opposite] A Village of Barking Prarie Squriels I walked out in the morn:g and Saw Several Villages of those little animals, also a great number of grous & 3 foxes, and observed Slate & Coal mixed, Some verry high hills on each Side of the river. Rains a little all day." The "grous" were likely sharp-tailed grouse, an undocumented species before Lewis and Clark. The Captains later attempted to send a live sharp-tailed grouse back to President Jefferson on the keelboat they sent from Fort Mandan in 1805. Although the sharp-tailed grouse died in the four-month voyage, one of the magpies they shipped survived.

Rough Blazing Star *Liatris aspera*

Rigid Goldenrod *Solidago rigida*

Canada Milkvetch

Astragalus canadensis L.
BEAN FAMILY (Fabaceae)

Plants: Perennial herbs that often form patches. Stems 1 to 4 feet tall. Leaves alternate, pinnately compound with fifteen to thirty-five leaflets. **Flowers:** Greenish white to cream colored. Arranged in dense racemes up to 8 inches long that contain many flowers. **Fruits:** Rounded pods, less than 1 inch long, with pointed tips. **Flowering Season:** May to August. **Habitat/Range:** Moist prairies, riverbanks, and open woods from British Columbia to Hudson's Bay and the Atlantic Coast, and south to California and Texas.

FROM THE JOURNALS: A specimen of Canada milkvetch still exists with an original label on which Lewis wrote, "No. 46 The growth of the open praries taken 15th of Septr. 1804." On this date Clark described passing the mouth of the White River in present-day Lyman County, South Dakota: "Capt Lewis and my Self went up this river a Short distance and Crossed, found that this differed verry much from the Plat or que Courre [Niobrara], threw out but little Sand . . . the water confind within 150 yards, the current regular & Swift much resemblig the Missourie . . . passed a Small (2) Island Covered with Ceeder on I Saw great numbers of Rabits & Grapes . . . Camped on the S. S. [starboard side] opposite the mouth of a large Creek on which there is more timber than is usial on Creeks this size . . . I killed a Buck Elk & Deer, this evening verry Cold, Great many wolves of Different Sorts howling about us." The next day they named the creek "Corvus Creek" in honor of the magpies they saw there. It was later renamed American or American Crow Creek. It flows near present-day Oacoma, South Dakota.

Silky Wormwood

Artemisia dracunculus L.
ASTER FAMILY (Asteraceae)

Plants: Perennial herbs with reddish, clustered or unbranched stems, 1 to 3 feet tall. Leaves green, ¾ to 3 ½ inches long, mostly entire but a few of the lower ones sometimes have one to three basal lobes. **Flowers:** In small, yellow, rayless heads arranged in open panicles with numerous lateral branches. **Fruits:** Small, smooth, oval achenes. **Flowering Season:** August to October. **Habitat/Range:** Dry prairies and mountain slopes from the Yukon to Baja, California, east to Manitoba, and south to northern Mexico.

FROM THE JOURNALS: A specimen of silky wormwood exists with an original label in Lewis's hand. He wrote: "No. 52 Sept. 15th 1804. growth of the open Plains." On this date the expedition passed the White River and camped on the Missouri opposite the mouth of "Corvus Creek" (now American or American Crow Creek) near present-day Oacoma, South Dakota (see *From the Journals* under *Canada Milkvetch*).

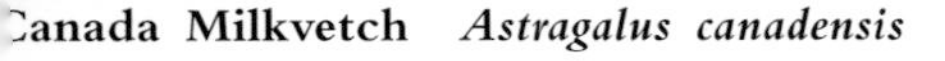

Canada Milkvetch *Astragalus canadensis*

Silky Wormwood *Artemisia dracunculus*

On September 14 Clark killed a male pronghorn antelope and expedition-member Shields killed a white-tailed jackrabbit. Both of these animals, common to the High Plains, were previously undocumented species. Lewis described the physical characteristics of the white-tailed jackrabbit in great detail in his notes that day. He also wrote, "it's food is grass or herbs—it resorts the open plains, is extreemly fleet and never burrows or takes shelter in the ground when pursued, I measured the leaps of one . . . and found them 21 feet . . . they apear to run with more ease and to bound with greater agility than any anamall I ever saw."

Spiny Goldenweed

Machaeranthera pinnatifida (Hook.) Shinners
Also *Haplopappus spinulosus* (Pursh) DC.
ASTER FAMILY (Asteraceae)

Plants: Perennial herbs 4 to 24 inches tall and usually covered with minute glandular and woolly hairs that give the plant a white or gray cast. Leaves are finely dissected into numerous segments with spiny tips. **Flowers:** Showy heads with twenty-five to thirty yellow rays surrounding a yellow disk. **Fruits:** Narrow, top-shaped achenes with pappus of a few yellowish brown bristles. **Flowering Season:** May to September. **Habitat/Range:** Open prairies and plains from Saskatchewan and Alberta, south to Texas and Baja, California.

FROM THE JOURNALS: A specimen of spiny goldenweed still exists with a label in Pursh's hand. He stated, "Prairies, Septb: 15, 1804." (See *From the Journals* under *Canada Milkvetch*.) On September 16, 1804, the expedition moved their camp across the Missouri River and camped 1¼ miles above the mouth of "Corvus Creek." Lewis recorded the observations of two of the men, Sergeant Gass and Reubin Fields, who had explored the White River and adjacent plains: "these extensive planes had been lately birnt and the grass had sprung up and was about three inches high. vast herds of Buffaloe deer Elk and Antilopes were seen feeding in every direction as far as the eye of the observer could reach."

Missouri Milkvetch

Astragalus missouriensis Nutt.
BEAN FAMILY (Fabaceae)

Plants: Perennial herbs, low and trailing on the ground. Leaves alternate and pinnately compound with nine to seventeen leaflets covered with fine, closely appressed, axe-shaped hair. **Flowers:** Rose to purple, arranged in loose racemes of three to nine flowers. **Fruits:** Legumes about 1 inch long, body cross-corrugated. **Flowering Season:** March to July. **Habitat/Range:** Prairies, plains, and rocky bluffs from southern Manitoba to Alberta and south to Oklahoma and New Mexico.

FROM THE JOURNALS: A specimen of Missouri milkvetch exists with an original label on which Lewis wrote: "No. 36 18th of Septr. The growth of the high Prarie." On this date the expedition was a few miles above the White River near present-day Oacoma, South Dakota. The day before, on September 17, Lewis left camp before sunrise with six of his best hunters, hoping to kill a female pronghorn antelope; he had already collected a male. On this outing Lewis described a grove of wild plum trees loaded with ripe fruit, and "immence herds of Buffaloe deer Elk and Antelopes which we saw in every direction feeding on the hills and plains. I do not think I exagerate when I estimate the number of Buffaloe which could be compreed at one view to amount to 3000." He also described a pronghorn antelope: "I had this day an opportunity of witnessing the agility and superior fleetness of this anamal which was to me really astonishing . . . I think I can safely venture the ascertion that the speed of this anamal is equal if not superior to that of the finest blooded courser."

Spiny Goldenweed *Machaeranthera pinnatifida*

Missouri Milkvetch *Astragalus missouriensis*

Tall Blazing Star

Liatris pycnostachya Michx.
ASTER FAMILY (Asteraceae)

Plants: Perennial herbs with stiff, single stems 1 to 5 feet tall. Leaves numerous, narrow, and up to 16 inches long but progressively smaller up the stem. **Flowers:** Pinkish purple disk-flowers in small heads arranged in long, cylinder-shaped spikes that each have five to seven heads. **Fruits:** Achenes with tiny barbs on the pappus bristles. **Flowering Season:** July to September. **Habitat/Range:** Moist prairies from the eastern one-third of the Great Plains east to Kentucky and south to Louisiana.

FROM THE JOURNALS: A specimen of tall blazing star still exists with the original label on which Lewis wrote, "No. 35 Sept. 18th growth of the praries." On September 18, 1804, the expedition was traveling near present-day Oacoma, South Dakota. Lewis wrote that he "saw the first brant [Canada geese] on their return from the north." Clark wrote about a walk on the shore: "Saw Goats, Elk, Buffalow, Black tail Deer, & the Common Deer, I Killed a Prarie Wollf, aboat the Size of a gray fox bushey tail head & ear like a wolf, Some fur Burrows in the ground and barks like a Small Dog. what has been taken heretofore for the Fox was those wolves, and no Foxes has been Seen." Clark's "prarie wollf" was a coyote.

Broom Snakeweed

Gutierrezia sarothrae (Pursh) Britton
ASTER FAMILY (Asteraceae)

Plants: Perennial shrubs, usually less than 2 feet tall, many branched with narrow, green, resinous leaves. **Flowers:** Small heads in flat-topped clusters on the ends of the stems. Heads have three to eight yellow rays surrounding a yellow disk. **Fruits:** Achenes with pappus of eight to ten pointed scales. **Flowering Season:** August to October. **Habitat/Range:** Dry plains from Manitoba to northern Mexico and west to Washington and California.

FROM THE JOURNALS: Two specimens of broom snakeweed exist. One has an original label on which Lewis wrote, "No. 59. 1804. 19th Septbr—the growth of high and bear praries which produce little grass, generally mineral with earth." The second specimen has a label with similar information that Pursh copied. On this date the expedition traveled about 26 miles and camped just below the "Commencemt of the Big bend" of the Missouri River near present-day Lower Brule, South Dakota. Clark's notes described their success in hunting that day: "I Killed a fat Buffalow Cow, and a fat Buck elk, york my Servent Killed a Buck, the Huntes Killed 4 Deer, & the boat Crew killed 2 Buffalow Swiming the river." Clark also described walking on shore past a "place that all nations who meet are at peace with each other, Called the Seaux pass of the 3 rivers [Crow, Elk, and Campbell Creeks]."

Tall Blazing Star *Liatris pycnostachya*

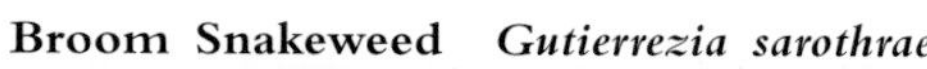

Broom Snakeweed *Gutierrezia sarothrae*

Slender Flowered Scurfpea

Psoralidium tenuiflorum (Pursh) Rydb.
Also *Psoralea tenuiflora* Pursh
BEAN FAMILY (Fabaceae)

Plants: Perennial herbs with many branched stems 1 to 3 feet tall. Leaves compound with three to five leaflets that radiate from a common point. Also known as *wild alfalfa,* which the plants resemble. **Flowers:** Arranged in loose racemes of widely spaced, small blue to purple flowers. Sepals have glandular dots. **Fruits:** Small, smooth pods with glandular dots and short beaks. **Flowering Season:** May to July. **Habitat/Range:** Prairies, plains, and open woodlands from Montana to northern Mexico and east to Minnesota and Indiana.

FROM THE JOURNALS: Two specimens of slender flowered scurfpea still exist. Each specimen has a label in Pursh's hand that places their collection on September 21, 1804, on the Big Bend of the Missouri River, above present-day Lower Brule, South Dakota. The expedition traveled 30 miles around the Big Bend on September 20, 1804, and camped on a sandbar. Clark's notes for September 21, 1804, described a near calamity while camped there: "This morng [morning] at a half past one oClock the Sand bar on which we Camped began to give way, which alarmed the Serjt on guard & the noise waked me, I got up and by the light of the moon observed that the Sand was giving away both above & beloy and would Swallow our Perogues [open boats] in a few minits, ordered all hands on board and pushed off we had not got to the opposite Shore before pt. of our Camp fel into the river. we proceeded on to the Gorge of the bend & brackfast, the Distance of this bend around is 30 miles, and 1¼ miles thro."

Four Wing Saltbush

Atriplex canescens (Pursh) Nutt.
GOOSEFOOT FAMILY (Chenopodiaceae)

Plants: Shrubs, woody throughout, 1 to 4 feet tall. Leaves alternate, narrow, grayish green, up to 2 inches long. **Flowers:** Unisexual. Male flowers in panicles of dense spikes, five stamens each. Female flowers in short spikes in the leaf axils. Below each tiny flower is a large four-winged bract. **Fruits:** Enclosed by the prominent four-winged bracts. **Flowering Season:** May to August. **Habitat/Range:** Dry, alkaline flats and bluffs from eastern Washington to Baja, California, east to Saskatchewan, and south to Texas and Mexico.

FROM THE JOURNALS: A specimen of four wing saltbush exists with an original Lewis label and a copy in Pursh's hand that place the collection on September 21, 1804. The expedition was camped near the present-day Joe Creek boat ramp across the Missouri River from Clark's "Tylors River," which is now known as Medicine Creek. Clark's notes for September 20 described a walk on shore: "the Prarie below & Sides of the hills containing great quantites of the Prickly Piar which nearly ruind my feet . . . I Saw Several Goats Elk Ders &c. & Buffalow in every Derection feeding. R. Fields Killed a Deer & 2 Goats one a female, which differs from the male as to Size being Something Smaller, Small Straight horns without any black about the neck."

Slender Flowered Scurfpea *Psoralidium tenuiflorum*

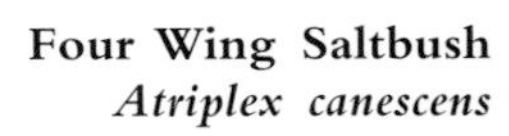

Four Wing Saltbush
Atriplex canescens

Rubber Rabbitbrush

Chrysothamnus nauseosus (Pall.) Britt.
Also *Ericameria nauseosa* (Pall. Ex Pursh) G. L. Nesom and Baird
ASTER FAMILY (Asteraceae)

Plants: Shrubs 1 to 3 feet tall. Twigs covered with dense, white, feltlike hair. Leaves narrow, less than 2½ inches long, grayish green in color. **Flowers:** Rayless heads with five yellow disk flowers per head. Bracts keeled and overlapping in vertical rows. **Fruits:** Achenes with pappus of slender, hairlike bristles. **Flowering Season:** June to September. **Habitat/Range:** Dry grasslands and open woods of plains, valleys, and foothills from southern British Columbia to Saskatchewan and south to California, Texas, and southern Mexico.

FROM THE JOURNALS: There are six specimens of rubber rabbitbrush in the Lewis and Clark Herbarium, more than any other species. The explorers collected two of the specimens on September 21, 1804, on the Big Bend of the Missouri River in either the present-day Crow Creek or Lower Brule Indian Reservation below Pierre, South Dakota. We believe they collected two additional specimens on October 2, 1804, above the mouth of the Cheyenne River in the present-day Cheyenne River Indian Reservation above Pierre. We think they collected the final two specimens in October 1804 in either North or South Dakota, but the exact place and date are unknown.

Original labels associated with two of these specimens, in Lewis's hand, provide some interesting information: "No. 32. Specimens of aromatic plants on which the a{n}telope feeds—these were obtained 21st of Sept. 1805 {1804}. at the upper part of the bigg bend of the Missouri . . . No. 54. October 2ed—grows from 18 inches to 2 ½ feet, many stalks from the same root, from which they issue near the groun{d}—the radix [root] perennial. The goat or antelope feed on it in the winter. It is the growth of the high bluffs."

Lance-Leaved Sage

Salvia reflexa Hornem.
MINT FAMILY (Lamiaceae)

Plants: Strongly scented annual herbs 4 to 28 inches tall. Stems square. Leaves entire or somewhat toothed, in opposite pairs less than 2½ inches long. **Flowers:** Blue, short-lived, arranged in slender racemes on the ends of branches. Petal tube has two lobes, the lower as long as the tube. Two stamens. **Fruits:** Smooth, round, light-tan nutlets. **Flowering Season:** June to July. **Habitat/Range:** Dry, disturbed places at low elevation from Wisconsin to Texas and west to Montana and Arizona.

FROM THE JOURNALS: Two specimens of lance-leaved sage exist with labels in Pursh's hand that place the collection on September 21, 1804, at the Big Bend of the Missouri River above present-day Lower Brule, South Dakota. Clark remarked in his journals for the day: "the Cat fish not So plenty . . . & much Smaller than usial, Great nunbers of Brant & plover, also goat and black tail [mule] Deer. . . . The Praries in this quarter Contains Great qts. of Prickley Pear."

Rubber Rabbitbrush *Chrysothamnus nauseosus*

Lance-Leaved Sage
Salvia reflexa

Aromatic Aster

Aster oblongifolius Nutt.
ASTER FAMILY (Asteraceae)

Plants: Fragrant perennial herbs, less than 2½ feet tall. Leaves narrow, linear, up to 3 inches long and less than 1 inch wide, with an entire margin and no petiole. Upper leaves, stems, and flower bracts have small glands. **Flowers:** Arranged in panicles of heads, each with about thirty purple ray-florets surrounding the yellow disk-florets. **Fruits:** Small, flattish achenes with yellowish white, hairlike bristles. **Flowering Season:** September to November. **Habitat/Range:** Prairies and savannahs from Pennsylvania to Alabama and west to eastern Montana and New Mexico.

FROM THE JOURNALS: A specimen of aromatic aster exists. The explorers collected it on September 21, 1804, at the Big Bend of the Missouri River above present-day Lower Brule, South Dakota. Clark's notes for the day described the scene: "both abov and below the bend is a butifull inclined Plain in which there is great numbers of Buffalow, Elk & Goats in view feeding & Scipping on those Plains Grouse, Larks & the Prarie bird is Common in those Plains. We proceeded on passed a (1) willow Island below the mouth of a Small river called Tylors R [Medicine Creek] about 35 yds. wide which coms in on the L. S. [larboard side] 6 miles above the Gorge of the bend."

Fragrant Sumac

Rhus aromatica Aiton
Also *Rhus trilobata* Nutt.
SUMAC FAMILY (Anacardiaceae)

Plants: Densely branching shrubs from 3 to 6 feet tall; skunky fragrance when broken or bruised. Leaves compound with three leaflets that vary from simple to lobed and/or toothed. **Flowers:** Yellow, small, and arranged in compact, spikelike clusters formed from the previous year's twigs. **Fruits:** Red, round, single-seeded drupes with glands on the skin giving them a sour, lemonlike flavor. **Flowering Season:** April to June. **Habitat/Range:** Plains, rocky hillsides, canyons, and open woods in much of the United States, adjacent Canada, and northern Mexico.

FROM THE JOURNALS: A specimen of fragrant sumac, with an original label, still exists. Lewis wrote, "No. 57. October 1st 1804 first discovered in the neighborhood of the Kancez River [which they reached on June 26, 1804]—now very common, the growth of the little cops which appear on the steep declivities of the hills where they are sheltered from the ravages of the fire." The expedition passed the mouth of the Cheyenne River on October 1, 1804, and camped near Lookout Creek (probably present-day No Heart Creek) in Dewey County, South Dakota. Clark's journal for the day described their campsite: "opposit a Tradeing house, where a Mr. Valles & 2 men had Some fiew goods to trade with the Soiux . . . Mr. Vallie informed us he wintered last winter 300 Legus [leagues] up the Cheymne River under the Black mountains. . . . The Chyenne Nation has about 300 Lodges hunt the Buffalow, Steel horses from the Spanish Settlements."

Aromatic Aster *Aster oblongifolius*

Fragrant Sumac *Rhus aromatica*

Silver Sagebrush

Artemisia cana Pursh
ASTER FAMILY (Asteraceae)

Plants: Aromatic shrubs usually less than 3 feet tall. Leaves up to 3 inches long, linear to lance shaped, and covered with fine, silvery hair. **Flowers:** Numerous, small, rayless heads arranged in small, spikelike clusters forming narrow, leafy panicles. **Fruits:** Very small, smooth achenes without a pappus. **Flowering Season:** August to September. **Habitat/Range:** Plains, foothills, and the bottoms of draws, especially on clayey soils, from Saskatchewan to Nebraska and New Mexico, and west to British Columbia and California.

FROM THE JOURNALS: Four specimens of silver sagebrush still exist. Lewis described the first specimen on a label as "No. 60 1804 October 1st another variety of wild sage growth of high and bottom prairies." On the second specimen's label, specimen number 55, he wrote, "October 2ed 1804 growth of the high Bluffs." The expedition collected the other two at the same time and in the same place as the October 2 specimen.

On April 14, 1805, while camped near the mouth of the Little Missouri River in present-day North Dakota, Lewis described several *Artemisia* species: "on these hills many aromatic herbs are seen; resembling in taste, smel and appearance, the sage, hysop, wormwood, southernwood, and two other herbs which are strangers to me; the one [big sagebrush, *A. tridentata*] resembling the camphor in taste and smell, rising to the hight of 2 or 3 feet; the other [silver sagebrush] about the same size, has a long, narrow, smooth, soft leaf of an agreeable smel and flavor; of this last the Atelope is very fond; they feed on it, and perfume the hair of their foreheads and necks with it by rubing against it."

Rocky Mountain Juniper or Cedar

Juniperus scopulorum Sarg.
CYPRESS FAMILY (Cupressaceae)

Plants: Small, aromatic, evergreen shrubs or trees up to 50 feet tall and 3 feet or more in diameter. Leaves scalelike, closely appressed, but barely overlap. **Flowers:** unisexual; female cones round and fleshy, like powdery blue berries with straight stalks; male cones much smaller and yellowish brown. **Fruits:** Blue to purple, fleshy, berrylike cones with one to three seeds each. **Flowering Season:** April to May. **Habitat/Range:** Dry, rocky canyons, bluffs, rivers, and open forests from North Dakota to British Columbia and south to New Mexico and Nevada.

FROM THE JOURNALS: A specimen of Rocky Mountain juniper, with an original label, still exists. On it Lewis wrote, "No. 58 found 2nd October 1804. A species of Cedar found on the Blufs, the trees of which are large some of them 6 feet in the girth." Lewis and Clark mentioned "cedar" or "red cedar" in the journals many times. For example, on September 18, 1804, near present-day Chamberlain, North Dakota, Clark wrote, "this Island is about a mile long, and

Silver Sagebrush
Artemisia cana

Rocky Mountain Juniper or Cedar

Rocky Mountain Juniper or Cedar *Juniperus scopulorum*

has a great perpotion of red Cedir on it." On October 1, 1804, Clark documented information he had obtained from Mr. Jon Vallie, who had wintered the previous year up the Cheyenne River near the Black Hills: "The Countrey from the Missourie to the black mountain [Black Hills] is much like the Countrey on the Missourie, less timber & a greatr perpotion of Ceder. . . . great quantities of Pine Grow on the mountains, a great noise is heard frequently on those mountains." Today we know that Rocky Mountain juniper is the common cedar or juniper that occurs in the Black Hills and along the Missouri River in North Dakota and Montana, while eastern red cedar *(Juniperus virginiana)* occurs along the Missouri in South Dakota and downriver to St. Louis.

Long-Leaved Sagewort

Artemisia longifolia Nutt.
ASTER FAMILY (Asteraceae)

Plants: Perennial herbs up to 2½ feet tall with silvery hair covering most of the foliage. Leaves up to 5 inches long, narrow, and gradually tapering to a long point. **Flowers:** In rayless heads arranged in narrow panicles. **Fruits:** Smooth achenes without a pappus. **Flowering Season:** July to September. **Habitat/Range:** Dry, open, alkaline sites in the High Plains from Saskatchewan and Alberta to South Dakota and Wyoming.

FROM THE JOURNALS: A specimen of long-leaved sagewort, with an original label, still exists. On it Lewis wrote, "No. 53 October 3rd flavor like the camomile radix [root] perennial growth of the high bluffs." Clark described an anxious encounter on October 2: "we observed some Indians on a hill on the S. S. [starboard side] one Came down to the river opposit to us and fired off his gun, & beckind. to us to Come too, we payed no attention to him. . . . we proceeded on (1) passed a large Island, the S. S. here we expected the Tetons would attempt to Stop us and under that idear we prepared our Selves for action which we expected every moment. . . . This Island we call Isd. Of *Caution* [today inundated by Lake Oahe] we took in Some wood on a favourable Situation where we Could defend our men on Shore & (2) Camped on a Sand bar."

Fire-on-the-Mountain

Euphorbia cyathophora Murray
SPURGE FAMILY (Euphorbiaceae)

Plants: Annual herbs up to 4 feet tall. Leaves up to 6 inches long, but highly variable in size and shape. Upper leaves and bracts blotched red or yellow near the base. **Flowers:** Clustered on stem ends. The small, unisexual flowers are in curious cuplike structures with glands. **Fruits:** Smooth capsules. **Flowering Season:** August to October. **Habitat/Range:** Moist, disturbed prairies and woodlands from Virginia to Florida and west to South Dakota and Texas.

FROM THE JOURNALS: A specimen of fire-on-the-mountain still exists with an original label on which Lewis wrote: "No. 38. 1804 October.the growth of the high Prairies or plain." A second label in Pursh's hand places the collection on October 4, 1804. On October 4 the expedition camped on an island above Teel Creek (now known as Stove or Cherry Creek) in present-day Dewey County, South Dakota, that had the remains of an old fortified Arikara Indian village. Clark described the village as "Circular and walled Containing 17 lodges and it appears to have been deserted about five years." On October 15, 1804, the expedition camped below present-day Fort Yates, North Dakota, according to Clark, near a "Camp of Ricares [Arikara] of 10 lodges on the S. S [starboard side] . . . Capt Lewis & my Self went with the Chief . . . to the Huts of Several of the men all of whome Smoked & gave us Something to eate . . . those people were kind and appeared to be much plsd. at the attentioned paid them. Those people are much pleased with my black Servent."

Long-Leaved Sagewort
Artemisia longifolia

Fire-on-the-Mountain
Euphorbia cyathophora
—Steven Foster photo

Indian Tobacco

Nicotiana quadrivalvis Pursh
NIGHTSHADE FAMILY (Solanaceae)

Plants: Strongly scented, annual herbs up to 4 feet tall and thickly covered with glandular hairs. Leaves entire, ovate to lance shaped, the largest basal ones up to 7 inches long and 2 inches wide. **Flowers:** Arranged in long, loose racemes. Sepals ¾ inches long. Petal tube 2 inches long and very narrow, white and sometimes with a greenish, bluish, or pinkish tinge. **Fruits:** Capsules with four valves, shorter than the sepals. **Flowering Season:** April to September. Blooms in the evening, closing midmorning. **Habitat/Range:** Open, dry, well-drained washes and disturbed soils of California, southern Oregon, and Nevada. Great Plains Indian tribes once cultivated it, and in 1814 Frederick Pursh reported it was "spontaneous," or growing wild on the Missouri River. Per Axel Rydberg (1860-1931), a famous Swedish-born American botanist and curator of the New York Botanical Garden, reported in his *Flora of the Prairies and Plains of Central North America* (1932) that the species had "escaped in North Dakota." However, no one has ever found a specimen to document Rydberg's claim, and more recently, no one has collected or even found the species in its native Great Plains habitat.

FROM THE JOURNALS: A specimen of Indian tobacco still exists with a label on which Lewis wrote, "No. 45. Specimen of the Ricara's [Arikara] tobacco—taken 12th of October 1804." On this date the expedition sat in council with the Arikara Indians above present-day Mobridge, South Dakota. Clark described the event in his journal for October 12: "there was many Chief and warriers & about 7 bushels of Corn, a pr Leagins a twist of their Tobacco & Seeds of 2 Kind of Tobacco we Set Some time before the Councill Commenced." Lewis's 1805 transmittal list included a lengthy discussion about Indian tobacco: "The recarres cultivate two species of tobacco *[Nicotiana quadrivalvis* and *N. rustica],* for the purpose of smoking . . . they prepare hills at the distance of about 2½ feet from each other . . . in these hills they sew the seed as early in the spring as the climate will permit them to prepare the earth say latter end of April . . . They esteem much more the carraller [flower] dryed for the purpose of smoking—and for this purpose leave some plant more widely seperated from each other—in which situation they produce a greater abundance of flowers & seed. . . . I found it very pleasant—it dose not affect the nerves in the same manner that the tobacco cultivated in the U' S. dose."

In 1814 Pursh named and described the species for botanical science using a specimen from Lewis's collection. Pursh stated: "Cultivated . . . principally among the Mandan and Ricara nations . . . The tobacco prepared from is excellent. The most delicate tobacco is prepared by the Indians from the dried flowers."

Indian Tobacco *Nicotiana quadrivalvis*

Inside reconstructed Hidatsa earthlodge,
Knife River Indian Villages,
Stanton, North Dakota

Creeping Juniper

Juniperus horizontalis Moench
CYPRESS FAMILY (Cupressaceae)

Plants: Aromatic, evergreen shrubs about 1 foot tall or less, with stems that trail on the ground forming large mats. Leaves small and scalelike, overlapping on the stems. **Flowers:** Unisexual; the female cones round, berrylike, bluish with white powdery coating and recurved stalks. Male cones much smaller, yellowish to purplish. **Fruits:** Berrylike cones with two to four seeds, maturing the second year. **Flowering Season:** May to June. **Habitat/Range:** Dry, rocky hillsides and washes from Nova Scotia to Alaska, south to New York and Nebraska, and northwest to British Columbia.

FROM THE JOURNALS: Two sheets of creeping juniper, both collected on October 16, 1804, still exist. On this day the expedition camped above the mouth of Big Beaver Creek in present-day Emmons County, North Dakota. They mentioned creeping juniper many times in the journals. Lewis described it in his transmittal list: "a dwarf cedar of the open praries seldom ever rises more than six inches high—it is said to be a stimilating shrub—it is used as a tea by the Indians to produce sweat—they would make a handsome edging to the borders of a gardin if used as the small *box* [boxwood, *Buxus* species] sometimes is." On April 9, 1805, Clark wrote, "juniper grows on the Sides of the hills and runs on the ground." Lewis also described creeping juniper in detail in his journal for April 12, 1805: "I found some of the dwarf cedar of which I preserved a specimen . . . this plant spreads it's limbs alonge the surface of the earth . . . on the upper there are a great number of small shoots which with their leaves seldom rise higher than 6 or eight inches. they grow so close as perfectly to conceal the eath [earth]."

Common Juniper or Dwarf Juniper

Juniperus communis L.
CYPRESS FAMILY (Cupressaceae)

Plants: Low, evergreen shrubs, usually less than 6 feet tall, forming large mats. Leaves needlelike, sharp pointed, arranged in whorls of three on the three-angled stems. **Flowers:** Unisexual cones; the female cones round and berrylike. Male cones smaller and oblong. **Fruits:** Dark blue, berrylike cone with white powdery coating and one to three seeds. **Flowering Season:** May to June. **Habitat/Range:** Dry grasslands and forests in northern latitudes around the earth. In North America from Alaska to California and east to Newfoundland and Georgia.

FROM THE JOURNALS: Four sheets of common juniper still exist, including two collected October 17, 1804, below the mouth of the Cannonball River in present-day North Dakota, and two more on July 7, 1806, probably collected by Lewis near Lewis and Clark Pass northeast of present-day Lincoln, Montana. On the label for specimen number 47, taken October 17, Lewis wrote that it was "a species of Juniper, common to the bluffs." Since both Rocky Mountain and common juniper are abundant in the area today, Lewis was likely referring to them both on August 1, 1805 (near present-day Cardwell, Montana), when he wrote, "on the

Creeping Juniper ***Juniperus horizontalis***

Common Juniper or Dwarf Juniper
Juniperus communis

river about the mountains wich Capt. C. passed today he saw some large cedar trees [Rocky Mountain juniper] and some [common] juniper also." In his journal for October 17, 1804, Clark noted "Great numbers of Goats [pronghorn antelope] in large gangues," and the previous day he wrote, "Great numbers of Goats in the river, and Indians on the Shore on each Side . . . boys in the water Killing the Goats with Sticks and halling them to Shore, Those on the banks Shot them with arrows and as they approachd. the Shore would turn them back[.] of this Gangue of Goats I counted 58 of which they had killed."

Silver-Leaved Scurfpea

Pediomelum argophyllum (Pursh) J. Grimes
Also *Psoralea argophylla* Pursh
BEAN FAMILY (Fabaceae)

Plants: Perennial herbs, usually less than 2 feet tall, often in colonies. Leaves compound with three to five leaflets each, and covered with silvery, silky hair. **Flowers:** Small, blue to purple flowers arranged in spikes having two to five whorls of three to six flowers each. **Fruits:** Small pods with a straight beak, mostly enclosed by the sepals. **Flowering Season:** June to September. **Habitat/Range:** Prairies and open woods from Manitoba to Alberta and south to Oklahoma and New Mexico.

FROM THE JOURNALS: Two specimens of silver-leaved scurfpea still exist. The expedition collected both below the mouth of the Cannonball River in present-day North Dakota. On a label Lewis wrote: "No. 48. No. 103. October 17th 1804. a decoction of this plant used by the Indians to wash their wounds." On the Fort Mandan transmittal list Lewis wrote, "No. 103. is the growth of the open praries—it seldom grows higher[.] it is said to be good for inflamed eyes[.] the leaves are immerced in water and being bruised with the fingers a little the water is squeezed from it and occasionally droped when could upon the eyes."

Canada Columbine

Aquilegia canadensis L.
BUTTERCUP FAMILY (Ranunculaceae)

Plants: Perennial herbs up to 2 feet tall. Basal leaves compound with nine leaflets in three sets of three leaflets. Stem leaves smaller with fewer leaflets. **Flowers:** Sepals red, petal blades yellow with red spurs, many yellow stamens. **Fruits:** Beaked follicles. **Flowering Season:** March to June. **Habitat/Range:** Woods, cliffs, and rock outcrops from Newfoundland to Manitoba and south to Georgia and Texas.

FROM THE JOURNALS: No specimen of Canada columbine exists, but botanists believe that Lewis's specimen number 100, which he collected near Fort Mandan and sent downriver to President Jefferson, was Canada columbine. The specimen was lost as were many of the specimens sent from Fort Mandan. In the transmittal list Lewis wrote about this specimen: "Novr. 17th the seed of a plant given me by the recaray [Arikara] chief [Piaheto] who accompanied us to the mandanes[.] he informed me that a tea of the seed was a strong diaerettic—and that the squaws chewed them and rubed their hair with them as a perfume." On November 17, 1804, the expedition was at Fort Mandan below the mouth of the Knife River in present-day North Dakota, where they stayed until April 7, 1805. Clark wrote in his journal that day, "a fine morning, last night was Cold, the ice thicker than yesterday, Several Indians visit us, one Chief Stayed all day[.] we are much engaged about our huts."

Silver-Leaved Scurfpea
Pediomelum argophyllum

Canada Columbine *Aquilegia canadensis*
—Steven Foster photo

Reconstructed Hidatsa earthlodge,
Knife River Indian Villages, Stanton, North Dakota

Narrow-Leaved Purple Coneflower

Echinacea angustifolia DC.
ASTER FAMILY (Asteraceae)

Plants: Perennial herbs. Stems single, up to 2 feet tall, covered with stiff hairs. Leaves 2 to 12 inches long, less than 1 ½ inches wide, prominently veined, and hairy. **Flowers:** Arranged in heads on the ends of the solitary stems. Pink to purple ray-flowers radiate downward from the spiny, brown to orange tinged, dome-shaped disk. **Fruits:** Achenes with four-angled sides and short, toothed crowns. **Flowering Season:** June to July. **Habitat/Range:** Open prairies and plains from eastern Montana to western Minnesota and south through the Great Plains to Texas.

FROM THE JOURNALS: No specimen of narrow-leaved purple coneflower exists, but the journals attest to the collection and importance of this medicinal plant. On February 28, 1805, while at Fort Mandan, Clark wrote: "a fine morning, two men of the N W Compy arrve with letters and a Sacka comah [kinnikinnick] also a Root and top of a plant [narrow-leaved purple coneflower] presented by Mr. Haney, for the Cure of mad Dogs Snakes &c [etc.], and to be found & used as follows vz [i.e.]: 'this root is found on high lands and asent of hills, the way of useing it is to Scarify the part when bitten to chu or pound an inch or more if the root is Small, and applying it to the bitten part renewing it twice a Day. the bitten person is not to chaw nor Swallow any of the Root for it might have contrary effect." On March 20, 1805, Clark wrote, "I also collected a Plant the root of which is a Cure for the Bite of a mad dog & Snake which I shall Send." Clark was writing about purple coneflower and his intention to send it to President Jefferson.

In his transmittal list, Lewis described specimen number 101 (narrow-leaved purple coneflower): "the root wen pounded in either green or dryed state makes an excellent poltice for swellings or soar throat.—information of the same chief." The "same chief" refers to the Arikara chief Piaheto who joined the explorers at his village on October 12 and remained with them as they traveled on to the Mandan and Hidatsa Villages. The specimen has since been lost.

Western Sagewort

Artemisia campestris L.
ASTER FAMILY (Asteraceae)

Plants: Biennial or perennial herbs with clusters of branching stems 1 to 2 feet tall. Leaves finely divided into numerous narrow segments except the uppermost leaves, which may be simple. **Flowers:** Arranged in small, rayless heads in narrow panicles on the upper stems. **Fruits:** Small, smooth achenes without pappus. **Flowering Season:** July to September. **Habitat/Range:** Dry places, especially on sandy soils from boreal Canada south to Florida and California.

FROM THE JOURNALS: No specimen of western sagewort exists. However, Frederick Pursh credited Lewis's collection as the source of the specimen that he used to describe western sagewort in his 1814 book. Pursh probably used Lewis's notes to describe its habitat and flowering season. He wrote, "On the plains of the Missouri . . . Sept.–Nov." This is one of at least six sage *(Artemisia)* species that Lewis and Clark collected.

Narrow-Leaved Purple Coneflower
Echinacea angustifolia

Western Sagewort
Artemisia campestris

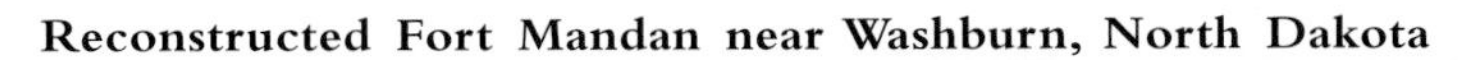

Reconstructed Fort Mandan near Washburn, North Dakota

Kinnikinnick or Bearberry

Arctostaphylos uva-ursi (L.) Spreng.
HEATH FAMILY (Ericaceae)

Plants: Low, trailing, evergreen shrubs that often form large mats. Leaves alternate, leathery, entire, rounded, and spatula shaped. **Flowers:** Pink, urn shaped, hanging downward. **Fruits:** Mealy or fleshy, red drupe. **Flowering Season:** April to July. **Habitat/Range:** Prairies and forests from Newfoundland to Alaska and south to New Jersey, New Mexico, and California; also Eurasia.

FROM THE JOURNALS: A specimen of kinnikinnick, with an original label in Lewis's hand, still exists. On it he wrote: "No. 33 An evergreen plant which grows in the open plains usually. the natives smoke it's leaves, mixed with tobacco Called by the French Engages [boatmen] *Sacacommis*—obtained at Fort Mandan." Native Americans also ate the kinnikinnick berries. On October 29, 1805, near present-day The Dalles, Oregon, Clark wrote, "This chief gave us to eate Sackacommis burries Hasel nuts fish Pounded, and a kind of Bread made of roots." On December 9, 1805, while near present-day Seaside, Oregon, among the Clatsop Indians, Clark wrote, "was invited to a lodge by a young Chief was treated great Politeness, we had new mats to Set on, and himself and wife produced for us to eate, fish, Lickorish, & black roots, on neet Small mats, and Cramberries & Sackacomey berries, in bowls made of horn, Supe made of a kind of bread made of berries common to this Country." On the Columbia Plains on March 2, 1806, Clark described the sage grouse and the importance of kinnikinnick berries in its diet.

Wood Lily

Lilium philadelphicum L.
LILY FAMILY (Liliaceae)

Plants: Perennial herbs up to 6 feet tall, uppermost leaves whorled, lower leaves alternate, up to 6 inches long. **Flowers:** Usually one flower per stem with six red to orange, purple-spotted petals, 2 to 3 inches long, and six stamens. **Fruits:** Capsule about 1 ½ inches long. **Flowering Season:** June to August. **Habitat/Range:** Prairies and open woods from Quebec to British Columbia and south to Virginia and Arizona.

FROM THE JOURNALS: A wood-lily specimen does not exist today, but Frederick Pursh credited Lewis's collection as one of two sources for his description of *Lilium umbellatum,* which we now recognize as a variety of wood lily. In *Flora Americae Septentrionalis,* Pursh wrote: "On the banks of the Missouri. *M. Lewis and Nuttall* . . . By all appearance the plant found by the above gentlemen, among the Mandan nation on the Missouri . . . the flowers are of an uniform deep scarlet colour, and are highly ornamental."

nnikinnick or Bearberry *Arctostaphylos uva-ursi*

Wood Lily
Lilium philadelphicum

The expedition was at Fort Mandan from October 27, 1804, to April 7, 1805, and then again on August 17, 1806. On that day Clark wrote in his journal: "Settled with Touisant Chabono for his Services as an enterpreter the pric of a horse and Lodge purchased of him for public Service in all amounting to 500$ 33⅓ cents . . . I offered to take his little Son a butifull promising Child who is 19 months old to which they both himself & wife wer willing provided the Child had been weened. they observed that in one year the boy would be Sufficiently old to leave his mother & he would then take him to me if I would be so freindly as to raise the Child for him." Clark did raise the child named Jean Baptiste Charbonneau.

Indian Corn

Zea mays L.
GRASS FAMILY (Poaceae)

Plants: Tall, robust, annual grasses with overlapping sheaths and broad blades. **Flowers:** Unisexual; the male spikelets in long racemes on the ends of the stems; female spikelets in numerous rows on a thickened, almost woody center (the cob), enclosed in large, leaflike bracts. The long styles (the silk) protrude from the bracts as a mass of silky threads. **Fruits:** The corn grains (kernels). **Flowering Season:** June to August. **Habitat/Range:** Believed to have originated in Mexico. Has been cultivated in the Americas since prehistoric times.

FROM THE JOURNALS: In his 1814 book Frederick Pursh wrote about Lewis's Indian corn specimen: "one of those [varieties] brought by M. Lewis, Esq. from the Mandan nation, on the Missouri, deserves particular attention, as it ripens sooner and produces as excellent ears as any sort I know. It would be calculated to cultivate in climates not quite so warm as all the other sorts require." Corn was important to the expedition and Lewis and Clark mentioned it in the journals many times. On October 12, 1804, above present-day Mobridge, South Dakota, Clark described the Arikara Indians: "they are tall Stout men corsily featured, their womin Small & industerous; raise great quantities of corn beans &c [etc.] also Tobacco for the men to Smoke." On July 13, 1805, near present-day Great Falls, Montana, Lewis wrote, "meat now forms our food prinsipally as we reserve our flour parched meal and corn as much as possible for the rocky mountains which we are shortly to enter, and where . . . game is not very abundant."

FORT MANDAN TO THE MARIAS RIVER

White Milkwort

Polygala alba Nutt.
MILKWORT FAMILY (Polygalaceae)

Plants: Perennial herbs up to 16 inches tall. Leaves narrow, lower ones taper toward the base. **Flowers:** White with greenish center, arranged in racemes on the stem ends. **Fruits:** Capsules with two hairy seeds. **Flowering Season:** May to August. **Habitat/Range:** Rocky prairies and ravines from Minnesota to Montana and south to Texas, Arizona, and northern Mexico.

FROM THE JOURNALS: A specimen of white milkwort, collected August 10, 1806, still exists. Lewis and his party camped that evening near present-day Williston, North Dakota. Clark was camped with his men about 25 miles downriver that evening near Tobacco Creek in present-day North Dakota. The next day, while out hunting, Peter Cruzatte accidentally shot Lewis. He mistook him for an elk. Lewis described the injury in his journal: "a ball struck my left thye about an inch below my hip joint, missing the bone it passed through the left thye and cut the thickness of the bullet across the hinder part of the right thye." On August 12, 1806, Lewis's party caught up with Clark about 6 miles south of present-day Sanish, North Dakota. They had been apart since leaving "Traveller's rest" near present-day Lolo, Montana, on July 3, 1806.

Indian Corn *Zea mays*

White Milkwort
Polygala alba
—Drake Barton photo

Chokecherry

Prunus virginiana L.
ROSE FAMILY (Rosaceae)

Plants: Shrubs or small trees up to 25 feet tall. Leaves alternate, simple, egg shaped, having serrate margins with the teeth directed towards the leaf tips. A pair of reddish glands is found at the leaf base or adjacent petiole. **Flowers:** White, arranged in long racemes of fifteen to thirty flowers. **Fruits:** Berries, each has a single, bony pit; dark red, purple, to nearly black when fully ripe. **Flowering Season:** April to July. **Habitat/Range:** Streams, canyons, draws, and woodlands from Newfoundland to British Columbia and south to North Carolina and California.

FROM THE JOURNALS: Lewis learned herbal medicine from his mother, an herbal healer. On June 11, 1805, Lewis was leading a small party searching for the "great falls of the Missouri," when he fell ill: "I was taken with such violent pain in the intestens that I was unable to partake of the feast of marrowbones. . . . I directed a parsel of the small twigs [of chokecherry] to be geathered striped of their leaves, cut into pieces of about 2 Inches in length and boiled in water until a strong black decoction of an astringent bitter tast was produced; at sunset I took a point {pint} of this decoction and abut an hour after repeated the dze[.] by 10 in the evening I was entirely releived from pain and in fact every symptom of the disorder forsook me; my fever abated, a gentle perspiration was produced and I had a comfortable and refreshing nights rest." The next morning Lewis took another portion of the chokecherry decoction and hiked 27 miles up the Missouri. On June 13, 1805, after another hike of 15 miles, he finally reached the "great falls," which he described as a "sublimely grand specticle."

Two specimens of chokecherry, both collected on the return trip from the Pacific Ocean, still exist. One was collected on May 29, 1806, near present-day Kamiah, Idaho, and the other on August 10, 1806, near present-day Williston, North Dakota. In his journal for May 29, 1806, Lewis wrote a detailed botanical description of chokecherry: "The Choke Cherry has been in blume since the 20th inst. . . . a single flower, which has five obtuse short patent white petals with short claws inserted on the upper edge of the calyx. . . . the stamens are upwards of twenty and are seated on the margin of the flower cup."

On August 11, 1806, Peter Cruzatte accidentally shot Lewis (see *From the Journals* under *White Milkwort*). Lewis wrote on August 12, "as wrighting in my present situation is extreemly painfull to me I shall desist until I recover . . . however I must notice a singular Cherry which is found on the Missouri in the bottom lands about the beaverbends and some little distance below the white earth river." Lewis's last journal entry of the expedition concluded with a lengthy botanical description of pin cherry, *Prunus pensylvanica,* which he contrasted with the more familiar chokecherry: "it rises to the hight of eight or ten feet seldom puting up more than one stem from the same root not growing in cops as the Choke Cherry dose. . . . the fruit is a globular berry about the size of a buck-shot of a fine scarlet red."

Chokecherry *Prunus virginiana*

Chokecherry flowers

Chokecherries

Indian Breadroot or White Apple

Pediomelum esculentum (Pursh) Rydb.
Also *Psoralea esculenta* Pursh
BEAN FAMILY (Fabaceae)

Plants: Perennial herbs up to 8 inches tall. Foliage covered with long, silky hairs. Leaves compound with five leaflets, which join at a common point. **Flowers:** Blue, fading to yellowish as they mature, arranged in dense, spikelike racemes. **Fruits:** Egg-shaped pods with slender beaks; enclosed by persistent sepals. **Flowering Season:** May to July. **Habitat/Range:** Prairies, plains, and open woodlands from Manitoba to Alberta and southeast to Louisiana and New Mexico.

FROM THE JOURNALS: A specimen of Indian breadroot still exists. We know it came from the Missouri River but it doesn't have a label, so we don't know the exact date and place of collection. Frederick Pursh named and described this species in his book and credited a specimen from Lewis's collection as the source of his description. Pursh described how the "American Western Indians" preserved Indian breadroot: "They collect them in large quantities, and if for present use, they roast them in the ashes . . . if intended for winter use, they are carefully dried, and preserved in a dry place in their huts."

On May 8, 1805, near the mouth of the Milk River in present-day Montana, Lewis wrote a detailed botanical description of white apple and continued with a discussion of its uses: "This root forms a considerable article of food with the Indians of the Missouri, who for this purpose prepare them in several ways. they are esteemed good at all seasons of the year, but are best from the middle of July too the latter end of Autumn when they are sought and gathered . . . for their winter store. when collected they are striped of their rhind and strung on small throngs . . . and exposed to the sun or placed in the smoke of their fires to dry; when well dryed they will keep for several years . . . in this situation they usually pound them between two stones . . . untill they reduce it to a fine powder[.] thus prepared they thicken their soope with it; sometimes they also boil these dryed roots with their meat without breaking them; when green they are generally boiled with their meat, sometimes mashing them . . . they also prepare an agreeable dish with them by boiling and mashing them and adding the marrow grease of the buffaloe and some buries, until the whole be of the consistency of a haisty pudding. they also eat this root roasted and frequently make hearty meals of it raw . . . The White or brown bear feed very much on this root . . . the white apple appears to me to be a tastless insipid food of itself tho' I have no doubt but it is a very healthy and moderately nutricious food. I have no doubt but our epicures would admire this root very much, it would serve them in their ragouts and gravies in stead of the truffles morella." On May 9, 1805, Lewis described in humorous detail Toussaint Charbonneau's preparation of the white pudding so esteemed by the men of the expedition. Perhaps the flour he used to prepare it was from white apple collected the day before.

Top: Indian Breadroot or White Apple
Pediomelum esculentum

Inset: Indian Breadroot illustration from Frederick Pursh's 1814 *Flora Americae Septentrionalis*

Right Indian Breadroot dried for winter storage. From the Lewis and Clark Interpretive Center, Great Falls, Montana

Wild Licorice

Glycyrrhiza lepidota Pursh
BEAN FAMILY (Fabaceae)

Plants: Perennial herbs less than 4 feet tall forming dense colonies. Leaves pinnately compound with nine to nineteen leaflets that have needlelike tips; arranged in opposite pairs. **Flowers:** White or yellowish with a slight tinge of purple; arranged in dense, spikelike racemes. **Fruits:** Pods covered with hooked prickles. **Flowering Season:** May to July. **Habitat/Range:** Streambanks, swales, and ravines from Ontario to British Columbia and south to Arkansas and southern California.

FROM THE JOURNALS: A wild-licorice specimen does not exist, and we have no evidence that they ever collected one, but Lewis and Clark did mention it several times in the journals. On May 8, 1805, near the mouth of the present-day Milk River in Montana, Clark wrote, "In walking on Shore with the Interpreter & his wife, the Squar [Sacagawea] Geathered on the Sides of the hills wild Lickerish, & the white apple as called by the angegies [French boatmen] and gave me to eat." On January 24, 1806, while at Fort Clatsop in Oregon, Lewis wrote: "I observe no difference between the licuorice of this countrey and that common to maney parts of the United States where it is sometimes cultivated in our gardens. . . . the natives roaste it in the embers and pound it slightly with a small stick in order to make it seperate more readily from the strong liggament which forms the center of the root. . . . this root when roasted possesses an agreeable flavour not unlike the sweet pittaitoe." Given Lewis's knowledge of plants and powers of observation, it is likely that this journal entry refers to the taller wild licorice and not the low-growing Chinook licorice *(Lupinus littoralis),* which also grows near Fort Clatsop (see *Chinook licorice* in the *Pacific Forest*).

Rusty Lupine

Lupinus pusillus Pursh
BEAN FAMILY (Fabaceae)

Plants: Annual herbs, up to 8 inches tall, covered with long silky hair. Leaves compound with five to seven leaflets attached at a common point on the end of the leafstalk. **Flowers:** Light blue to bluish purple, arranged in racemes of five to forty flowers. **Fruits:** Pods up to ¾ inch long covered with long, shaggy hair, containing two seeds each. **Flowering Season:** April to July. **Habitat/Range:** Dry sandy soil of plains, badlands, and dunes from Central Washington to California and east to Saskatchewan and Kansas.

FROM THE JOURNALS: The Royal Botanic Gardens at Kew, near London, houses a specimen of rusty lupine. The label, in Pursh's hand, gives the plant name but not the date and place of collection. In his 1814 book Frederick Pursh named and described this species crediting one of Lewis's specimens as the source of the material he examined. Pursh placed it "On the banks of the Missouri . . . June." In June 1805 the expedition did travel from the white cliffs of the Missouri River near Eagle Creek to present-day Great Falls, Montana, where this plant species is still found. However, since the plants Lewis collected in June of 1805 were destroyed by moisture in the Great Falls caches, we assume Lewis collected the existing specimen on his return trip in 1806.

Wild Licorice *Glycyrrhiza lepidota*

Wild Licorice flowers

Rusty Lupine
Lupinus pusillus

Narrow-Leaved Cottonwood

Populus angustifolia James
WILLOW FAMILY (Salicaceae)

Plants: Trees up to 65 feet tall with lance-shaped leaves that are two to five times longer than wide, and up to 5 inches long and 1½ inches wide. Leafstalks ⅜ inch long or less. **Flowers:** Unisexual, nonshowy (without petals), arranged in drooping catkins, and have a cup-shaped disk below each flower. **Fruits:** Capsules, usually release their cottony seed before full leaf-development. **Flowering Season:** April to May. **Habitat/Range:** Streams from Montana and Idaho south to Texas and Arizona.

FROM THE JOURNALS: Although no specimen of narrow-leaved cottonwood still exists, the explorers mentioned the species several times in the journals. Cottonwood trees were important to the expedition's success (see *From the Journals* under *plains cottonwood*). On June 3, 1805, Lewis described the observations of the Fields brothers along the Teton River near present-day Loma, Montana, when he wrote: "they came down this little river and found it a boald runing stream of about 40 yds. wide containg much timber in it's bottom, consisting of the narrow and wide leafed cottonwood with some birch and box alder undrgrowth willows rosebushes currents &c." Then on June 12, 1805, between the mouth of the Marias River and the lowest of the "great falls" of the Missouri River, Lewis provided a botanical description: "The narrow leafed cottonwood differs only from the other [plains cottonwood] in the shape of it's leaf and greater thickness of it's bark . . . the beaver appear to be extremely fond of this tree and even seem to scelect it from among the other species of Cottonwood, probably from it's affording a deeper and softer bark than the other species."

Pennsylvania Cinquefoil

Potentilla pensylvanica L.
ROSE FAMILY (Rosaceae)

Plants: Low, perennial herbs up to 2 feet tall. Leaves compound and have five to nineteen leaflets, which are arranged in opposite pairs. Leaflets have lobes cut halfway or more to the midrib, green on upper surface and whitish underneath. **Flowers:** Yellow, arranged in a compact cyme. **Fruits:** Achenes with a style about the same length (or shorter) attached at the end, or nearly at the end, of the achene. **Flowering Season:** June to August. **Habitat/Range:** Dry, sandy or rocky prairies, open woodlands, and alpine tundra from Greenland to Alaska and south to New Hampshire and California.

FROM THE JOURNALS: This is another species we know Lewis and Clark collected because of Frederick Pursh's 1814 book. Pursh credited Lewis's collection as the source of the plant specimen he used to describe a variety of this species. He wrote: "on the Missouri. June, July . . . Flowers yellow." The specimen has since been lost. The explorers did not mention it in the journals either. They were traveling along the Missouri River near present-day Great Falls, Montana, in June and July 1805, but plants collected then were ruined by water that entered their caches. Perhaps Lewis collected the specimen in July 1806 as he descended the Missouri on the return trip.

Narrow-Leaved Cottonwood
Populus angustifolia

Pennsylvania Cinquefoil
Potentilla pensylvanica

Confluence of Missouri and Marias Rivers near Loma, Montana

Wax Currant

Ribes cereum Dougl.
CURRANT FAMILY (Grossulariaceae)

Plants: Shrubs without thorns, less than 6 feet tall. Leaves with three to five shallow lobes and a wavy margin, often covered with sticky hairs. **Flowers:** In clusters of two to eight, greenish white to white with a pink tinge, tubular, and have sticky hairs on outer surface. **Fruits:** Red to orange berries with sticky hairs; unpalatable. **Flowering Season:** April to June. **Habitat/Range:** Rocky places in sagebrush deserts to subalpine ridges from British Columbia to North Dakota and south to California and Oklahoma.

FROM THE JOURNALS: No specimen of wax currant exists, but we know that plant specimens cached at present-day Great Falls, Montana, were damaged beyond repair by moisture. Lewis wrote a botanical description of wax currant in his journal for June 18, 1805, while camped below the mouth of "Portage Creek" (Belt Creek) down the Missouri River from Great Falls, Montana: "There is a species of gooseberry which grows very common about here in open situations among the rocks on the sides of the clifts. they are now ripe of a pale red colour, about the size of a common goosberry, and like it is an ovate pericarp of soft pulp invelloping a number of smal whitish coloured seeds; the pulp is a yelloish slimy muselaginous substance of a sweetish and pinelike tast, not agreeable to me. the surface of the berry is covered with a glutinous adhesive matter, and the fruit altho' ripe retains it's withered corollar."

Plains Prickly Pear

Opuntia polyacantha Haw.
CACTUS FAMILY (Cactaceae)

Plants: Succulent, leafless shrubs with smooth, flat, segmented stems about 5 inches long that have numerous weakly barbed spines. **Flowers:** Yellow, pink, or red; 6½ inches wide; numerous petals, numerous stamens, and a single style. **Fruits:** Round to egg shaped, spiny, about ¾ to 1½ inches long, dry, tan in color. **Flowering Season:** May to July. **Habitat/Range:** Sandy plains, foothills, and lower mountains from British Columbia to Saskatchewan and south to California, Texas, and Mexico.

FROM THE JOURNALS: Lewis and Clark mentioned plains prickly pear often in the journals. On September 19, 1804, near present-day Lower Brule, South Dakota, Clark wrote, "a Creek of about 10 yards wide Coms in passing thro a plain in which great quantities of the Prickley Pear grows. I call this Creek *Prickley Pear Creek* . . . it is Situated at the Commencement of . . . Big Bend of the Missourie." Near present-day Great Falls, Montana, on June 14, 1805, Lewis spent the day alone exploring the various falls, and was threatened by a grizzly bear, a catlike creature, and charging bull buffalo. Lewis wrote, "did not think it prudent to remain all night at this place which really from the succession of curious adventures wore the impression on my mind of inchantment; at sometimes for a moment I thought it

Top left: Wax Currant flowers
Ribes cereum

Top right: Wax Currant berries

Bottom right: Plains Prickly Pear
Opuntia polyacantha

might be a dream, but the prickley pears which pierced my feet very severely once in a while, particularly after it grew dark, convinced me that I was really awake." The expedition passed the Smith River above Great Falls on July 15, 1805, and Lewis wrote, "the prickly pear is now in full blume and forms one of the beauties as well as the greatest pests of the plains."

Common Sunflower

Helianthus annuus L.
ASTER FAMILY (Asteraceae)

Plants: Annual herbs up to 7 feet tall with rough, hairy foliage. Lower leaves heart shaped, those above egg shaped, 4 to 16 inches long and about half as wide. **Flowers:** Large, flat heads, 1 inch or more in diameter, with yellow rays surrounding a reddish brown disk. **Fruits:** Smooth achenes with a pappus of two awns, sometimes with secondary scales. **Flowering Season:** June to September. **Habitat/Range:** Disturbed places in the plains, valleys, and foothills across southern Canada, the United States, and northern Mexico.

FROM THE JOURNALS: While no specimen of sunflower exists, the explorers mentioned it often in the journals. In his journal for July 17, 1805, near the "pine island rapids," where the Missouri River flows out of the Rocky Mountains into the High Plains near present-day Hardy, Montana, Lewis wrote: "The sunflower is in bloom and abundant in the river bottoms. The Indians of the Missouri particularly those who do not cultivate maze make a great uce of the seed of this plant for bread, or use it in thickening their soope. they most commonly first parch the seed and then pound them between two smooth stones until they reduce it to fine meal. to this they sometimes mearly add a portion of water and drink it in that state, or add a sufficient quantity of marrow grease to reduce it to the consistency of common dough and eate it in that manner. the last composition I think much best and have eat it in that state heartily and think it a pallateable dish." Then on August 26, 1805, in the present-day Lemhi Valley of Idaho, Lewis wrote, "The sunflower is very abundant near the watercourses the seeds of this plant are now rip and the natives collect them in considerable quantities and reduce them to meal . . . this meal is a favorite food [of the Native Americans]." Wild sunflower is the state flower and floral emblem of Kansas.

Needle-and-Thread Grass

Stipa comata Trin. and Rupr.
Also *Hesperostipa comata*
(Trin. and Rupr.) Barkworth
GRASS FAMILY (Poaceae)

Plants: Perennial bunchgrasses less than 3 feet tall and often 1 foot or less. **Flowers:** In narrow, dense panicles; one sharp-pointed floret per spikelet with a long (4 to 8 inches), twisted, bristlelike awn. **Fruits:** Long, narrow grain. **Flowering Season:** May to July. **Habitat/Range:** Sandy plains from Manitoba to the Yukon and south to Michigan, Texas, and California.

FROM THE JOURNALS: A specimen of needle-and-thread grass, collected on July 8, 1806, in either Lewis and Clark or Teton County, Montana, still exists. Lewis and his small party crossed the Continental Divide that day, dropped out of the Rocky Mountains onto the High Plains, and camped 8 miles below the confluence of Elk Creek and the Sun River. Lewis wrote in his journal that day: "the Shishiquaw mountain [Haystack Butte] is a high insulated conic mountain standing several miles

Top: Common Sunflower
Helianthus annuus

Bottom: Needle-and-Thread Grass
Stipa comata

in advance of the Eastern range of the rocky mountains . . . Josh. Fields saw two buffaloe below us some distance which are the first that have been seen. . . . much rejoiced at finding ourselves in the plains of the Missouri which abound with game. . . . the land of neither the plains nor bottoms is fertile. It is of a light colour intermixed with a considerable proportion of gravel the grass generally about 9 inghes high . . . I killed a very large and the whitest woolf I have seen."

Lewis's Blue Flax

Linum lewisii Pursh
Also *Linum perenne* L. var. *lewisii* (Pursh) Eat. and Wright
FLAX FAMILY (Linaceae)

Plants: Perennial herbs, 8 to 32 inches tall, with numerous, closely spaced stems. Alternate, narrow leaves with parallel margins, less than 1¼ inches long. **Flowers:** Arranged in racemes or panicles with few branches; five sepals, five bright blue petals, five stamens, and five styles per flower. **Fruits:** Capsules with ten cells. **Flowering Season:** May to August. **Habitat/Range:** Sandy or rocky soil of prairies, open mountain-slopes, and alpine ridges throughout western North America.

FROM THE JOURNALS: Two specimens of Lewis's blue flax still exist. The label of one places its collection on July 9, 1806, along the Sun River above present-day Simms, Montana. July 9 was cold and rainy, and Lewis's party only traveled 8 miles, spending the day feasting on buffalo meat and taking shelter from the weather. The next day the party traveled 24 miles and camped 4 to 5 miles above the confluence of the Sun and Missouri Rivers near present-day Great Falls, Montana. On July 10, 1806, Lewis wrote in his journal: "I sent the packhorses on with Sergt. Gass. . . . they informed us that they had seen a very large bear in the plains which had pursued Sergt. Gass and Thomson some distance but their horses enabled them to keep out of it's reach. they were afraid to fire on the bear least their horses should throw them as they were unaccustomed to the gun. we killed five deer 3 Elk and a bear today; saw vast herds of buffaloe . . . we hered them bellowing about us all night. vast assemblages of wolves. . . . both species of prickly pears just in blume."

Foxtail Barley

Hordeum jubatum L.
GRASS FAMILY (Poaceae)

Plants: Perennial bunchgrasses less than 32 inches tall with flat blades. **Flowers:** Arranged in a spike of spikelets with numerous long, fine, bristlelike awns. A close look at the parts of the inflorescence shows three spikelets coming together at a common point; the central one has both pistils and stamens (fertile), and the lateral ones neutral or have only stamens. **Fruits:** Oblong grain furrowed on the back. **Flowering Season:** June to August. **Habitat/Range:** Moist to wet meadows and disturbed places throughout most of North America, except the southeastern states.

FROM THE JOURNALS: Two specimens of foxtail barley still exist. Lewis collected one near Fort Clatsop on the Pacific Coast in present-day Oregon on March 13, 1806, and the other one near present-day Great Falls, Montana. On the label associated with the latter specimen, Frederick Pursh wrote: "Calld the golden or Silken Rye. On the white bear Islands on the Missouri. Jul. 12th 1806." Lewis didn't mention foxtail barley in his journal on that day, but when the expedition was at the White Bear Islands near Great Falls, Montana, the previous year on June 25, Lewis described the grass: "there is a species of wild rye which is now heading it rises to the hight of 18 or 20 inches, the beard is remarkably fine and soft[.] it is a very handsome grass; the culm is jointed and is in every rispect the wild rye in minuture. great quantities of mint also are here."

Lewis's Blue Flax *Linum lewisii*

Foxtail Barley *Hordeum jubatum*

Crooked Falls of the Missouri River near Great Falls, Montana

Gumbo Evening Primrose

Oenothera caespitosa Nutt.
EVENING PRIMROSE FAMILY (Onagraceae)

Plants: Perennial herbs growing in low tufts less than 1 foot tall. Leaves broad and taper towards the base. **Flowers:** Bloom at dusk, white when fresh but turn pink and purple as they age. **Fruits:** Woody capsules, angled, but do not have wings at their margins. **Flowering Season:** May to July. **Habitat/Range:** Dry and rocky, gravelly, or clayey soils from Manitoba to Nebraska and Texas, and west to Washington and California.

FROM THE JOURNALS: Two sheets of gumbo evening primrose still exist. Pursh's labels place the collection "Near the Falls of Missouri Jul. 17th 1806." A few days before, on July 13, while at their White Bear Islands camp near present-day Great Falls, Montana, Lewis wrote, "had the cash [cache] opened found my bearskins entirely destroyed by the water. . . . all my specimens of plants also lost." Lewis may have been replacing some of the lost plant specimens when he collected gumbo evening primrose on July 17. Lewis wrote in his journal on that day: "I arrose early this morning and made a drawing of the falls. after which we took breakfast and departed. it being my design to strike Maria's river about the place at which I left it on my return to it's mouth in the begining of June 1805." For the next eleven days Lewis explored the Marias River and its tributaries up to Camp Disappointment beyond present-day Cut Bank, Montana.

Greasewood

Sarcobatus vermiculatus (Hook.) Torr.
GOOSEFOOT FAMILY (Chenopodiaceae)

Plants: Shrubs up to 6 feet tall with white bark and spine-tipped branches. Leaves fleshy and rounded in cross section. **Flowers:** Unisexual; male flowers arranged in dense spikes on the ends of branches; female flowers in the leaf axils with two styles. Flowers nonshowy (without petals). **Fruits:** Shaped like a small top with a flared skirt at midline. **Flowering Season:** May to August. **Habitat/Range:** Eroded hills, floodplains, in clayey, saline, or alkaline soils from Saskatchewan to Texas and west to Washington and California.

FROM THE JOURNALS: Lewis's specimen of greasewood, collected on July 20, 1806, while he was exploring the Marias River south of present-day Shelby, Montana, still exists (see *From the Journals* under *Moundscale*). On May 11, 1805, Lewis described greasewood while traveling up the Missouri River near present-day The Pines Recreation Area in Valley County, Montana: "there is another growth that begins now to make it's appearance in the bottom lands and is becoming extreemly troublesome; it is a shrub which rises to the hight of from two to four feet, much branched . . . the branches beset with a great number of long, shap, strong, wooddy looking thorns; the leaf is about ¾ or an inch long, and one ⅛ of an inch wide . . . veinless fleshy and gibbose; has no perceptable taste or smell, and no anamal appears to eat it . . . I shall call it the *fleshey leafed thorn.*"

Gumbo Evening Primrose *Oenothera caespitosa*

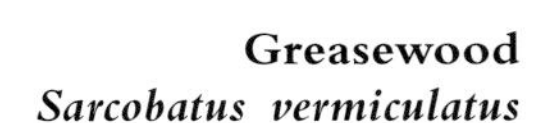

Greasewood
Sarcobatus vermiculatus

Moundscale

Atriplex gardneri (Moq.) Dietr.
Also *Atriplex nuttallii* S. Wats.
GOOSEFOOT FAMILY (Chenopodiaceae)

Plants: Perennial half-shrubs, woody only at the base, 4 to 20 inches tall. Leaves alternate, egg shaped, grayish green, and covered with small, branlike scales. **Flowers:** Nonshowy, unisexual, arranged in dense clusters; the male and female flowers on separate plants. **Fruits:** Bladderlike, with odd-shaped, spongy bracts. **Flowering Season:** June to August. **Habitat/Range:** Plains, valleys, and badlands on saline soil from Manitoba to Alberta and south to Nebraska and Arizona.

FROM THE JOURNALS: A specimen of moundscale still exists. Pursh wrote on the label, "A half Shrub from the high plains of Missouri Jul. 20th 1806." In Lewis's journal for the day, he described the habitat that is characteristic of greasewood and moundscale: "the plains are more broken than they were yesterday and have become more inferior in point of soil; a great quanty of small gravel is every where distributed over the surface of the earth which renders travling extreemly painfull to our bearfoot horses. the soil is generally a white or whiteish blue clay . . . the mineral salts common to the plains of the missouri has been more abundant today than usual." Lewis's party was exploring the Marias River on July 20. They were camped about 5 miles southwest of present-day Shelby, Montana.

Scarlet Globemallow

Sphaeralcea coccinea (Nutt.) Rydb.
MALLOW FAMILY (Malvaceae)

Plants: Low-growing perennial herbs less than 20 inches tall, usually trailing on the ground. Leaves grayish green, divided into three to five segments, which are further lobed. **Flowers:** Orange to red or pink, arranged in a raceme on the branch ends. Lower portion of filaments join to form a tube. **Fruits:** Capsule with ten or more cells and one seed per cell. **Flowering Season:** April to August. **Habitat/Range:** Dry plains and valleys from Manitoba to Alberta and south to Iowa, Texas, and Arizona.

FROM THE JOURNALS: Two sheets of scarlet globemallow, which Lewis collected on July 20, 1806, along the Marias River south of present-day Shelby, Montana, still exist. In Lewis's journal for the day he wrote, "the wild liquorice and sunflower are very abundant in the plains and river bottoms, the latter is now in full blume; the silkgrass and sand rush are also common." A few days later, on July 26, 1806, Lewis left Camp Disappointment and described the vegetation along the Two Medicine River about a mile below Badger Creek: "the rose, honeysuckle [snowberry] and redberry [buffaloberry] bushes constitute the undergrowth there being but little willow." Later that day, Lewis's party of four encountered eight Indians and camped with them that evening. Early the next morning the Indians tried to steal the party's guns and horses, which resulted in a fight. R. Fields stabbed one Indian to death and Lewis shot another. Lewis and his party fled. They rode hard all day and most of the night and reached the safety of their boats on the Missouri River the next morning. Lewis estimated that they fled over 120 miles.

Moundscale *Atriplex gardneri*

Scarlet Globemallow
Sphaeralcea coccinea

Winterfat

Krascheninnikovia lanata (Pursh) A. Meeuse and A. Smit.
Also *Ceratoides lanata* (Pursh) Howell
GOOSEFOOT FAMILY (Chenopodiaceae)

Plants: Low shrubs with woody bases and many erect, annual stems up to 20 inches long. Stems and foliage covered with white, woolly hair. Leaves narrow with parallel sides, up to 1½ inches long. Leaf margins rolled towards the lower side of the leaf. **Flowers:** Arranged in the leaf axils, each flower has four woolly bracts but no petals. Unisexual, the male flowers on the upper part of the stems in short clusters and the female flowers below with larger woolly bracts. **Fruits:** Oval and flat with white, woolly hair. **Flowering Season:** May to July. **Habitat/Range:** Plains and foothills, often in saline or alkaline soil from Saskatchewan to Alberta and Washington, and south to Texas and California.

FROM THE JOURNALS: No specimen of winterfat exists, but in his 1814 book Frederick Pursh initially named the species *Diotis lanata* using a specimen from Lewis's collection. Pursh placed winterfat's collection "On the banks of the Missouri, in open prairies M. Lewis . . . Aug. Sept." Perhaps Lewis collected the specimen along the Marias River in July 1806 near where he collected moundscale and greasewood, which share the same habitat, or later as he descended the Missouri in August or September 1806.

Wooly Groundsel

Senecio canus Hook.
Also *Packera cana* (Hook) W. A. Weber and A. Love
ASTER FAMILY (Asteraceae)

Plants: Perennial herbs up to 14 inches tall covered with dense, white, woolly hair. Lower leaves have long stalks while the upper leaves are stalkless and progressively smaller towards the top of the plant. Leaf blades egg shaped, often tapering towards the base. **Flowers:** Eight to thirteen yellow ray-flowers surrounding a yellow disk with black-tipped bracts. Arranged in cymes of six to twelve heads. **Fruits:** Smooth achenes with numerous long, white, pappus bristles. **Flowering Season:** May to August. **Habitat/Range:** Dry, rocky plains, foothills, and mountains from British Columbia to Manitoba and south to California, New Mexico, and Nebraska.

FROM THE JOURNALS: A wooly-groundsel specimen does not exist, but Frederick Pursh described and named *Cineraria intergifolia* var. *minor* using a specimen from Lewis's collection that we believe was wooly groundsel. The specimen has since been lost. In crediting Lewis's specimen, Pursh wrote: "On the banks of the Missouri. *M. Lewis* . . . Aug. Sept. . . . About a foot high; flowers the size of *Senecio Jacobaea,* yellow ; the rays very short." Given the sparse information above, Lewis could have collected wooly groundsel in the Tallgrass Prairie, the High Plains, or the Rocky Mountains.

Winterfat *Krascheninnikovia lanata*

Wooly Groundsel *Senecio canus*

Pulse Milkvetch

Astragalus tenellus Pursh
BEAN FAMILY (Fabaceae)

Plants: Perennial herbs, 4 to 18 inches tall, covered with short, stiff hairs. Leaves pinnately compound with eleven to twenty-five small leaflets. **Flowers:** White, cream, pinkish, rarely purple; arranged in open racemes of two to twenty flowers. **Fruits:** Downward-hanging, flat pods. **Flowering Season:** May to July. **Habitat/Range:** Gravelly plains, badlands, and open woodlands from Ontario to the Yukon and south to Nebraska, New Mexico, and west to Nevada and Idaho.

FROM THE JOURNALS: Pulse milkvetch was a species new to science when Frederick Pursh named and described it in his 1814 book. Pursh credited a specimen from Lewis's collection as the source of his information. He wrote: "On the banks of the Missouri. *M. Lewis* . . . Flowers small, yellowish-white." The specimen has since been lost. If collected on the Missouri in August, Lewis might have found it in the Tallgrass Prairie in 1804, the valleys of the Rocky Mountains in 1805, or more likely the High Plains in 1806.

Textile Onion

Allium textile A. Nels. and Macbr.
LILY FAMILY (Liliaceae)

Plants: Small, perennial herbs less than 1 foot tall with a strong onion or garlic odor. Two very narrow, channeled leaves as long or longer than the flowering stem. **Flowers:** Each plant has a single, upright umbel of fifteen to thirty flowers. Six tepals, white with a reddish brown midrib. Six stamens, shorter than the tepals. **Fruits:** Capsules have six or fewer black, shiny seeds. **Flowering Season:** May to July. **Habitat/Range:** Dry plains, hills, and open pine-woods from central Canada and Minnesota to Idaho and Washington, and south to Kansas, Nevada, and New Mexico.

FROM THE JOURNALS: A specimen of onion still exists but it is only leaves, so it is difficult to identify the species. On this specimen's label Frederick Pursh wrote, "Allium Kuskuskiense. On the waters of Kookooskee [Clearwater River in Idaho] Aprl. 30th 1806." In the past, botanists thought this incomplete onion specimen was textile onion, but now they believe it's Geyer's onion, *Allium geyeri* (Reveal, Moulton, and Schuyler, 1999), which is discussed in the *Rocky Mountains.*

Pursh described a species of onion in his 1814 book using a specimen from Lewis's collection. Pursh wrote: "On the banks of the Missouri. *M. Lewis and Nuttall* . . . July. . . . Flowers white." Although this white-flowered onion specimen has been lost, botanists believe that it was textile onion. On April 12, 1805, near the confluence of the Little Missouri River and Missouri River in present-day North Dakota, Lewis described textile onion in his journal: "found a great quantity of small onions in the plain where we encamped; had some of them collected and cooked, found them agreeable. the bulb grows single, is of an oval form, white, and about the size of a small bullet; the leaf resem{bles} that of the shive [chive]."

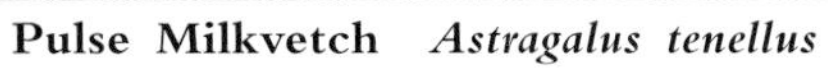

Pulse Milkvetch *Astragalus tenellus*

Textile Onion *Allium textile*

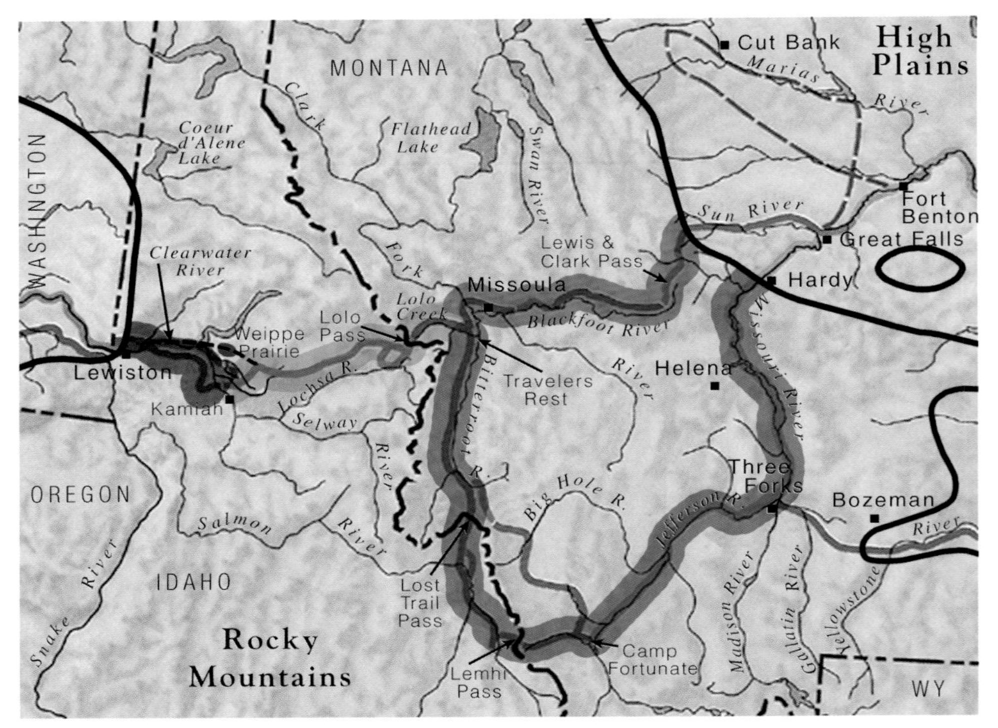

Ribes aureum
Mimulus lewisii
Acer glabrum
Symphoricarpos albus
Perideridia montana
Lonicera utahensis
Sorbus scopulina
Angelica arguta

Philadelphus lewisii
Chrysothamnus viscidiflorus
Lomatium triternatum
Erigeron compositus
Ceanothus velutinus
Phlox speciosa
Amelanchier alnifolia[1]
Pinus ponderosa
Fritillaria pudica
Erythronium grandiflorum
Calochortus elegans
Penstemon wilcoxii
Achillea millefolium
Clematis hirsutissima
Rhamnus purshiana
Holodiscus discolor
Prunus emarginata
Prunus virginiana[2]
Allium douglasii
Allium geyeri
Erysimum capitatum
Clarkia pulchella
Lonicera ciliosa

Sedum lanceolatum
Scutellaria angustifolia
Lupinus sericeus
Eriophyllum lanatum
Phacelia heterophylla

Festuca idahoensis
Pseudoroegneria spicata
Poa secunda
Koeleria macrantha
Lomatium dissectum
Rosa nutkana
Geum triflorum
Matricaria matricarioides
Polygonum bistortoides
Camassia quamash
Frasera fastigiata
Camissonia subacaulis

Trillium petiolatum
Anemone piperi
Penstemon fruticosus
Xerophyllum tenax
Cornus canadensis
Paxistima myrsinites[3]
Ribes viscosissimum
Calypso bulbosa
Aquilegia formosa
Thermopsis montana
Asarum caudatum
Veratrum californicum

Ipomopsis aggregata
Synthyris missurica
Lewisia triphylla
Polemonium pulcherrimum
Claytonia lanceolata
Ceanothus sanguineus
Menziesia ferruginea
Phyllodoce empetriformis
Larix occidentalis
Thuja plicata
Cypripedium montanum
Populus trichocarpa
Bazzania trilobata
Lewisia rediviva
Orthocarpus tenuifolius
Sedum stenopetalum
Trifolium microcephalum

Mimulus guttatus
Iris missouriensis
Purshia tridentata
Elaeagnus commutata
Pentaphylloides floribunda
Pedicularis groenlandica
Pedicularis cystopteridifol
Juniperus communis[2]
Balsamorhiza sagittata[3]
Oxytropis besseyi
Lonicera involucrata
Gaillardia aristata
Lupinus argenteus
Zigadenus elegans

1. *See* Columbia Plains.

2. *See* High Plains.

3. *See* Pacific Forest

The Rocky Mountains

The North American Rocky Mountains span the continent from Alaska to Mexico. Lewis and Clark crossed the Rocky Mountains in present-day western Montana and northern Idaho. This is an area of forested mountain ranges interspersed with broad, grassy valleys and deep, rocky canyons. Elevations range from over 10,000 feet on some of the mountain ranges that the explorers passed by to less than 750 feet above sea level at the confluence of the Clearwater and Snake Rivers, where they exited the Rocky Mountains.

The climate in the dry, mountainous region east of "Travellers rest" (Travelers Rest) near present-day Lolo, Montana, is temperate and semiarid, with an annual precipitation of 10 to 40 inches. West of Travelers Rest in northern Idaho the climate is wetter, influenced by maritime patterns, and annual precipitation ranges from 20 to 100 inches. Most precipitation falls as snow, which remains on the highest north-facing slopes year-round.

The vegetation of the Rocky Mountains is distributed in elevation-zones starting with the grasslands and shrublands in the valleys, ponderosa pine and Douglas-fir forests on lower mountain-slopes, and subalpine fir and spruce forests at higher elevations below the treeless alpine-zone, the summits of the highest peaks. Tree diversity is greater in the moist, humid forests west of Travelers Rest. In addition to the coniferous trees I have already mentioned, larch, white pine, red cedar, and western hemlock grow at lower and middle elevations, and mountain hemlock occurs at higher elevations along the Lolo Trail. There are diverse flowering shrubs and herbaceous plants in the Rocky Mountains. Meadows filled with blue camas, pink elephant's head, shooting stars, and yellow arrowleaf-balsamroot are common. Glacier lilies and trillium brighten the forest floor while wild ginger flowers are more subtle.

On July 17, 1805, Lewis and Clark first entered the Rocky Mountains above the "pine island" rapids near present-day Hardy, Montana. The explorers traversed the region for almost three months. They pulled their boats up the Missouri River to Camp Fortunate (now inundated by Lewis and Clark Canyon Reservoir) near present-day Dillon, Montana, where they obtained horses. Then they traveled on horseback over the Continental Divide at Lemhi Pass on August 26, Lost Trail Pass on September 4, and Lolo Pass on September 13, reaching the forks of the Clearwater River on September 26, 1805, where they established a camp and built canoes below present-day Orofino, Idaho. The party exited the Rocky Mountains by canoe at the confluence of the Clearwater and Snake Rivers on October 10, 1805.

The travelers reentered the Rocky Mountains at the confluence of the Snake and Clearwater Rivers on May 5, 1806. They established Camp Chopunnish along the Clearwater River near present-day Kamiah, Idaho, and camped there from May 13 to June 10. The party then camped at the "quawmash flatts" (Weippe Prairie) near present-day Weippe, Idaho, for several days. After an aborted attempt to traverse the snow-clad Lolo Trail, they returned to Weippe Prairie and enlisted three

Chopunnish (Nez Perce) Indian guides. With the guides showing the way, they crossed over the Lolo Trail and arrived at Travelers Rest on June 30, 1806.

Here the Captains divided the party into two groups. Lewis's party traveled northeast past present-day Missoula, Montana, and up the Blackfoot River, exiting the Rocky Mountains east of Lewis and Clark Pass on July 8, 1806, between present-day Lincoln and Simms, Montana. Clark's party went south up the Bitterroot Valley, over the Continental Divide at Gibbon's Pass, and back to Camp Fortunate. There they raised their boats. Some rode horseback while others paddled down the Beaverhead and Jefferson Rivers. Near present-day Three Forks, Montana, the party split into two groups. One, with Sergeant Ordway in charge, continued in boats down the Missouri River and joined Captain Lewis at the "great falls of the Missouri" River. Clark led the other group on horseback over Bozeman Pass near present-day Bozeman, Montana, where they exited the Rocky Mountains on July 15, 1806.

While at Camp Fortunate in 1805, they cached the plants they had collected in the Rocky Mountains on the outbound journey. They intended to retrieve the cache on the return trip. On August 20, 1805, Lewis wrote in his journal, "I made up a small assortment of medicines, together with the specemines of plants, minerals, seeds &c. [etc.] which, I have collected betwen this place and the falls of the Missouri which I shall deposit here." Captain Clark opened the cache on July 8, 1806, and even though he observed, "I found every article Safe, except a little damp," we presume that moisture (and mildew) destroyed the plant specimens that Captain Lewis had deposited there since only a single specimen from this period (golden currant, *Ribes aureum*) resides in the Lewis and Clark Herbarium today. Since no records for these plants have been found, we don't know how many plants were lost in the cache or what species they were.

We do know what plants they collected between Camp Fortunate and the mouth of the Clearwater River in Idaho during the hurried and arduous outbound journey in the fall of 1805, and we know what plants they collected on their return trip in the spring of 1806. The party camped at Camp Chopunnish along the Clearwater River for almost a month during the peak of plant blooming in 1806. Here, and on the way to Travelers Rest, Lewis preserved many plant species.

We know the expedition collected at least eighty-one plant species in the Rocky Mountains, more than from any other geographic region they traveled through. We can identify seventy-eight of these species from specimens that are still intact in the Lewis and Clark Herbarium in Philadelphia. Using references in Pursh's 1814 book, botanists have also identified three plants that were lost.

I included all eighty-one of these (collected) species in this book. However, five of them were duplicate specimens of species that I discussed in other regions: *common juniper* and *chokecherry* in the *High Plains; mountain lover* and *arrow-leaved balsamroot* in the *Pacific Forest;* and *western serviceberry* in the *Columbia Plains.* I also included ten species that are mentioned in the journals, but we don't know if Lewis and Clark actually collected them.

Creek below Hungery Creek in Idaho

Western Larch in the fall

The Rocky Mountains

Golden Currant

Ribes aureum Pursh
CURRANT FAMILY (Grossulariaceae)

Plants: Shrubs 3 to 10 feet tall. Leaves alternate with three lobes. Stems smooth (no prickles). **Flowers:** Yellow, arranged in racemes of five to eighteen flowers. Each flower consists of a cylindrical tube attached to the top of the ovary with five showy lobes that flare from the end of the tube. **Fruits:** Edible, smooth berries that vary in color from orange, yellow, red, to black. **Flowering Season:** April to May. **Habitat/Range:** Along streams of the grasslands and dry forests from British Columbia to California and east to Quebec and Texas.

FROM THE JOURNALS: Two specimens of golden currant, mounted on a single herbarium sheet, still exist at the Lewis and Clark Herbarium in Philadelphia. The explorers collected the first specimen on July 29, 1805, near present-day Three Forks, Montana, and the second one on April 16, 1806, at "rockfort camp" near present-day The Dalles, Oregon. A duplicate of the April 16 specimen from "rockfort camp" is kept at the Royal Botanic Gardens at Kew near London.

Lewis first described golden currant on July 17, 1805, the day after the explorers entered the Rocky Mountains near present-day Hardy, Montana: "there are a great abundance of red yellow perple & black currants, and service berries now ripe and in great perfection. I find these fruits very pleasent particularly the yellow currant which I think vastly preferable to those of our gardens. the shrub which produces this fruit rises to the hight of 6 or 8 feet . . . they grow closely ascociated in cops either in the oppen or timbered lands near the watercourses. . . . the perianth [sepals and petals] of the fructification is one leaved, five cleft, abbreviated and tubular, the corolla is monopetallous funnel-shaped . . . and of a fine orrange colour. . . . the fruit is a berry. . . . it is quite as transparent as the red current of our gardens, not so ascid, & more agreeably flavored."

On April 16, while at "rockfort camp," Lewis collected golden currant and described it in his journal: "I also met with sundry other plants which were strangers to me which I also preserved, among others there is a currant which is now in blume and has yellow blossom something like the yellow currant of the Missouri but is a different species." Lewis showed keen powers of observation when he noticed the subtle differences between the golden currants found on the Missouri River and those along the Columbia River. In his 1814 book, Frederick Pursh considered both the Missouri and Columbia populations one species and named it *Ribes aureum*. Today, most botanists agree that both populations fit into one species, *Ribes aureum,* with two varieties: the variety *villosum* from the Missouri River has larger flowers, leaves with varying amounts of hair, and a slightly different flower morphology than the variety *aureum,* which is found on the Columbia River.

olden Currant flowers *Ribes aureum*

Golden Currant berries

The Missouri River exits the Rocky Mountains near Hardy, Montana

Lewis's Red Monkey-Flower

Mimulus lewisii Pursh
FIGWORT FAMILY (Scrophulariaceae)

Plants: Perennial herbs 1 to 3 ½ feet tall. Leaves opposite, entire, without leafstalks, palmately veined, have coarsely toothed margins, long hairs, and sticky glands on the surface. **Flowers:** Pink to purple, yellow marks in the throat; arranged singly on long stalks from the leaf axils. The large flowers have two lips; the upper lip has two lobes and the lower lip has three. **Fruits:** Capsules with numerous seeds. **Flowering Season:** July to September. **Habitat/Range:** Along (and in) streams and seeps from British Columbia to California and east to Alberta and Colorado.

FROM THE JOURNALS: A specimen of Lewis's red monkey-flower does not exist today, but Frederick Pursh described it in his 1814 book and credited Lewis's collection as the source of the specimen he used to describe this species. Pursh was the first person to describe this species for science, and he named the plant *Mimulus lewisii* in honor of Meriwether Lewis. He also featured this plant as one of the twenty-three illustrations in his book.

Pursh wrote of this species, "On the head springs of the Missouri, at the foot of Portage hill . . . flowers two or three, larger than any other known species [of *Mimulus*], of a beautiful pale purple." From this information we know that Lewis collected his red monkey-flower specimen in the spring-fed headwaters of Trail Creek in present-day Montana, just below Lemhi Pass, where it still grows today. Lewis crossed Lemhi Pass on August 12 and 15, 1805, with a small party searching for the Shoshone Indians and horses to purchase. On August 12 he wrote, "McNeal had exultingly stood with a foot on each side of this little rivulet [Trail Creek] and thanked his god that he had lived to bestride the mighty & heretofore deemed endless Missouri." On August 26 they crossed Lemhi Pass the last time as the party proceeded on towards the Pacific Ocean.

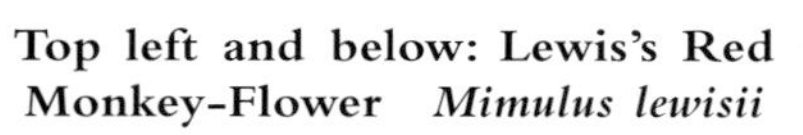

Top left and below: Lewis's Red Monkey-Flower *Mimulus lewisii*

Top right: Illustration of Lewis's Red Monkey-Flower from Frederick Pursh's 1814 *Flora Americae Septentrionalis*

Mountain Maple

Acer glabrum Torrey
MAPLE FAMILY (Aceraceae)

Plants: Tall shrubs or small tree 8 to 30 feet tall. Leaves are opposite, sharply toothed on the margin, and have three lobes. Young twigs smooth and cherry red. Buds valvelike with only two bud scales. **Flowers:** Greenish, small, and inconspicuous; consist of five sepals, five petals, and eight to ten stamens. **Fruits:** A pair of broadly winged samaras joined where they attach to the plant. **Flowering Season:** April to June. **Habitat/Range:** Along streams and on wooded slopes from Alaska to California, east to Alberta and New Mexico, and in Nebraska.

Common Snowberry

Symphoricarpos albus (L.) Blake
HONEYSUCKLE FAMILY (Caprifoliaceae)

Plants: Shrubs 3 to 6 feet tall. Spring growth starts at lateral buds, not end (terminal) buds, resulting in dense twig-arrangement; twigs have many branches. Leaves opposite, elliptical, entire; on new, rapidly growing shoots, the leaves often toothed and lobed. **Flowers:** White to pink, bell shaped, arranged in few-flowered racemes. **Fruits:** White, round, and berrylike. **Flowering Season:** May to August. **Habitat/Range:** Shaded woods from Alaska to California and east to Quebec and North Carolina.

FROM THE JOURNALS: Lewis, with an advance party, first crossed the Continental Divide at Lemhi Pass on August 12, 1805. They were trying to make contact with the Shoshone Indians to acquire horses to carry their baggage and equipment to a navigable branch of the Columbia River. The next day Lewis described two new plants he encountered on a tributary of the Lemhi River in Idaho: "the road . . . brought us to a large creek [Pattee Creek?] . . . I saw near the creek some bushes of the white maple [mountain maple] . . . and a species of honeysuckle [common snowberry] much in it's growth and leaf like the small honeysuckle of the Missouri [western snowberry, *Symphoricarpos occidentalis*] only reather larger and bears a globular berry as large as a garden pea and as white as wax. this berry is formed of a thin smooth pellicle [delicate membrane] which envellopes a soft white musilagenous substance in which there are several small brown seed irregularly scattered or intermixed without any sell [cell] or perceptible membranous covering." A common-snowberry specimen still exists, but it doesn't have a label so we don't know the date and place of its collection. However, Lewis often collected specimens on or near the date he described them in his journal.

A mountain maple specimen does not exist, but this species is mentioned in the journals several times. On June 16, 1806, while traveling along the Lolo Trail, Lewis wrote, "the dogtooth violet [glacier lily] is just in blume, the honeysuckle, huckburry and a small speceis of white maple [mountain maple] are beginning to put fourth their leaves." Lewis also mentioned common snowberry while traveling along the Lolo Trail on September 20, 1805: "saw the hucklebury, honeysuckle, and alder . . . also a kind of honeysuckle which bears a white bury and rises about 4 feet high not common but to the western side of the rockey mountains."

Mountain Maple *Acer glabrum*

Common Snowberry flowers
Symphoricarpos albus

Common Snowberry fruit

Yampah

Perideridia montana (Blank.) Dorn
Also *Perideridia gairdneri* (H. and A.) Math.
PARSLEY FAMILY (Apiaceae)

Plants: Perennial herbs 1 to 4 feet tall. Leaves compound with several long, narrow leaflets; the upper leaves sometimes simple. Leaves often withering during flowering and fruiting. **Flowers:** White, arranged in compound umbels on the end of the stems and in the upper leaf axils. **Fruits:** Schizocarps, round and slightly flattened. **Flowering Season:** July to August. **Habitat/Range:** Meadows and open woods from British Columbia to California and east to Saskatchewan and New Mexico.

FROM THE JOURNALS: No specimen exists, but on August 26, 1805, while in the Lemhi Valley of Idaho, Lewis wrote a detailed description of yampah: "I observe the indian women collecting the root of a speceis of fennel which grows in the moist grounds and feeding their poor starved children; it is really distressing to witness the situation of those poor wretches. the radix [root] of this plant is of the knob kind, of a long ovate form terminating in a single radicle [root], the whole b[e]ing about 3 or four inches in length and the thickest part about the size of a man's little finger. it is white firm and crisp in it's present state, when dryed and pounded it makes a fine white meal; the flavor of this root is not unlike that of annis-seed but not so pungent; the stem rises to the hight of 3 or four feet is jointed smooth and cilindric; from 1 to 4 of those knobed roots are attatched to the base of this stem. the leaf is sheathing sessile [without a stalk], & pultipartite {multipartite}, the divisions long and narrow; the whole is of a deep green. it is now in blume; the flowers are numerous, small, petals white, and are of the umbellaferous [arranged in compound umbels] kind . . . the root of the present year declines when the seeds have been matured and the succeeding spring other roots of a similar kind put fourth from the little knot which unites the roots."

On May 18, 1806, while the party was at Camp Chopunnish on the Clearwater River in present-day Idaho, Lewis again mentioned yampah: "our indian woman [Sacagawea] was busily engaged today in laying in a store of the fennel roots for the Rocky mountains. these are called by the Shoshones *year-pah*."

Right: Yampah *Perideridia montana*

Below: Looking west from Lemhi Pass
—United States Forest Service
photo by K. R. Bump

Utah Honeysuckle

Lonicera utahensis S. Wats.
HONEYSUCKLE FAMILY (Caprifoliaceae)

Plants: Erect shrubs 3 to 6 feet tall. Leaves opposite, egg shaped, about 2 inches long and 1 inch wide. Twigs have large, purplish buds. **Flowers:** Yellowish white, trumpet shaped, arranged in pairs from the leaf axils. **Fruits:** Pairs of red, juicy berries from a common stalk. **Flowering Season:** May to July. **Habitat/Range:** Mountain forests from British Columbia to Oregon and east to Alberta and New Mexico.

Cascade Mountain-Ash

Sorbus scopulina Greene
ROSE FAMILY (Rosaceae)

Plants: Shrubs 3 to 12 feet tall. Leaves alternate and compound. Each leaf has nine to thirteen pinnately arranged leaflets, which have toothed margins and sharp, pointed tips. **Flowers:** White to yellowish, arranged in flat-topped corymbs of seventy to over one-hundred flowers. **Fruits:** Orange, berrylike pomes in large, flat-topped clusters. **Flowering Season:** May to July. **Habitat/Range:** Mountain forests from Alaska to California and east to Alberta and New Mexico.

Angelica

Angelica arguta Nutt.
Or *Angelica dawsonii* Wats.
PARSLEY FAMILY (Apiaceae)

Plants: Perennial herbs 1 to 6 feet tall. Leaves twice compound with eleven to twenty-three leaflets per leaf. The lateral veins run to the end of the tooth on the leaf margin. **Flowers:** White to pinkish, arranged in two or more compound umbels, usually don't have bracts at the juncture of the rays. Dawson's angelica *(Angelica dawsonii)* has yellow flowers arranged in a single umbel and conspicuous leafy bracts at the juncture of the rays. **Fruits:** Smooth schizocarps with winged ribs on the back and margins (sides). **Flowering Season:** June to August. **Habitat/Range:** Along streams, in seeps and marshes from British Columbia to California and east to Alberta and Colorado.

FROM THE JOURNALS: The explorers collected a specimen of Utah honeysuckle on September 2, 1805, near Lost Trail Pass. They collected Cascade mountain-ash on September 2, 1805, and June 27, 1806, on the Lolo Trail. These specimens still exist with original labels. Two labels document when the explorers collected angelica specimens: September 3, 1805, and another on June 25, 1806, along the Lolo Trail. It appears that insects ate the angelica specimens, and therefore botanists aren't sure which species they were.

On September 2, 1805, the expedition was struggling over the divide between the North Fork Salmon River of Idaho and the East Fork Bitterroot River of Montana near Lost Trail Pass. Clark's journal clearly shows the hazards and difficulties they faced: "we Set out early and proceeded on up the Creek [North Fork Salmon River] . . . and at 8 miles left the roade on which we were pursuing and which leads over to the Missouri; and proceeded up a West fork without a roade proceeded on thro'

Utah Honeysuckle *Lonicera utahensis*

Cascade Mountain-Ash *Sorbus scopulina*

Angelica *Angelica arguta*

thickets in which we were obliged to Cut a road, over rockey hill Sides where our horses were in pitial danger of Slipping to Ther certain distruction ... Several horses fell, Some turned over, and others Sliped down Steep hill Sides, one horse Crippeled & 2 gave out. with the greatest dificuelty risqué &c. [etc.] we made five miles." On September 3 he wrote: "A Cloudy morning, horses verry Stiff Sent 2 men back with the horse on which Capt Lewis rode for the load left back last night . . . The Country is timbered with Pine Generally the bottoms have a variety of Srubs & the fur trees in Great abundance. . . . This day we passed over emence hils and Some of the worst roade that ever horses passed our horses frequently fell ... Snow about 2 inches deep when it began to rain which termonated in a Sleet."

Mockorange or Syringa

Philadelphus lewisii Pursh
HYDRANGEA FAMILY (Hydrangeaceae)

Plants: Shrubs 4 to 8 feet tall with stiff and erect stems; older stems have cross-checked bark that flakes off. Leaves opposite, simple, with three main veins from the leaf base. **Flowers:** White, with the fragrance of orange blossoms. Each flower has four petals, four styles, and many stamens. Arranged in racemes of three to eleven flowers on lateral branches. **Fruits:** Hard capsule that remains on shrub for extended period. **Flowering Season:** May to July. **Habitat/Range:** Streamsides, rocky cliffs and slopes from the Pacific Coast to the Rocky Mountains, from British Columbia to California and east to Montana and Idaho.

FROM THE JOURNALS: Two specimens of mockorange were mounted on a single herbarium sheet. The expedition collected the first one on May 6, 1806, along the Kooskooske (Clearwater) River between Colters Creek (Potlatch River) and Pine Creek in Idaho. Lewis and his party collected the second specimen on July 4, 1806, while they traveled between Grant Creek near Missoula, Montana, and the Cokahlarishkit (Blackfoot) River. On May 6, 1806, Lewis wrote: "I exchanged horses with We-ark'-koomt and gave him a small flag with which he was much gratifyed. the sorrel I obtained is an eligant strong active well broke horse perfictly calculated for my purposes. at this place we met with three men of a nation called the Skeets-so-mish who reside at the falls of a large river disharging itself into the Columbia on it's East side. . . . this river they informed us headed in a large lake in the mountains and that the falls below which they resided was at no great distance from the lake." Lewis was writing about the Coeur d'Alene Indians who were describing Lake Couer d'Alene, Idaho, and their home at present-day Spokane, Washington. Syringa is now the state flower of Idaho.

Green Rabbitbrush

Chrysothamnus viscidiflorus (Hook.) Nutt.
ASTER FAMILY (Asteraceae)

Plants: Shrubs, usually less than 3 feet tall. Twigs brittle and smooth, or with fine, spreading hairs. Leaves alternate, long, narrow, and usually twisted; spiral like. **Flowers:** Yellow, arranged in flat-topped, cymelike clusters of heads covering the top of the plant. Each small head has about five disk flowers, about fifteen bracts, and no rays. **Fruits:** Achenes with numerous capillary bristles. **Flowering Season:** August to October. **Habitat/Range:** Dry plains and foothills from British Columbia to California and east to Montana and New Mexico.

FROM THE JOURNALS: On the label of the of green-rabbitbrush specimen, Frederick Pursh wrote, "A low Shrub growing in the rocky dry hills on the Kooskooskee [Clearwater River] May 6th 1806." Lewis wrote in his journal for May 7, 1806: "the face of the country when you have once ascended the river hills is perfectly level

Mockorange or Syringa
Philadelphus lewisii

Green Rabbitbrush
Chrysothamnus viscidiflorus

and partially covered with the longleafed [ponderosa] pine. the soil is a dark rich loam thickly covered with grass and herbatious plants which afford a delightfull pasture for horses. in short it is a beautifull fertile and picteresque country."

Nine-Leaved Bisquit-Root

Lomatium triternatum (Pursh) Coult. and Rose
PARSLEY FAMILY (Apiaceae)

Plants: Perennial herbs 8 to 32 inches tall. Leaves compound, having many narrow segments ½ to 4 inches long. **Flowers:** Yellow, arranged in compound umbels on the ends of the stems. Rays of the flower arrangement are of unequal lengths. Narrow bractlets join together just below where the flower stalks come together. **Fruits:** Dry schizocarp, oblong to elliptic, with wings on the margin. **Flowering Season:** May to July. **Habitat/Range:** Grasslands and meadows from British Columbia and Alberta south to California, Utah, and Colorado.

FROM THE JOURNALS: A specimen of nine-leaved bisquit-root has a label on which Frederick Pursh wrote: "A root 5 or 6 inches long eaten raw or boiled by the natives. On the Kooskooske [Clearwater River] My. 6th 1806." Clark may have been describing this species while at Camp Fortunate on July 9, 1806: "The Squar [Sacagawea] brought me a Plant the root of which the nativs eat. this root most resembles a Carrot in form and Size and Something of its colour, being of a pailer yellow than that of our Carrot, the Stem and leaf is much like the Common Carrot, and the taste not unlike. it is a native of moist land." However, several other species of desert-parsley have leaves more like the common carrot than nine-leaved bisquit-root, and they are also edible.

Cut-Leaved Daisy

Erigeron compositus Pursh
ASTER FAMILY (Asteraceae)

Plants: Perennial herbs 1 to 10 inches tall. Basal leaves consist of many narrow segments in groups of three often covered with hair. Leaves on the stems are few, small, and entire. **Flowers:** Arranged in solitary heads on the stem ends. Ray flowers usually white, but may be pink, blue, or absent altogether. Disk flowers yellow. **Fruits:** Achenes have twelve to twenty bristles. **Flowering Season:** May to August. **Habitat/Range:** Open slopes on sandy or stony soil from Alaska to Greenland and south to California, Arizona, South Dakota, and Quebec.

FROM THE JOURNALS: The specimen of cut-leaved daisy is in a nonflowering condition. The label with it states that the expedition collected it on the "Kooskoosky" (Clearwater) River, but it doesn't have a date. Botanists believe it was collected in the fall of 1805.

Buckbrush Ceanothus

Ceanothus velutinus Dougl. ex Hook.
BUCKTHORN FAMILY (Rhamnaceae)

Plants: Evergreen, aromatic shrubs 2 to 6 feet tall. Leaves alternate, entire, with three prominent veins that radiate from the leaf base. Upper leaf-surface shiny, dark green; lower surface dull gray. **Flowers:** White to cream colored. Arranged in panicle clusters on long stalks from the leaf axils. **Fruits:** Hard capsule that separates into three sections. **Flowering Season:** June to August. **Habitat/Range:** Well-drained slopes from British Columbia to California and east to Alberta, South Dakota, and Colorado.

Top left: Nine-Leaved Bisquit-Root
Lomatium triternatum

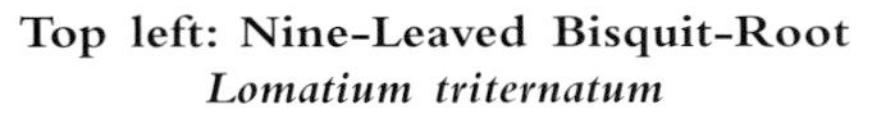

Top right: Cut-Leaved Daisy
Erigeron compositus

Bottom right: Buckbrush Ceanothus
Ceanothus velutinus

FROM THE JOURNALS: On the label of an undated specimen of buckbrush ceanothus, Frederick Pursh wrote: "An Evergreen A Shrub about 8 or 9 f. high. On the Rocky mountains Waters of the Kooskooskee [Clearwater River]." This specimen is in a nonflowering condition, and botanists believe Lewis and Clark collected it in the fall of 1805.

Showy Phlox

Phlox speciosa Pursh
PHLOX FAMILY (Polemoniaceae)

Plants: Perennial herbs 6 to 16 inches tall, erect, with a woody base. Leaves opposite, long and narrow, up to 2¾ inches long and ⅜ inch wide. **Flowers:** Pink to white, the petal lobes notched at the tip; arranged cymelike on the ends of the stems. **Fruits:** Capsules. **Flowering Season:** April to June. **Habitat/Range:** Dry slopes associated with sagebrush and ponderosa pine from interior British Columbia to California and east to Montana, Nevada, and New Mexico.

FROM THE JOURNALS: Lewis and Clark collected a specimen of showy phlox on May 7, 1806. The expedition traveled about 12 miles on that day from the vicinity of present-day Cherry Lane, Idaho, to Peck, Idaho. Today, portions of this specimen still exist on two herbarium sheets, one in the Lewis and Clark Herbarium and the other at the Royal Botanic Gardens at Kew near London. On May 7 the party crossed the Kooskooske (Clearwater) River at an Indian lodge near Bedrock Creek. Lewis wrote in his journal: "a man of this lodge produced us two canisters of powder which he informed us he had found by means of his dog where they had been buried in a bottom near the river some miles above, they were the same which we had buryed as we decended the river last fall. as he had kept them safe and had honesty enough to return them to us we gave him a fire steel by way of compensation."

Ponderosa Pine

Pinus ponderosa Dougl. ex Laws. and Laws.
PINE FAMILY (Pinaceae)

Plants: Large trees 30 to 50 inches in diameter and 90 to 130 feet tall. Bark in flat, scaly plates and deep furrows; brownish black on young trees and orangish brown on older trees. Leaves 5 to 8 inches long, usually in bundles of three, but sometimes two. **Flowers:** Male cones yellow to purple, about 1 inch long. Female cones reddish purple when young and mature to brown; 3 to 6 inches long with prickly-tipped scales. **Fruits:** Naked, winged seeds develop on the inner surface of the female-cone scales. **Flowering Season:** May to June. **Habitat/Range:** Dry slopes from British Columbia to California and east to North Dakota and Nebraska, and south through the Rocky Mountains to Mexico.

FROM THE JOURNALS: Two herbarium sheets of ponderosa pine still exist, both from material collected, according to Frederick Pursh, "On the Kooskooskee [Clearwater] On River bottoms in rich land, west of the mountains. Octbr: 1st 1805." On October 1, 1805, the explorers were at their "canoe camp" at the mouth of the North Fork Clearwater River constructing five canoes from large ponderosa pines. On October 2 Clark wrote, "day excesively hot in the river bottom wind North, Burning out the hotter {hollow?} of our canoes." The party first observed ponderosa pine on May 11, 1805, near present-day The Pines Recreation Area on Fort Peck Lake in Montana. That day Lewis remarked: "saw today some high hills on the Stard. whose summits were covered with pine. Capt Clark went on shore and visited them; he brought with him on his return som of the boughs of this

Ponderosa Pine ***Pinus ponderosa***

Showy Phlox ***Phlox speciosa***

pine it is of the pitch kind but I think the leaves somewhat longer than ours in Virginia." Throughout their journals the explorers referred to ponderosa pine as "long-leafed pine."

Ponderosa Pine needles and cones

Yellow Bell

Fritillaria pudica (Pursh) Spreng.
LILY FAMILY (Liliaceae)

Plants: Perennial herbs, 4 to 12 inches tall, with two to six narrow leaves ½ to 6½ inches long. **Flowers:** Yellow, facing downward, found singly (or two to three) on the stem ends with six stamens and one style hidden by six straight tepals. **Fruits:** Round or egg-shaped capsules, about 1 inch long. **Flowering Season:** March to June. **Habitat/Range:** Grasslands to dry forests from British Columbia to California and east to Alberta and New Mexico.

FROM THE JOURNALS: The explorers collected duplicate specimens of yellow bell, according to Frederick Pursh, on the "Plains of Columbia near the Kooskooskee [Clearwater River] May 8th 1806. the bulb in the Shape of a bisquit, which the natives eat." In the afternoon of May 8, 1806, the explorers left their camp just south of present-day Peck, Idaho, as described by Clark in his journal: "we assended the hills which was Steep and emencely high to a leavel rich Country thinly timbered with pine. we had not proceeded more than 4 miles before we . . . were verry coolly recved by the [Chief] twisted hair. he Spoke aloud and was answered by the [Chief] Cut Nose. we Could not learn what they Said. but plainly discovered that a missunderstanding had taken place between them. . . . [later, in counsel with them] it appears that the Cause of the quarrel between those two men is about our horses. . . . twisted hair Says the horses were taken from him &c [etc.]. . . . the cut nose said that the twisted hair was a bad man and wore two fases, that he had not taken care of our horses as was expected. that himself an the [Chief] broken arm had Caused our horses to be Watered in the winter and had them drove together."

Glacier Lily

Erythronium grandiflorum Pursh
LILY FAMILY (Liliaceae)

Plants: Perennial herbs, 4 to 12 inches tall, with a single stem and single pair of opposite leaves near the base. Leaves 4 to 8 inches long and ½ to 2 inches wide. **Flowers:** Yellow to white, facing downward, with one to four flowers on the stem ends. Each flower has six stamens and a style with three lobes clearly visible outside the six, reflexed tepals. **Fruits:** Cylindrical capsule about 2 inches long. **Flowering Season:** May to July. **Habitat/Range:** Moist slopes from foothills to high mountains from British Columbia to California and east to Alberta and New Mexico.

FROM THE JOURNALS: The explorers collected the first specimen of glacier lily southeast of present-day Peck, Idaho. Frederick Pursh wrote on this specimen's label: "From the plains of Columbia near Kooskooskee [Clearwater] R. May 8th 1806. the natives reckon this root as unfitt for food." They collected the second specimen on June 15, 1806—the party's first day along the Lolo Trail—somewhere between the "quawmash flatts" and Eldorado Creek where they camped that night. The next day the party paused in a meadow and Lewis noted, "the dogtooth violet [glacier lily] is just in blume, the honeysuckle, huckburry and a small speceis of white maple are beginning to put fourth their leaves." Along the Lolo Trail on June 27, near present-day Spring Mountain, Lewis wrote: "neare our encampment we

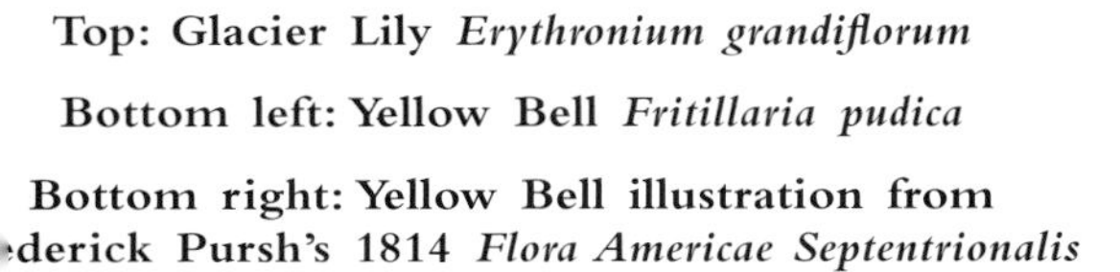

Top: Glacier Lily *Erythronium grandiflorum*

Bottom left: Yellow Bell *Fritillaria pudica*

Bottom right: Yellow Bell illustration from
derick Pursh's 1814 *Flora Americae Septentrionalis*

saw a great number of the yellow lilly with reflected petals in blume; this plant was just as forward here at this time as it was in the plains on the 10th of may."

Cat's Ear Mariposa Lily

Calochortus elegans Pursh
LILY FAMILY (Liliaceae)

Plants: Perennial herbs, 2 to 6 inches tall; each plant has a single, grasslike, basal leaf, 4 to 8 inches long and less than ⅜ inch wide. **Flowers:** White, with a purple blotch and long white to purple hair on the surface and along the margin of the petals. Each plant has one or two flowers on the end of a flower stalk that is 2 to 6 inches tall. **Fruits:** Nodding capsules with three wings. **Flowering Season:** May to June. **Habitat/Range:** Grassy hillsides and open woods from northern California and eastern Washington and Oregon, into Idaho and Montana.

FROM THE JOURNALS: On the label with a specimen of cat's ear mariposa lily, Frederick Pursh wrote: "A Small bulb of a pleasant flavour, eat by the natives. On the Kooskooske [Clearwater River]. May 17th 1806." Rain had soaked the party day and night on May 17 when Lewis remarked: "it rained moderately the greater part of the day and snowed as usual on the plain. Sergt. Pryor informed me that it was shoe deep this morning when he came down. it is somewhat astonishing that the grass and a variety of plants which are now from a foot to 18 inches high on these plains sustain no injury from the snow or frost; many of those plants are in blume and appear to be of a tender susceptable texture."

Wilcox's Beardtongue

Penstemon wilcoxii Rydb.
FIGWORT FAMILY (Scrophulariaceae)

Plants: Perennial herbs 12 to 40 inches tall. Leaves opposite, simple, 2 to 4 inches long and ½ to 1½ inches wide, with coarse teeth on the margin. **Flowers:** Blue to bluish purple, arranged in open panicles. Each flower is funnel shaped with a lobed margin, has four fertile stamens and one sterile stamen with yellow hair on the tip. **Fruits:** Capsules up to ¼ inch long. **Flowering Season:** May to July. **Habitat/Range:** Open woods from the foothills to mountain slopes of eastern Washington and Oregon, and into Idaho and northwestern Montana.

FROM THE JOURNALS: The explorers collected a specimen of Wilcox's beardtongue on May 20, 1806, near Camp Chopunnish. In his journal for May 20 Lewis complained: "It rained the greater part of last night and continued this morning untill noon when it cleared away about an hour and then rained at intervals untill 4 in the evening. our covering is so indifferent that Capt C. and myself lay in the water the greater part of the last night. . . . Frazier who had been permitted to go to the village this morning returned with a pasel of Roots and bread which he had purchased. brass buttons is an article of which these people are tolerably fond, the men have taken advantage of their prepossession in favour of buttons and have devested themselves of all they had in possesson which they have given in exchange for roots and bread."

Cat's Ear Mariposa Lily *Calochortus elegans*

[Wil]cox's Beardtongue *Penstemon wilcoxii*

Landscape south of Camp Chopunnish near Kamiah, Idaho

Yarrow

Achillea millefolium L.
ASTER FAMILY (Asteraceae)

Plants: Aromatic, perennial herbs, 8 to 24 inches tall, with lacy, fernlike leaves divided into many small, ultimate segments. **Flowers:** White, composed of many small heads in a flat-topped, corymb-like arrangement. **Fruits:** Small, flat, smooth achenes without a pappus. **Flowering Season:** April to October. **Habitat/Range:** Ubiquitous. Found from sea level to alpine slopes throughout the temperate northern hemisphere.

FROM THE JOURNALS: The explorers collected yarrow on May 20, 1806, near Camp Chopunnish. On May 21 Lewis referred to the many plants with lacy leaves in the area: "today we divided the remnant of our store of merchandize among our party with a view that each should purchase therewith a parsel of roots and bread from the natives as his stores for the rocky mountains for there seems but little probability that we shall be enabled to make any dryed meat for that purpose. . . . we would make the men collect these roots themselves but there are several species of hemlock which are so much like the cows [cous bisquit-root] that it is difficult to discriminate them from the cows and we are affraid that they might poison themselves." This was a wise decision since the poisonous water-hemlock does grow along the Clearwater River, as do many other plants with finely divided leaves such as yarrow and cous.

Sugarbowls

Clematis hirsutissima Pursh
BUTTERCUP FAMILY (Ranunculaceae)

Plants: Upright, hairy, perennial herbs, 6 to 26 inches tall. Leaves opposite on the stems and pinnately divided into many narrow, ultimate segments. **Flowers:** Purple, shaped like an upside-down vase, and found singly on the ends of the stems. **Fruits:** Achenes with long, featherlike, persistent styles. **Flowering Season:** April to July. **Habitat/Range:** Grasslands from Washington and Oregon, east to Montana, and south in the Rocky Mountains to New Mexico.

FROM THE JOURNALS: Frederick Pursh wrote on the label with sugarbowls specimen, "One of the most common plants of the plains of Columbia May 27th 1806." That day Lewis wrote in his journal: "[Chief] Hohastillpilp told us that most of the horses we saw running at large in this neighbourhood belonged to himself and his people, and whenever we were in want of meat he requested that we would kill any of them we wished; this is a peice of liberallity which would do honour to such as bost [best?] of civilization; indeed I doubt whether there are not a great number of our countrymen who would see us fast many days before their compassion would excite them to a similar act of liberallity."

Top left: Yarrow
Achillea millefolium

Top right: Sugarbowls
Clematis hirsutissima

Bottom right:
Sugarbowls fruit

Cascara Buckthorn

Rhamnus purshiana DC.
Also *Frangula purshiana* (DC.) J. G. Cooper
BUCKTHORN FAMILY (Rhamnaceae)

Plants: Large shrubs up to 33 feet tall. Leaves alternate, simple, with prominent, lateral veins. Buds naked and lack bud scales. **Flowers:** Clusters of eight to fifty small, green to yellow flowers in the axils of the leaves. Both bisexual and unisexual flowers may be present. **Fruits:** Purplish black berries. **Flowering Season:** April to June. **Habitat/Range:** British Columbia to California and east through Idaho and northwestern Montana.

Creambush Oceanspray

Holodiscus discolor (Pursh) Maxim.
ROSE FAMILY (Rosaceae)

Plants: Shrubs 3 to 10 feet tall with arching branches. Leaves alternate, simple, hairy, paler green on the lower surface. Margins of leaves slightly lobed and have fine teeth. **Flowers:** Numerous tiny, cream colored flowers arranged in pyramid-shaped panicles that are 4 to 7 inches long. **Fruits:** Single-seeded achene. **Flowering Season:** June to August. **Habitat/Range:** Gravelly and rocky soils from British Columbia to California and east to northern Idaho and northwestern Montana.

Bittercherry

Prunus emarginata (Dougl. Ex Hook.) Walpers
ROSE FAMILY (Rosaceae)

Plants: Shrubs, 3 to 50 feet tall, that often form thickets. Leaves alternate, simple, with finely toothed margins and rounded tips. Leaf tips sometimes pointed, but the tips not elongated like chokecherry *(Prunus virginiana)*. **Flowers:** White, arranged in corymbs of five to eight flowers. **Fruits:** Red, edible berries. **Flowering Season:** April to June. **Habitat/Range:** Streamsides and moist slopes from British Columbia to California and east to Montana and New Mexico.

FROM THE JOURNALS: Lewis and Clark collected specimens of these shrub species on May 29, 1806, near Camp Chopunnish. There are two cascara buckthorn specimens, one with a label on which Frederick Pursh wrote: "A Shrub apparently a Species of Rhamnus About 12 feet high, in Clumps. fruit a 5-valved purple berry which the natives eat & esteen highly; the berry depressed globous." On the label accompanying one of the two oceanspray specimens Pursh wrote, "A Shrub growing much in the manner of Nine bark." Pursh wrote on the label with the bittercherry specimen, "Prunus A Smaller Shrub than the Choak cherry, the natives count it a good fruit."

Lewis often collected contrasting plants on the same day. He collected both bittercherry and chokecherry *(Prunus virginiana)* on May 29 (see *chokecherry* in the *High Plains*). He waited until June 7 to write a botanical description of bittercherry: "There is a speceis of cherry which grows in this neighbourhood in sitations like the Choke cherry . . . it seldom grows in clumps or from the same cluster of roots as the choke cherry dose. . . . the leaf . . . margin so finely serrate that it is scarcely perseptable . . . the parts of fructification are much like those discribed of the choke cherry except that the petals are reather longer as is the calix [sepals] reather deeper."

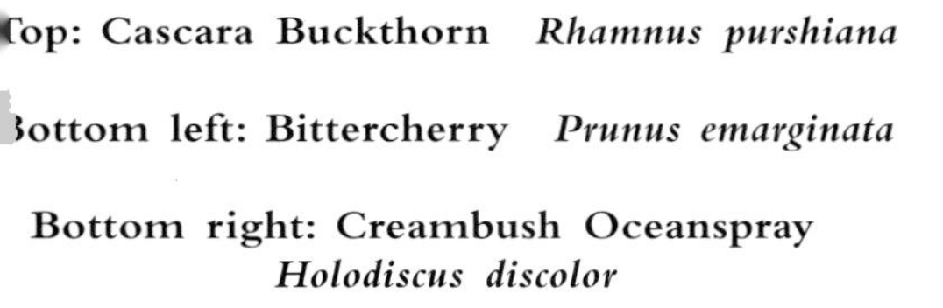

Top: Cascara Buckthorn *Rhamnus purshiana*

Bottom left: Bittercherry *Prunus emarginata*

Bottom right: Creambush Oceanspray *Holodiscus discolor*

Douglas's Onion

Allium douglasii Hook.
LILY FAMILY (Liliaceae)

Plants: Perennial herbs with a distinct onion odor. Each plant has a single, round, leafless stem 8 to 12 inches tall, and a pair of basal leaves. Leaves solid, often wide, flat, and curved inward, but may also be narrow and straight. **Flowers:** Pink, arranged in a many-flowered umbel on the ends of the stems. **Fruits:** Capsules with black seeds. **Flowering Season:** May to July. **Habitat/Range:** Openings where soil is moist in the winter in eastern Washington, eastern Oregon, Idaho, and northwestern Montana.

Geyer's Onion

Allium geyeri Wats.
LILY FAMILY (Liliaceae)

Plants: Perennial herbs with an onion odor that often grow in colonies. Each plant has a single, leafless stem 4 to 20 inches tall, and three (or more) basal leaves. The leaves are solid, narrow, and concave in cross section. **Flowers:** White, arranged in an umbel on the ends of the stems. Sometimes a few or all of the flowers in the umbels are replaced by small bulblets for asexual reproduction. **Fruits:** Capsules with black seeds. **Flowering Season:** May to June. **Habitat/Range:** Streamsides, seeps, and other moist places from British Columbia to Arizona and east to Manitoba and Texas.

FROM THE JOURNALS: The explorers collected a specimen of what botanists now identify as Geyer's onion on May 30, 1806, near Camp Chopunnish. That day Clark wrote about a sweat-bath treatment the explorers gave an Indian chief who had been paralyzed for three years: "we gave the Sick Chief a Severe *Swet* to day, Shortly after which he could move one of his legs and thy's and work his toes pritty well, the other leg he can move a little; his fingers and arms Seem to be almost entirely restored. he Seems highly delighted with his recovery. I begin to entertain Strong hope of his recovering by these sweats."

On May 30 Clark also wrote about a new onion species he saw: "one of the men brought me to day Some Onions from the high plains of a different Species [Douglas's onion] from those [Geyer's onion] near the borders of the river as they are also from the Shive [chive, *Allium schoenoprasum*] or Small Onion noticed below the Falls of Columbia. these [Douglas's] Onions were as large as an nutmeg, they generally grow double or two bulbs connected by the same tissue of radicles [roots]; each bulb has two long liner flat solid leaves. the pedencle is solid celindric and cround [crowned] with an umble of from 20 to 30 flowers. this Onion is exceedingly crisp and delicately flavoured indeed. I think more Sweet and less strong than any I ever tasted, it is not yet perfectly in blume, the parts of the flower are not distinct." On May 24, 1806, Clark applied an onion poultice to the swollen neck of Sacagawea's child. Just down the Missouri River from present-day Three Forks, Montana, on July 22, 1805, Lewis named an island "Onion Island" for the great quantities of pleasantly flavored onions and onion seed the expedition collected there.

Top left: Douglas's Onion
Allium douglasii

Top right: Geyer's Onion
Allium geyeri

Bottom: Site of Camp Chopunnish near Kamiah, Idaho

Rough Wallflower

Erysimum capitatum (Dougl. ex Hook.) E. Greene
Also *Erysimum asperum* (Nutt.) DC.
MUSTARD FAMILY (Brassicaceae)

Plants: Perennial herbs 8 to 40 inches tall. Leaves up to 5 inches long, arranged alternately on the stems; basal leaves arranged radially. **Flowers:** Yellow to orange, arranged in a raceme on the ends of the stems. **Fruits:** Long, narrow, upward-reaching pods 1 to 4 inches long. **Flowering Season:** May to July. **Habitat/Range:** Dry meadows from British Columbia to California, east to Quebec and Texas.

Elkhorns

Clarkia pulchella Pursh
EVENING PRIMROSE FAMILY (Onagraceae)

Plants: Annual herbs 4 to 20 inches tall. Leaves alternate, narrow, linear, ¾ to 3 inches long. The slender stems arch downward while the flowers are in bud and turn upward as they bloom. **Flowers:** Pink to lavender, arranged in short racemes of a few flowers. The four petals each have three lobes and a very narrow base with two small teeth. There are four fertile stamens and four smaller, sterile ones. The stigma has four white, petal-like lobes and looks like a tiny, white flower. **Fruits:** Capsules about ¾ inch long. **Flowering Season:** May to June. **Habitat/Range:** Dry grasslands or open woods east of the Cascade Mountains from British Columbia to Oregon and east through Idaho and western Montana.

FROM THE JOURNALS: The explorers collected specimens of rough wallflower and elkhorns near Camp Chopunnish on June 1, 1806. The wallflower specimen was not mentioned in the journals, but Lewis wrote a long and detailed botanical description of elkhorns that day: "I met with a singular plant today in blume of which I preserved a specemine; it grows on the steep sides of the fertile hills near this place . . . the stem is simple branching ascending, 2½ feet high celindric, villose [with silky hairs] and of a pale red colour. . . . The leaf is sissile, scattered thinly, nearly linear tho' somewhat widest in the middle, two inches in length. . . . a leaf is placed underneath eah branch, and each flower. . . . the corolla superior consists of four pale perple petals which are tripartite, the central lobe largest and all terminate obtusely; they are inserted with a long and narrow claw on the top of the germ. . . . there are two distinct sets of stamens the 1st or principal consist of four . . . the second set of stamens are very minute are also four and placed within and opposite to the petals, these are scarcely persceptable while the 1st are large and conspicuous. . . . it cannot be said where the style ends, or the stigma begins; jointly they are as long as the corolla, white, the limb is four cleft, sauser shaped, and the margins of the lobes entire and rounded. this has the appearance of a monopetallous flower growing from the center of a four petalled corollar, which is rendered more conspicuous in consequence of the 1st being white and the latter of a pale perple. I regret very much that the seed of this plant are not yet ripe and it is proble will not be so during my residence in this neighbourhood." Frederick Pursh named this plant *Clarkia pulchella* in honor of William Clark.

Rough Wallflower
Erysimum capitatum

Bottom left: Elkhorns
Clarkia pulchella

Bottom right: Elkhorns illustration from Frederick Pursh's 1814
Flora Americae Septentrionalis

Trumpet Honeysuckle

Lonicera ciliosa (Pursh) Poir. ex DC.
HONEYSUCKLE FAMILY (Caprifoliaceae)

Plants: Vines that climb trees to a height of 20 feet. Stems hollow. Leaves opposite, wide, and egg shaped. Uppermost leaf pairs on the twigs are fused near their bases forming bracts below the flowers. **Flowers:** Orange, trumpet shaped, 1 to 1½ inches long, densely hairy within the tubes. Flowers arranged in dense clusters on the ends of the twigs. **Fruits:** Red berries. **Flowering Season:** May to July. **Habitat/Range:** Wooded slopes from British Columbia to California and east to western Montana and Arizona.

Lance-Leaved Stonecrop

Sedum lanceolatum Torr.
STONECROP FAMILY (Crassulaceae)

Plants: Perennial herbs 2 to 8 inches tall. Leaves alternate, succulent, narrow, spear shaped, round to somewhat flattened in cross section, but not keeled. Many or most of the leaves fall from the plant at flowering. **Flowers:** Yellow, star shaped, arranged in compact cymes. **Fruits:** Erect follicles joined at the base. **Flowering Season:** May to August. **Habitat/Range:** Open, rocky places from Alaska to California and east to Alberta and New Mexico.

Narrow-Leaved Skullcap

Scutellaria angustifolia Pursh
MINT FAMILY (Lamiaceae)

Plants: Perennial herbs 4 to 12 inches tall. Leaves opposite, entire, narrow, and often slightly folded. **Flowers:** Purple to deep bluish violet, arranged solitary in the leaf axils. Petals form a two-lipped tube with white hair on the palate of the spreading lower lip. Sepals also have two lips with a red, raised appendage on, or near, the upper lip. **Fruits:** Hard nutlets. **Flowering Season:** May to June. **Habitat/Range:** Dry, rocky slopes in the foothills and lowlands from British Columbia to California and east into Idaho.

FROM THE JOURNALS: The explorers collected specimens of trumpet honeysuckle, lance-leaved stonecrop, and narrow-leaved skullcap near Camp Chopunnish on June 5, 1806. Frederick Pursh wrote on the lance-leaved stonecrop's label that Lewis and Clark collected it "on the naked rocks on the Kooskooskee [Clearwater River]." In his journal of June 5 Lewis listed a large number of plants that grew near Camp Chopunnish. The plant names in brackets are the current common names for the plants we believe Lewis described: "seven bark [ninebark], wild rose [woods rose or Nootka rose], vining honeysickle [trumpet honeysuckle], sweet willow [Pacific willow], red willow [red osier dogwood], longleafed pine [ponderosa pine], Cattail or cooper's flag [common cattail], lamsquarter [lambsquarter], strawberry [woods or mountain strawberry], raspberry [red raspberry] . . . sinquefield [silverweed or other cinquefoil] . . . elder [blue elderberry], and shoemate [mountain ash]."

Trumpet Honeysuckle *Lonicera ciliosa*

Lance-Leaved Stonecrop
Sedum lanceolatum

Narrow-Leaved Skullcap
Scutellaria angustifolia

Silky Lupine

Lupinus sericeus Pursh
BEAN FAMILY (Fabaceae)

Plants: Perennial herbs 10 to 32 inches tall; the foliage covered with silky or velvety hair. Leaves alternate, palmately compound, and have about seven leaflets joined together at a common point. **Flowers:** Pale blue, pale lavender, yellowish, or white; arranged in many-flowered racemes on the ends of the stems. There is a wide V-opening of about 60 degrees or more between the banner petal and the keel. The back surface of the banner normally covered with hair. **Fruits:** Pods with three to six seeds. **Flowering Season:** May to August. **Habitat/Range:** Grasslands and open woods from British Columbia to Oregon and Arizona and east to Alberta and New Mexico.

Oregon Sunshine

Eriophyllum lanatum (Pursh) Forbes
ASTER FAMILY (Asteraceae)

Plants: Perennial herbs, 4 to 24 inches tall, covered with dense, woolly hair. Leaves up to 3¼ inches long, entire or deeply cut into three or more segments. **Flowers:** Arranged in heads with golden yellow rays and disk. **Fruits:** Slender, four-sided achenes crowned with six to twelve scales. **Flowering Season:** May to August. **Habitat/Range:** Dry, open slopes from British Columbia to California and east to Montana and Utah.

Virgate Phacelia

Phacelia heterophylla Pursh
WATERLEAF FAMILY (Hydrophyllaceae)

Plants: Biennial or perennial herbs; usually have a single, erect stem, 8 to 48 inches tall, and sometimes have several short, secondary stems. Leaves entire, or lobed near the base of the blade. Foliage covered with long, bristly hairs; the stems covered with fine, short hairs. **Flowers:** Whitish flowers clustered on bowed stems that unwind as flowers bloom. Stamens and stigma lobes protrude from the flower petals. **Fruits:** Capsules split open on the back between the partitions. **Flowering Season:** May to July. **Habitat/Range:** Dry, open places at lower elevations from British Columbia to California and east to Montana and New Mexico.

FROM THE JOURNALS: The explorers collected specimens of silky lupine, Oregon sunshine, and virgate phacelia in early June 1806. They were at Camp Chopunnish waiting for enough snow to melt so they could travel over the Lolo Trail. They collected silky lupine on June 5, Oregon sunshine on June 6, and virgate phacelia on June 9. Silky lupine was probably one of "the pea blume flowering plants" Lewis mentioned while listing plants "common to our contry" in his journal on June 5. On June 6 Lewis noted, "we find that our whole party have an ample store of bread and roots for our voyage, a circumstance not unpleasing . . . The Kooskooske [Clearwater River] is about 150 Yds. wide at this place and discharges a vast body of water; notwithstanding it[s] high state the water remains nearly transparent, and it's temperature appea[r]s to be quite as cold as that of our best springs." Then, on June 9, the last day the expedition stayed at Camp Chopunnish,

y Lupine *Lupinus sericeus*

Oregon Sunshine *Eriophyllum lanatum*

Virgate Phacelia
Phacelia heterophylla

Lewis wrote:"our party seem much elated with the idea of moving on towards their friends and country . . . they have every thing in readiness for a move . . . have been amusing themselves very merrily today in runing footraces . . . &c. [etc.] the river has been falling for several days and is now lower by near six feet than it has been; this we view as a strong evidence that the great body of snow has left the mountains."

Idaho Fescue

Festuca idahoensis Elmer
GRASS FAMILY (Poaceae)

Plants: Perennial bunchgrasses with stems 16 to 26 inches tall. Leaves mostly basal, blades finely rolled and bluish green. Basal cluster of leaves 6 to 10 inches tall. **Flowers:** Arranged in open panicles of spikelets; each spikelet has five to six florets. Lemmas have straight, bristlelike appendages about 3⁄16 inch long. **Fruits:** Grains that separate above the glumes. **Flowering Season:** May to August. **Habitat/Range:** Sagebrush plains and grasslands from the Yukon to California and east to Alberta and New Mexico.

Bluebunch Wheatgrass

Pseudoroegneria spicata (Pursh) A. Love
Also *Agropyron spicatum* (Pursh) Scribn. and Smith
GRASS FAMILY (Poaceae)

Plants: Perennial bunchgrasses with stems 16 to 36 inches tall. Leaves mostly on the stems. Leaf blades flat, or slightly rolled inward, bluish green. **Flowers:** Arranged in spikes of spikelets; each spikelet has four to six florets. Lemmas usually have a long, bent, bristle tip about ½ inch long. **Fruits:** Grains that separate above the glumes. **Flowering Season:** June to August. **Habitat/Range:** Sagebrush plains and grasslands from Alaska to California and east to Saskatchewan and Texas.

Sandberg's Bluegrass

Poa secunda Presl
Also *Poa canbyi* (Scribn.) Howell
GRASS FAMILY (Poaceae)

Plants: Perennial bunchgrasses with stems 6 to 40 inches tall. Leaves form a basal cluster 6 to 12 inches tall, green to bluish green; bottom of leaves often tinged purple. Leaf blades flat or folded with a prowlike tip. **Flowers:** Arranged in erect, narrow, and often one-sided panicles of spikelets. Each spikelet has two to five florets. Lemmas without awns. **Fruits:** Grains that separate above the glumes. **Flowering Season:** June to August. **Habitat/Range:** Sagebrush plains and grasslands from Alaska to California and east to Quebec and New Mexico.

FROM THE JOURNALS: The explorers collected specimens of Idaho fescue, bluebunch wheatgrass, and Sandberg's bluegrass on June 10, 1806. They collected them as they moved from Camp Chopunnish along the Kooskooske (Clearwater) River to where they camped at the "quawmash flatts," or in Clark's words, "the Eastern boarders of the Quawmash flatts where we encamped near the place I first met with the Chopunnish [Nez Perce] Nation last fall." In their journals the Captains described the trees and undergrowth they saw along the way but did not mention grasses. However, on June 5, Lewis did describe four grasses, which botanists believe are common reedgrass *(Phragmites communis),* basin wildrye *(Elymus cinereus),* a brome grass *(Bromus* species), and a bluegrass, probably *Poa secunda.* Of the bluegrass Lewis

Top left: Idaho Fescue
Festuca idahoensis

Top right: Bluebunch Wheatgrass
Pseudoroegneria spicata

Bottom right: Sandberg's Bluegrass
Poa secunda

wrote:"a fourth and most prevalent speceis is a grass which appears to be the same called the blue grass common to many parts of the United States; it is common to the bottom as well as the uplands, is now seeding and is from 9 inches to 2 feet high; it affords an excellent pasture for horses and appears to bear the frosts and snow better than any grass in our country; I therefore regret very much that the seed will not be ripe before our probable departure. this is a fine soft grass and would no doubt make excellent hay if cultivated."

Prairie Junegrass

Koeleria macrantha (Ledeb.) Schultes
Also *Koeleria cristata* Pers.
GRASS FAMILY (Poaceae)

Plants: Perennial bunchgrasses with stems 10 to 26 inches tall. Leaves mostly basal. Leaf sheaths often covered with downy hair. Leaf blades 1½ to 5 inches long, usually folded or rolled, and have prowlike tips. **Flowers:** Arranged in dense, cylinder-shaped panicles of spikelets. Each spikelet has two to four florets. Lemmas may have short bristle-tips. **Fruits:** Grains that separate above the glumes. **Flowering Season:** June to August. **Habitat/Range:** Sagebrush plains to open, subalpine slopes from the Northwest Territories to Mexico, and east to Quebec and Florida.

Fern-Leaved Desert-Parsley

Lomatium dissectum (Nutt.) Math. and Const.
PARSLEY FAMILY (Apiaceae)

Plants: Perennial herbs 2 to 6 feet tall. Leaves compound, 4 to 12 inches long, and divided into many, lacelike segments. Leaf surfaces have short, bristly hairs. **Flowers:** Yellow or purple, arranged in compound umbels on the stem ends; each umbel has ten to thirty rays. **Fruits:** Very flat schizocarp with corky, winged margins. **Flowering Season:** April to June. **Habitat/Range:** Open, rocky slopes of the foothills and mountains from British Columbia to California and east to Alberta, Colorado, and Arizona.

Nootka Rose

Rosa nutkana Presl
ROSE FAMILY (Rosaceae)

Plants: Shrubs 3 to 10 feet tall; usually have prickles on the stems. Leaves compound with five to seven toothed-leaflets. **Flowers:** Pink to deep rose colored. Petals 1 to 1½ inches long. **Fruits:** Purple hips ½ to ⅞ inch long and about as thick. **Flowering Season:** May to July. **Habitat/Range:** Woods in the mountains from Alaska to California and east to Montana and New Mexico.

FROM THE JOURNALS: Lewis and Clark collected specimens of prairie junegrass and fern-leaved desert-parsley on June 10, 1806. Lewis described Nootka rose on June 10, but if he collected a specimen it has since been lost. On the label with the desert-parsley specimen, Frederick Pursh wrote, "A great horse medicine among the natives . . . grows on rich upland." On June 10 the explorers were traveling from Camp Chopunnish along the Kooskooske (Clearwater) River to the "quawmash flatts" and Lewis described the vegetation in the area: "a species of dwarf pine [lodgepole pine, *Pinus contorta*] which grows about ten or twelve feet high. bears a globular formed cone with small scales, the leaves are about the length and much the appearance of the common pitch [lodgepole] pine having it's leaves in fassicles of two . . . there are two speceis of the wild rose both quinqui petallous [five petals] and of a damask red but the one is as large as the common red rose of our gardens. I observed the apples [hips] of this speceis [Nootka rose] last fall to be more than triple the size of those of the ordinary wild rose [woods rose, *Rosa woodsii*]; the stem of this [Nootka] rose is the same with the other tho' the leaf is somewhat larger."

Prairie Junegrass *Koeleria macrantha*

Fern-Leaved Desert-Parsley
Lomatium dissectum

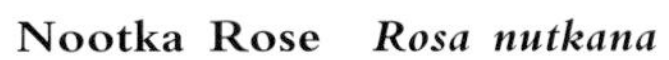

Nootka Rose *Rosa nutkana*

Prairie Smoke or Old Man's Whiskers

Geum triflorum Pursh
ROSE FAMILY (Rosaceae)

Plants: Perennial herbs with stems 12 to 16 inches tall. Leaves compound, mostly basal, and each cut into as many as thirty unequal, toothed segments. **Flowers:** Reddish purple sepals and yellow- to reddish-tinged petals; often arranged three on the ends of the stems. **Fruits:** Pear-shaped achenes with long, bearded styles. **Flowering Season:** April to August. **Habitat/Range:** Sagebrush plains to open, subalpine ridges from British Columbia to California and east to Newfoundland, Illinois, Nebraska, and New Mexico.

Pineapple Weed

Matricaria matricarioides (Less.) Porter
ASTER FAMILY (Asteraceae)

Plants: Annual herbs, 2 to 16 inches tall, with sweet, pineapple-like aroma. Leaves cut into many short, linear segments. **Flowers:** Yellowish green, arranged in conical heads with only disk flowers (no showy rays). The bracts have a thin, translucent margin and surround the head. **Fruits:** Achenes with a short crown. **Flowering Season:** May to August. **Habitat/Range:** Disturbed, open places from Alaska to California and east to Newfoundland and South Carolina.

American Bistort

Polygonum bistortoides Pursh
BUCKWHEAT FAMILY (Polygonaceae)

Plants: Perennial herbs with stems 8 to 24 inches tall. Leaves have long stalks and the blade is up to 6 inches long. Most leaves are basal; those on the stem are much smaller. **Flowers:** White to pinkish, arranged in densely flowered, headlike racemes on the stem ends. **Fruits:** Three-sided, shiny achenes. **Flowering Season:** May to August. **Habitat/Range:** Moist meadows and streambanks from British Columbia to California and east to Alberta and New Mexico.

FROM THE JOURNALS: The explorers collected specimens of prairie smoke, pineapple weed, and American bistort on June 12, 1806. The label with the pineapple weed specimen notes that the plant has "an agreable Smell." Frederick Pursh wrote on the label with American bistort, "In moist grounds On the quamash flats." The explorers were camped at the "quawmash flatts" on June 12. They arrived at this campsite on June 10, which Lewis described: "after we encamped this evening we sent out our hunters; Collins killed a doe on which we suped much to our satisfaction. . . . we find a great number of burrowing squirels about our camp of which we killed several; I eat of them and found them quite as tender and well flavored as our grey squirel. saw many sand hill crains and some ducks in the slashey glades about this place." On June 12 he wrote: "our camp is agreeably situated in a point of timbered land on the eastern border of an extensive level and beautifull prarie which is intersected by several small branches near the bank of one of which our camp is placed. the quawmash [camas] is now in blume and from the [pale blue] colour of its bloom at a short distance it resembles lakes of fine clear water, so complete is this deseption that on first sight I could have swoarn it was water."

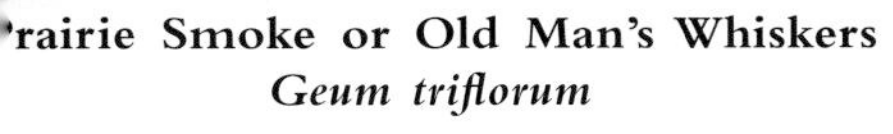

Prairie Smoke or Old Man's Whiskers
Geum triflorum

American Bistort
Polygonum bistortoides

Pineapple Weed *Matricaria matricarioides*

Blue Camas

Camassia quamash (Pursh) Greene
LILY FAMILY (Liliaceae)

Plants: Perennial herbs with solitary stems 12 to 28 inches tall. All leaves basal, narrow, flat, lance shaped, 4 to 16 inches long, and ⅜ to 1 inch wide. **Flowers:** Pale blue to purple, arranged in loose racemes. Each flower has six blue tepals, six stamens, and a single style. **Fruits:** Oval capsules up to 1 inch long. **Flowering Season:** April to early July. **Habitat/Range:** Seasonally moist meadows from British Columbia to California and east to Alberta and Utah.

FROM THE JOURNALS: Frederick Pursh wrote on the label with the blue-camas specimen, "Near the foot of the Rocky mountain on the Quamash flats—June 23rd 1806." Blue camas (quamash) was one of the most important food plants and trade items of the Northwest Native Americans, and the explorers' journals offer more information about this plant than any other they encountered. On September 20, 1805, Clark and an advance party of hunters were searching for food for the starving men behind them who were struggling over the Lolo Trail. Clark wrote that the hunting party arrived at "a Small Plain [Weippe Prairie] in which I found maney Indian lodges. . . . great numbers of women geathered around me . . . gave us a Small piece of Buffalow meat, Some dried Salmon[,] beries & roots . . . Some round and much like an onion which they call quamash the Bread or Cake is called Pas-she-co Sweet, of this they make bread & Supe they also gave us the bread made of this root all of which we eate hartily."

Later that day Clark described how the "Chopunnish" (Nez Perce) Indians prepared "quamash": "Emence quantity of the quawmash or *Pas-shi-co* root gathered & in piles about the plains, those roots grow much an onion in marshey places the seed are triangular Shell on the Stalk. they Sweat them in the following manner i. e. dig a large hole 3 feet deep Cover the bottom with Split wood on the top of which they lay Small Stones of about 3 or 4 Inches thick, a Second layer of Splited wood & Set the whole on fire which heats the Stones, after the fire is extinguished they lay grass & mud mixed on the Stones, on that dry grass which Supports the Pash-Shi-co root a thin Coat of the Same grass is laid on the top, a Small fire is kept when necessary in the Center of the kile &c. [etc.] I find myself verry unwell all the evening from eateing the fish & roots too freely." Clark wasn't the only one who became ill from this sudden shift in their diet. Most members of the party complained of intestinal problems, which lasted for days.

On June 11, 1806, the party returned to the "quawmash flatts." While there Lewis wrote a long description of camas, much shortened here: "As I have had frequent occasion to mention the plant which the Chopunnish call quawmash I shall here give a more particular discription of that plant and the mode of preparing it for food as practiced by the Chopunnish . . . it delights in a black rich moist soil . . . most luxuriantly where the land remains from 6 to nine inches under water untill the seed are nearly perfect which . . . is about the last of this month. . . . soon after the seeds are mature the . . . foliage of this plant perishes, the grownd becomes dry . . . and the root encreases in size and shortly becomes fit for use; this happens about the middle of July when the natives begin to collect it for use which they

“quawmash flatts” near Weippe, Idaho

Blue Camas *Camassia quamash*

continue until the leaves of the plant attain some size in the spring of the year.” Lewis continued with a detailed description of how the Chopunnish people steamed the roots in pits and further prepared them: “[the roots are] exposed to the sun in scaffoalds untill they become dry, when they are black and of a sweet agreeable flavor. . . . if the design is to make bread or cakes of the roots they undergo a second process . . . reduced to the consistency of dough and then rolled in grass in cakes of eight or ten lbs are returned to the sweat . . . when taken out the second time the women make up this dough into cakes . . . usually from ½ to ¾ of an inch thick and expose it on sticks to dry in the sun, or place it over the smoke of their fires.—the bread this prepared . . . will keep sound for a great length of time. this bread or the dryed roots are frequently eaten alone by the natives with further preparation, and when they have them in abundance they form an ingredient in almost every dish they prepare. this root is palateable but disagrees with me in every shape I have ever used it.”

Clustered Elkweed

Frasera fastigiata (Pursh) A. Heller
GENTIAN FAMILY (Gentianaceae)

Plants: Perennial herbs with a single stem 2 to 5 feet tall. Leaves 8 to 18 inches long and 2 to 5 inches wide; stem leaves in whorls of three or four. **Flowers:** Blue, arranged in dense clusters on the ends of the stems. A tiny, fringed membrane surrounds a circular, nectar gland found near the base of each petal. **Fruits:** Oval capsules. **Flowering Season:** May to July. **Habitat/Range:** Moist meadows and open woods in the Blue Mountains of eastern Washington and Oregon, and in northern Idaho.

Long-Leaved Evening Primrose

Camissonia subacaulis (Pursh) Raven
Also *Oenothera heterantha* Nutt.
EVENING PRIMROSE FAMILY (Onagraceae)

Plants: Perennial herbs without stems. Basal leaves 2 to 12 inches long. Leaves are widest well above the middle, and taper to a narrow leafstalk. Most leaves are entire, but some have a few lobes near the base. **Flowers:** Four yellow petals; four green sepals that turn away from the petals. Flower parts attached to the top of a long, narrow extension of the ovary that looks like a flower stalk. **Fruits:** Four-sided capsules. **Flowering Season:** May to July. **Habitat/Range:** Moist meadows from Washington to California and east to Montana and Colorado.

FROM THE JOURNALS: The explorers collected specimens of clustered elkweed and long-leaved evening primrose on June 14, 1806. This was the last day the expedition was camped at the "quawmash flatts." In his journal for June 13 Lewis wrote: "about noon seven of our hunters returned with 8 deer. . . . we directed the meat to be cut thin and exposed to dry in the sun. we made a digest of the Indian Nations West of the Rocky Mountains which we have seen and of whom we have been repeated informed by those with whom we were conversent. they amount by our estimate to 69,000 Souls." On June 14 Lewis described their preparations for their Lolo-Trail journey the next day: "we had all our articles packed up and made ready for an early departure in the morning. our horses were caught and most of them hubbled and otherwise confined in order that we might not be detained. from hence to traveller's rest we shall make a forsed march; at that place we shal probably remain one or two days to rest ourselves and horses and procure some meat. we have now been detained near five weeks in consequence of the snows; a serious loss of time at this delightfull season for traveling. I am still apprehensive that the snow and the want of food for our horses will prove a serious imbarrassment to us as at least four days journey of our rout in these mountains lies over hights and along a ledge of mountains never intirely destitute of snow."

Clustered Elkweed *Frasera fastigiata*

Long-Leaved Evening Primrose *Camissonia subacaulis*

Purple Trillium

Trillium petiolatum Pursh
LILY FAMILY (Liliaceae)

Plants: Perennial herbs with short stems largely hidden underground. Each plant has a whorl of three leaves, 3 to 5 inches in diameter, with long leafstalks that thrust the leaves above the flower. **Flowers:** Purple, solitary, at ground level without a flower stalk. Each flower has three green sepals, three purple petals, and six purple anthers. **Fruits:** Fleshy, berrylike capsules. **Flowering Season:** April to June. **Habitat/Range:** Streambanks and moist meadows east of the Cascade Mountains in Washington and Oregon and into adjacent northern Idaho.

Piper's Anemone

Anemone piperi Britt. ex Rydb.
BUTTERCUP FAMILY (Ranunculaceae)

Plants: Perennial herbs, 6 to 14 inches tall, with one or two basal leaves and a whorl of three leaves a few inches below the flower. Each leaf is compound, having three toothed leaflets. **Flowers:** White or sometimes pinkish, solitary on the stem ends. **Fruits:** Numerous small, oval achenes with short beaks. **Flowering Season:** May to July. **Habitat/Range:** Moist, shaded woods from interior British Columbia to Oregon and east to Idaho, Montana, and Utah.

Shrubby Penstemon

Penstemon fruticosus (Pursh) Greene
FIGWORT FAMILY (Scrophulariaceae)

Plants: Shrubs or half-shrubs 6 to 16 inches tall. Leaves opposite, shiny, and evergreen; the larger ones occur on sterile stems at the base of the current-season's growth. **Flowers:** Lavender; arranged in one-sided clusters with a pair of large flowers at each node. The four fertile anthers are covered with long, woolly hair. The sterile stamen is much shorter than the fertile ones, and it has yellow hair on the tip. **Fruits:** Capsules up to ½ inch long. **Flowering Season:** May to August. **Habitat/Range:** Dry, rocky woods in the mountains from interior British Columbia and Alberta, south to Oregon, Idaho, and Wyoming.

FROM THE JOURNALS: Specimens of purple trillium, Piper's anemone, and shrubby penstemon, collected on June 15, 1806, still exist. The explorers collected them as they traveled roughly 22 miles from the "quawmash flatts" to their camp on Eldorado Creek near the mouth of Lunch Creek. On this day Lewis described the landscape: "the rains have rendered the road very slippery insomuch that it is with much difficulty our horses can get on; several of them fell but sustained no injury. . . . the fallen timber in addition to the slippry roads made our march slow and extreemly laborious on our horses. the country is exceedingly thickly timbered with long leafed [ponderosa] pine, some pitch [lodgepole] pine, larch, white pine, white [western red] cedar or arborvita of large size, and a variety of firs. the undergrowth principally reed root [red root, *Ceanothus* species] from 6 to 10 feet high . . . the soil is good; in some plaices it is of a red cast like our lands in Virginia

Purple Trillium *Trillium petiolatum*

Piper's Anemone *Anemone piperi*

Shrubby Penstemon *Penstemon fruticosus*

about the S. W. mountains. Saw the speckled [hairy] woodpecker, bee martin [western kingbird] and log cock or large [pileated] woodpecker. found the nest of a humming bird, it had just began to lay its eggs."

Beargrass

Xerophyllum tenax (Pursh) Nutt.
LILY FAMILY (Liliaceae)

Plants: Perennial herbs with large clumps of evergreen, basal leaves, and a single, leafy, flower stem up to 5 feet tall. Leaves grasslike, tough, and wiry. **Flowers:** Creamy white, arranged in dense racemes on the stem ends. **Fruits:** Three-lobed capsules. **Flowering Season:** May to August. **Habitat/Range:** Mountain forests and openings from British Columbia to California and east to Alberta and northwestern Wyoming.

FROM THE JOURNALS: Two specimens of beargrass still exist: one at the Lewis and Clark Herbarium and the other at the Royal Botanic Gardens at Kew near London. The explorers collected these specimens on June 15, 1806, along the Lolo Trail between the "quawmash flatts" and Eldorado Creek in present-day Idaho. On September 2, 1804, along the Missouri River above present-day Yankton, South Dakota, Clark wrote in his journal, "I observe *Bear grass* [yucca] & Rhue [sumac] in the Sides of the hills." On the Missouri River plains and eastward, "bear grass" is a common name for yucca *(Yucca glauca)*. Yucca resembles the beargrass *(Xerophyllum tenax)* of the Rocky Mountains, which may explain why Lewis and Clark applied the name "beargrass" to this plant when they encountered it in the Rockies. On June 26, 1806, along the Lolo Trail at their campsite near Bald Mountain in Idaho, Lewis described the vegetation: "there is a great abundance of a speceis of bear-grass *[Xerophyllum tenax]* which grows on every part of these mountains it's growth is luxouriant and continues green all winter but the horses will not eat it."

On January 17, 1806, while wintering at Fort Clatsop in Oregon, Lewis described how Clatsop Indians used beargrass for making baskets: "their baskets are formed of cedar bark and beargrass so closely interwoven with the fingers that they are watertight without the aid of gum or rosin; some of these are highly ornamented with strans of beargrass which they dye of several colours and interweave in a great variety of figures; this serves them the double perpose of holding their water or wearing on their heads; and are of different capacites from that of the smallest cup to five or six gallons; they are generally of a conic form or reather the segment of a cone of which the smaller end forms the base or bottom of the basket. these they make very expediciously and dispose off for a mear trifle. it is for the construction of these baskets that the beargrass becomes an article of traffic among the natives[.] this grass grows only on their high mountains near the snowey region; the blade is about ⅜ of an inch wide and 2 feet long smoth pliant and strong; the young blades which are white from not being exposed to the sun or air, are those most commonly employed, particularly in their neatest work."

Near Fort Clatsop on January 19, 1806, Lewis wrote: "we also purchased . . . a hat for some fishinghooks. these hats are of their own manufactory and are composed of Cedar bark and bear grass interwoven with the fingers and ornimented with various colours and figures, they are nearly waterproof, light, and I am convinced are more durable than either chip or straw. These hats form a small article of traffic with the Clatsops and Chinnooks who dispose of them to the whites. the form

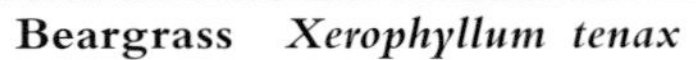

Beargrass *Xerophyllum tenax*

Beargrass illustration m Frederick Pursh's 1814 ***'lora Americae Septentrionalis***

of the hat is that which was in vogue in the Ued States and great Britain in the years 1800 & 1801 with a high crown reather larger at the top than where it joins the brim; the brim narrow or about 2 or 2½ inches."

Bunchberry

Cornus canadensis L.
DOGWOOD FAMILY (Cornaceae)

Plants: Perennial herbs or shrublike plants 2 to 8 inches tall; spreads by runners and forms colonies of low groundcover. Leaves in whorls of four to seven. Main lateral veins bend and run parallel with the leaf margin. **Flowers:** Four large, white, petal-like bracts surround a cluster of tiny, white to purplish tinged, true flowers. **Fruits:** A cluster of bright, coral red, berrylike drupes. **Flowering Season:** June to August. **Habitat/Range:** Moist, shady woods from Alaska to California, east to Greenland, Pennsylvania, and Minnesota, and south in the Rocky Mountains to New Mexico.

Sticky Currant

Ribes viscosissimum Pursh
CURRANT FAMILY (Grossulariaceae)

Plants: Aromatic shrubs, without prickles, 3 to 6 feet tall. Leaves alternate, maplelike, with three to five rounded lobes and palmate veins. Foliage covered with downy hair and glands that exude a sticky fluid. **Flowers:** Creamy white, often tinged pink, arranged in racemes of six to twelve flowers. **Fruits:** Unpalatable, bluish black berries with sticky, smelly glands. **Flowering Season:** May to June. **Habitat/Range:** Forested slopes from British Columbia to California and east to Alberta and Colorado.

Fairy Slipper

Calypso bulbosa (L.) Oakes
ORCHID FAMILY (Orchidaceae)

Plants: Perennial herbs, 2 to 6 inches tall. Each plant has a single, broad, basal leaf about 2 inches long with prominent, parallel veins. **Flowers:** Solitary, pink to purple with white or yellow hair on the apron of the inflated, slipperlike lip petal. **Fruits:** Erect capsules with many seeds the size of dust particles. **Flowering Season:** May to July. **Habitat/Range:** Cool, moist, shaded forests from Alaska to Labrador, south to Maine and Minnesota, south in the Rocky Mountains to New Mexico, and south along the Pacific Coast to California.

FROM THE JOURNALS: The explorers collected specimens of bunchberry, sticky currant, and fairy slipper on June 16, 1806. The explorers were struggling along the Lolo Trail between their camps on Eldorado Creek and Hungery Creek (a tributary of Fish Creek) in present-day Idaho. From the information provided on the labels, it appears that the explorers collected bunchberry along Eldorado Creek, sticky currant on the ridge between Eldorado and Fish Creeks, and fairy slipper near Hungery Creek.

On June 16 the party paused in a meadow along a tributary of Fish Creek, which Lewis described in his journal: "before we reached this little branch on which we dined we saw in the hollows and N. hillsides large quatities of snow yet undisolved; in some places it was from two to three feet deep. vegetation is proportionably backward; the dogtooth violet [glacier lily] is just in blume, the honeysuckle, huckburry and a small speceis of white maple are beginning to put fourth their leaves; these

Bunchberry flowers *Cornus canadensis*

Sticky Currant *Ribes viscosissimum*

Bunchberry fruit

Fairy Slipper *Calypso bulbosa*

appearances in this comparatively low region augers but unfavourably with rispect to the practibility of passing the mountains." The following day the Captains decided to turn back and recruit Chopunnish (Nez Perce) Indian guides to help them find their way over the snow-clad mountains.

Red Columbine

Aquilegia formosa Fisch. ex DC.
BUTTERCUP FAMILY (Ranunculaceae)

Plants: Perennial herbs 1 to 3 feet tall. Leaves mostly basal and compound. Each basal leaf has nine leaflets arranged in three sets of three leaflets. The single leaf on the stem is smaller and only has three leaflets. **Flowers:** Each nodding flower has five red, petal-like sepals, five straight, red spurs, and five yellow petals. Flowers arranged in one- to ten-flowered cymes. **Fruits:** Follicles about 1 inch long with beaks ⅜ inch long. **Flowering Season:** May to August. **Habitat/Range:** Mountain meadows from Alaska to California and east to western Montana and Utah.

Mountain Goldenpea

Thermopsis montana Nutt.
BEAN FAMILY (Fabaceae)

Plants: Perennial herbs 2 to 3 feet tall. Leaves alternate and compound. Each leaf has three leaflets up to 4 inches long and two large, leaflike stipules attached to the base of the leafstalk. **Flowers:** Yellow, arranged in racemes of ten to sixty flowers on the stem ends. **Fruits:** Straight, erect, hairy pods with two to five seeds. **Flowering Season:** May to August. **Habitat/Range:** Moist meadows from Washington to Arizona and east to Montana and New Mexico.

Wild Ginger

Asarum caudatum Lindl.
BIRTHWORT FAMILY (Aristolochiaceae)

Plants: Perennial herbs that creep along the ground and often form leafy mats. Leaves opposite, heart shaped, up to 4 inches long and 6 inches wide, with long leafstalks. Foliage has distinct gingerlike aroma when crushed. **Flowers:** The flowers usually rest on the ground, often concealed by the leaves. Each solitary flower has three brownish purple, petal-like sepals with long tail-like tips. **Fruits:** Fleshy capsules. **Flowering Season:** April to July. **Habitat/Range:** Moist, shaded forests from British Columbia to California and east to Idaho and northwestern Montana.

FROM THE JOURNALS: No specimens of red columbine, mountain goldenpea, or wild ginger exist today, but Lewis and Clark mentioned all of them in the journals. On June 16, 1806, Lewis described the plants he saw near Hungery Creek, a tributary of Fish Creek in present-day Idaho: "Hungry creek is but small at this place but is deep and runs a perfect torrent; the water is perfectly transparent and as cold as ice. the pitch [lodgepole] pine, white pine some larch and firs constite the timber; the long leafed [ponderosa] pine extends a little distance on this side of the main branch of Collins [Lolo] creek, and the white [western red] cedar not further than the branch of hungry [Fish] creek on which we dined . . . in the fore part of the day I observed the Cullumbine *[Aquilegia formosa]* the blue bells *[Mertensia paniculata]*, and the yelow flowering pea *[Thermopsis montana]* in blume."

Red Columbine *Aquilegia formosa*

Mountain Goldenpea *Thermopsis montana*

Wild Ginger *Asarum caudatum*

On June 27 the party camped along the Lolo Trail, high on the watershed divide between the North Fork Clearwater and Lochsa Rivers near Spring Hill in the present-day Clearwater National Forest. Here Lewis wrote: "Potts's legg which has been much swolen and inflamed for several days is much better this evening and gives him but little pain. we applyed the pounded roots and leaves of the wild ginger & from which he found great relief."

California False Hellebore

Veratrum californicum Dur.
LILY FAMILY (Liliaceae)

Plants: Perennial herbs 4 to 6 feet tall. Leaves alternate, parallel veined, pleated, 9 to 16 inches long and 4 to 8 inches wide; they don't have leafstalks but clasp the stem where they attach. **Flowers:** White to greenish white, arranged in erect panicles on the stem ends. **Fruits:** Oval capsules tipped with persistent styles. **Flowering Season:** June to August. **Habitat/Range:** In wet meadows and along streams from Washington to California and east to Montana and New Mexico.

Scarlet Gilia

Ipomopsis aggregata (Pursh) Grant
Also *Gilia aggregata* (Pursh) Spreng.
PHLOX FAMILY (Polemoniaceae)

Plants: Biennial herbs that grow as a cluster of radiating basal leaves at ground level the first year and have stems 8 to 40 inches tall the second year. Leaves divided into many narrow segments that are pinnately arranged. **Flowers:** Red to pink, often speckled white, trumpet shaped with five, pointed lobes. **Fruits:** Capsules. **Flowering Season:** May to August. **Habitat/Range:** Open, rocky, disturbed slopes from British Columbia to California and east to Montana and Texas.

Mountain Kittentails

Synthyris missurica (Raf.) Pennell
FIGWORT FAMILY (Scrophulariaceae)

Plants: Perennial herbs 4 to 24 inches tall. Leaves round or kidney shaped, cut with coarse teeth on the margin, and have veins that radiate from where the leaf attaches to the long leafstalk. Mostly basal leaves with only a few small leaves or bracts on the stem. **Flowers:** Blue to pink or lavender, four uneven lobes, arranged in racemes. **Fruits:** Capsules, almost round in outline. **Flowering Season:** April to July. **Habitat/Range:** Along streams and in moist meadows from Washington to California and east to Idaho and northwestern Montana.

FROM THE JOURNALS: The explorers collected specimens of California false hellebore, scarlet gilia, and mountain kittentails while traveling along the Lolo Trail in present-day Idaho with their three Chopunnish (Nez Perce) Indian guides. According to the label, they collected California false hellebore on June 25, 1806, that was "growing in wet places . . . On the Kooskooskee [Clearwater River watershed]," probably along Eldorado Creek. They collected scarlet gilia and mountain kittentails the next day along Hungery Creek.

Lewis wrote in his journal for June 25: "last evening the indians entertained us with seting the fir trees on fire. they have a great number of dry lims near their bodies which when set on fire creates a very suddon and immence blaze from bottom to top of those tall trees. they are a beatifull object in this situation at night. this exhibition reminded me of a display of fireworks. the natives told us that their object in seting those trees on fire was to bring fair weather for our journey . . . one of our guides complained of being unwell. . . . I gave the sik indian a buffaloe robe he having no other covering except his mockersons and a dressed Elkskin

Top left: California False Hellebore ***Veratrum californicum***

Top right: Scarlet Gilia ***Ipomopsis aggregata***

Bottom right: Mountain Kittentails ***Synthyris missurica***

without the hair." In his journal Clark described the morning of June 26: "We collected our horses and Set out early and proceeded on Down hungary Creek a fiew miles and assended to the Summit of the mountain where we deposited our baggage on the 17th inst. found every thing Safe and as we had left them. the Snow which was 10 feet 10 inches deep on the top of the mountain [on June 17], had sunk to 7 feet tho' perfectly hard and firm." The expedition had been unable to proceed further on June 17 and had been forced to return to the "quawmash flatts."

Three-Leaved Lewisia

Lewisia triphylla (Wats.) Robins.
PURSLANE FAMILY (Portulacaceae)

Plants: Small, perennial herbs 1 to 4 inches tall. Plants do not have basal leaves, instead they have a whorl of two or three (up to five) narrow, linear leaves, less than 2½ inches long, attached to the stem. **Flowers:** White with pink veins, in corymb-like arrangements of two to twenty-five on the stem ends. Each flower has two sepals, five to nine petals, three to five stamens, and three to five stigmas. **Fruits:** Round, one-celled capsules. **Flowering Season:** May to August. **Habitat/Range:** Moist soils, often blooming near melting snowbanks, from Washington to California and east to Montana and Colorado.

Showy Jacob's Ladder

Polemonium pulcherrimum Hook.
PHLOX FAMILY (Polemoniaceae)

Plants: Perennial herbs, 2 to 12 inches tall, with several erect, clustered stems. Leaves compound with eleven to twenty-five leaflets pinnately arranged in rows on the leafstalks. **Flowers:** Blue with a yellow eye; the lobes of the flowers equal to or longer than the tubes; arranged in cymes. **Fruits:** Capsules. **Flowering Season:** May to August. **Habitat/Range:** Moderate to high elevations in the mountains from Alaska to California and east to Alberta and New Mexico.

Western Spring Beauty

Claytonia lanceolata Pursh
PURSLANE FAMILY (Portulacaceae)

Plants: Perennial herbs 2 to 8 inches tall. Each plant has a pair of opposite, lance-shaped leaves midlength on the stem, and sometimes one or more basal leaves. **Flowers:** White to pink with pink veins, arranged in racemes of three to twenty. Each flower has two sepals, five petals with notched tips, five stamens with pink anthers, and three stigma lobes. **Fruits:** Egg-shaped capsules with three to six shiny, black seeds. **Flowering Season:** April to July. **Habitat/Range:** Foothills to high mountains from British Columbia to California and east to Alberta and New Mexico.

FROM THE JOURNALS: According to Lewis, the explorers rode their horses over 28 miles of snowpacked trail on June 27, 1806, along "the dividing ridge between the Waters of the Kooskooske [here Lewis refers to the Lochsa River] and Chopunnish [North Fork Clearwater] rivers." The explorers collected specimens of three-leaved lewisia, showy Jacob's ladder, and western spring beauty along this route in present-day Idaho.

On June 25 Lewis described western spring beauty in his journal: "we arrived at the branch of hungary [Fish] creek . . . here we halted and dined and our guides overtook us. at this place I met with a plant the root of which the Shoshones eat. it is a small knob root a good deel in flavor an consistency like the Jerusalem Artichoke. it has two small oval smooth leaves placed opposite on either side of the peduncle just above the root. the scape [main flower stem] is only about 4 inches long is round and smooth. the roots of this plant formed one of those collections of roots which Drewyer [Drouillard] took from the Shoshones last summer [August 21,

Top left: Three-Leaved Lewisia
Lewisia triphylla

Top right: Showy Jacob's Ladder
Polemonium pulcherrimum

Bottom right: Western Spring Beauty *Claytonia lanceolata*

1805] on the head of Jefferson's river [Shoshone Cove]." In this dangerous encounter, Drouillard chased a young Shoshone man (who stole his gun) for about ten miles, caught him, and according to Lewis, "seized his gun and wrest her out of his hands." An illustration of *Claytonia lanceolata,* drawn using one of Lewis's plant specimens, is one of the thirty plates in Frederick Pursh's 1814 book.

Redstem Ceanothus

Ceanothus sanguineus Pursh
BUCKTHORN FAMILY (Rhamnaceae)

Plants: Deciduous shrubs, 3 to 9 feet tall, with reddish purple bark. Leaves alternate, egg shaped, with fine teeth and glands on their margins; dull (not shiny) on upper surface. **Flowers:** White, arranged in panicles from the previous-year's twigs. **Fruits:** Capsules have three deep lobes but don't have the crests of some related species. **Flowering Season:** May to July. **Habitat/Range:** Forest openings and thin woods from British Columbia to California and east to Idaho and northwestern Montana.

Fool's Huckleberry

Menziesia ferruginea Smith
HEATH FAMILY (Ericaceae)

Plants: Deciduous shrubs, 3 to 7 feet tall, with a skunklike aroma when the foliage is brushed. Leaves alternate, ovate, with fine teeth on the margin and soft hair and sticky glands on both surfaces. A small, white point protrudes from the midvein at the leaf tip. **Flowers:** Pink, urn shaped, arranged in clusters on the end of previous-year's growth. **Fruits:** Egg-shaped capsules with many seeds. **Flowering Season:** May to August. **Habitat/Range:** Cool, moist, mountain slopes from Alaska to California and east to Alberta and Wyoming.

Red Mountain Heather

Phyllodoce empetriformis (Sm.) D. Don
HEATH FAMILY (Ericaceae)

Plants: Evergreen shrubs, 4 to 16 inches tall, with many narrow leaves that look like the needles of a fir tree. Plants form colonies and often extensive mats. **Flowers:** Red to pink, bell shaped, petal lobes recurved, arranged in clusters on the branch ends. **Fruits:** Capsules open at terminal slits. **Flowering Season:** July to August. **Habitat/Range:** High mountain slopes from Alaska to California and east to Alberta, Montana, and northwestern Wyoming.

FROM THE JOURNALS: Frederick Pursh wrote on the redstem ceanothus's label: "Ceanothus atropurpureus. Near the foot of the Rocky mountain, on Collins [Lolo] Creek. Jun. 27, 1806." The explorers were traveling along the ridge between the Lochsa and North Fork Clearwater Rivers of Idaho on this day—a full day and a half east of "Collins" Creek. It's likely that Pursh had the date wrong since this species is more common at the lower elevations along Lolo Creek in Idaho (not to be confused with Lolo Creek in Montana) than it is along the high ridges of the Lolo Trail. On June 10, 1806, Lewis mentioned "a large speceis of redroot *[Ceanothus sanguineus]*" that was blooming under ponderosa pine, larch, and "several speceis of fir" as they traveled from Camp Chopunnish to the "quawmash flatts." They crossed Collins Creek along the way, so they may have collected the "redroot" specimen then.

Specimens of fool's huckleberry and red mountain heather do not exist, but Frederick Pursh credited Lewis's collection as the source of the specimens Pursh used to describe these two species in his 1814 book. The date and place that the

Redstem Ceanothus *Ceanothus sanguineus*

Red Mountain Heather
Phyllodoce empetriformis

Fool's Huckleberry
Menziesia ferruginea

explorers collected these specimens are not clear in Pursh's book, but both species are present today on the high ridges of the Lolo Trail that the party traversed on June 27.

Western Larch or Tamarack

Larix occidentalis Nutt.
PINE FAMILY (Pinaceae)

Plants: Large coniferous trees, up to 175 feet tall and 3 feet or more in diameter, that shed their needles yearly. Much of the lower trunk often has no branches. Bark reddish brown with deep furrows and flat, flaky plates. Clusters of fourteen to thirty needles attached to short shoots. **Flowers:** Male (pollen) cones solitary, yellow. Female (seed) cones purple red to reddish brown, 1 to 1½ inches long. **Fruits:** Cones have a pair of naked, winged seeds that form on the inner surface of each cone scale. **Flowering Season:** May. **Habitat/Range:** Deep, porous soils of mountain valleys and lower slopes from interior British Columbia to Oregon and east to Idaho and Montana.

Western Red Cedar

Thuja plicata Donn ex D. Don
CYPRESS FAMILY (Cupressaceae)

Plants: Large, evergreen trees up to 175 feet tall and 8 feet or more in diameter. They often live a long time, some over 1,000 years. Bark reddish brown, fibrous, and fissured. Leaves opposite in four rows, scalelike and overlapping, forming flat, branched sprays. **Flowers:** Male cones reddish. Female cones brown, up to ½ inch long, with two to three pairs of fertile scales. **Fruits:** Cones have eight to fourteen seeds. **Flowering Season:** April to June. **Habitat/Range:** Moist forests of valleys and lower slopes from Alaska to California and east into Idaho and Montana.

FROM THE JOURNALS: On September 14, 1805, Joseph Whitehouse was the first explorer to mention western red cedar in the journals: "the most of these mountains are covred with pine. Saw Some tall Strait Siprass [cypress], or white ceeder [western red cedar] today." In his course-and-distance journal that day Clark wrote, "6 miles over a high mountain . . . this Mountain is covered with Spruce & Pitch pine fir, & what is called to the Northard Hackmatack & Tamerack [western larch]." That day the explorers traveled from Packer Meadows near Lolo Pass to their camp on the Lochsa River near the present-day Powell Ranger Station in Idaho, where large cedar and larch trees are still common.

In the journals, the explorers mentioned often the different items Native Americans constructed using western red cedar: canoes, clothing, and lodging. As the party descended the Columbia River near present-day The Dalles, Oregon, on October 28, 1805, Clark wrote, "The wind which is the cause of our delay, does not retard the motions of those people at all, as their canoes are calculated to ride the highest waves, they are built of white cedar [western red cedar] or Pine verry light wide in the middle and tapers at each end, with aperns [aprons, rims on the gunnels], and heads of animals carved on the bow, which is generally raised." On March 19, 1806, Lewis described the clothing of the coastal Native Americans: "the most esteemed and valuable of these robes are made of strips of the skins of the Sea Otter net together with the bark of the white cedar. . . . The garment which occupys the waist, and from thence as low as nearly to the knee before and the

Along the Lolo Trail

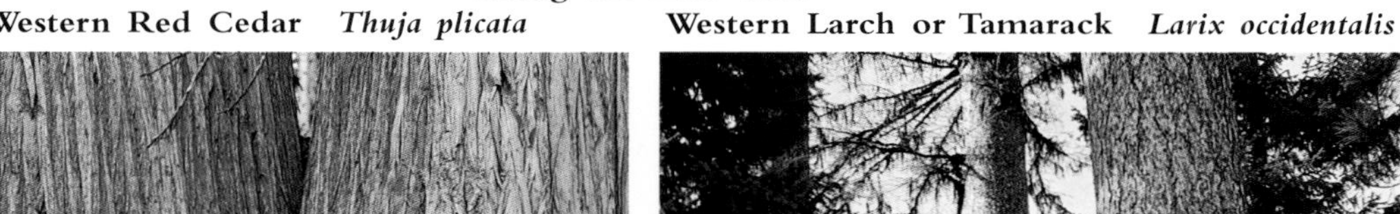

Western Red Cedar *Thuja plicata*

Western Larch or Tamarack *Larix occidentalis*

ham, behind . . . is a tissue of white cedar bark, bruised or broken into small shreds . . . they also cover their heads from the rain sometimes with a common water cup or basket made of the cedar bark and beargrass."

Mountain Lady's Slipper

Cypripedium montanum Dougl. ex Lindl.
ORCHID FAMILY (Orchidaceae)

Plants: Perennial herbs, 8 to 24 inches tall, with broad leaves 2 to 6 inches long. Leaves have obvious parallel veins. **Flowers:** Each large flower has a white, lipped petal that is inflated and pouchlike, and usually has a few purple stripes within the pouch; lateral petals twisted and purple, as are the petal-like sepals. One to three flowers arranged in racemes on the ends of the stems. **Fruits:** Dry capsules. **Flowering Season:** May to June. **Habitat/Range:** Mountain woods from Alaska to California and east to Alberta and Wyoming.

FROM THE JOURNALS: A specimen of mountain lady's slipper does not exist, but the explorers discussed it in the journals. On June 30, 1806, the party traveled from the present-day Lolo Hot Springs to "Travellers rest," stopping for dinner along the way at Graves Creek. Lewis wrote in his journal: "this morning on the steep side of a high hill my horse sliped with both his hinder feet out of the road and fell, I also fell off backwards and slid near 40 feet . . . fortunately . . . we both escaped unhirt. . . . I also met with the plant in blume which is sometimes called the lady's slipper or mockerson flower. it is in shape and appearance like ours only that the corolla is white, marked with small veigns of pale red longitudinally on the inner side. After dinner we resumed our march."

Black Cottonwood

Populus trichocarpa Torr. and A. Gray
Also *Populus balsamifera* L.
WILLOW FAMILY (Salicaceae)

Plants: Large trees up to 150 feet tall and 6 feet in diameter. Bark sharply furrowed. Leaves 3 to 7 inches long and 3 to 4 inches wide, rounded at base, and taper to a sharp tip. Bud scales very resinous. **Flowers:** Without sepals or petals. Male and female flowers occur on separate trees. Male flowers are arranged in catkins about 1 inch long, and each flower has numerous stamens; female flowers are in catkins 3 to 8 inches long. Each flower has a single pistil. **Fruits:** Capsules with numerous seeds covered with long, white hairs for wind dispersal. **Flowering Season:** April to June. **Habitat/Range:** Along streams from Alaska to California and east to Alberta and Utah.

FROM THE JOURNALS: On the label with this specimen, which still exists, Frederick Pursh wrote: "Cotton tree of the Columbia River. Jun: 1806." As suggested by this label, black cottonwood is common throughout the Columbia River watershed. The explorers were either in the Kooskooske (Clearwater) River drainage or the Clark's (Bitterroot) River drainage, both tributaries of the Columbia River, when they collected the specimen of black cottonwood in June 1806. On July 2, 1806, while at "Travellers rest," Lewis wrote about black cottonwood: "The leaf of the cottonwood on this river is like that common to the Columbia [black cottonwood] narrower than that common to the lower part of the Missouri and Mississippi [plains cottonwood] and wider than that on the upper part of the Missouri [narrow-leaved cottonwood]."

Top left: Mountain Lady's Slipper
Cypripedium montanum

Top right: Black Cottonwood
Populus trichocarpa

Bottom: Black Cottonwoods along the Bitterroot River below Travelers Rest

Braided Liverwort

Bazzania trilobata (L.) S. F. Gray
(Lepidoziaceae)

Plants: Liverworts with leaves that have three equal-sized lobes; the leaves overlap closely, like shingles, concealing the stems. The plants form mosslike, dense tufts 2 to 8 inches deep. The tuft color varies from grass green to olive green, even yellowish green. **Flowers:** No true flowers. Antheridia produce sperm and archegonia produce eggs. The sperm-producing, male branches are small, budlike, and whitish, arising from the axils of the small leaves on the underside of the stems. The egg producing, female branches are often abundant in a series along the stems. **Fruits:** Four-valved capsules containing single-celled spores. **Flowering Season:** Spores produced from June to July. **Habitat/Range:** They live on humus or peaty soil, very decayed logs, and the bark of trees in shaded streambanks, gorges, and ravines. They occur near the ocean and are rare or absent in the interior of continents. This species is widely distributed in Europe and the eastern half of North America, but in the West it is only found from Alaska to British Columbia.

FROM THE JOURNALS: The Lewis and Clark Herbarium includes a liverwort specimen that botanists have identified as braided liverwort. Frederick Pursh wrote on its label: "A moss used by the natives as a yellow dye. Grows on the Pines of the Rocky mountain Jul. 1st 1806." According to Pursh's label, the explorers collected this specimen while they were camped at "Travellers rest." Liverwort expert Dr. Won Shic Hong of Great Falls, Montana, confirms that *Bazzania trilobata* is not found in Montana or any place along the route Lewis and Clark traveled. Perhaps the specimen has been misidentified and/or mislabeled. It might be a related species of liverwort, like *Lepidozia reptans,* which is common in Montana, or another species of *Bazzania* that occurs along the route the explorers traveled in Idaho, Oregon, or Washington.

This is the only liverwort specimen Lewis and Clark collected and one of only three nonvascular plants. The other nonvascular plants are feather boa kelp *(Egregia menziesii)* and Oregon moss *(Eurhynchium oreganum),* both collected in the *Pacific Forest.*

Braided Liverwort *Bazzania trilobata*

Lepidozia reptans

Bitterroot

Lewisia rediviva Pursh
PURSLANE FAMILY (Portulacaceae)

Plants: Low-growing, perennial herbs about 2 inches tall. Leaves all basal, up to 2 inches long, narrow, round in cross-section, and fleshy. Leaves begin to wither by the time plant flowers. **Flowers:** Pink, rose, or white, large and showy, solitary. Each flower has six to nine sepals, twelve to eighteen petals, many stamens, and four to eight styles. **Fruits:** One-celled capsules with six to twenty seeds each. **Flowering Season:** May to July. **Habitat/Range:** Dry, exposed, gravelly or rocky soils from the plains to lower mountain slopes of interior British Columbia, south to California, and east to Montana and Colorado.

FROM THE JOURNALS: The explorers collected a specimen of bitterroot while they camped at "Travellers rest." On this specimen's label Frederick Pursh wrote, "The Indians eat the root of this Near Clark's R. [Bitterroot River] Jul. 1st 1806." Named in honor of Meriwether Lewis, *Lewisia* was one of three new genera that Pursh named in his 1814 *Flora Americae Septentrionalis.* Pursh wrote about bitterroot in this volume: "This elegant plant would be a very desirable addition to the ornamental perennials, since, if once introduced, it would be easily kept and propagated, as the following circumstance will clearly prove. The specimen with roots taken out of the Herbarium of M. Lewis, Esq. was planted by Mr. M'Mahon of Philadelphia, and vegetated for more than one year: but some accident happening to it, I had not the pleasure of seeing it in flower." Most likely Pursh applied the epithet *rediviva* to this plant because of M'Mahon's attempt to cultivate it; the Latin *redivivus* means "reviving from a dry state, living again."

On August 22, 1805, at Camp Fortunate, Lewis tasted bitterroot that came from "a bushel of roots of three different kinds dryed and prepared for uce," which George Drouillard had acquired in an altercation with some Shoshone Indians. Lewis wrote in his journal: "another speceis [bitterroot] was much mutilated but appeared to be fibrous; the parts were brittle, hard of the size of a small quill, cilindric and as white as snow throughout, except some small parts of the hard black rind which they had not seperated in the preperation. this the Indians with me informed were always boiled for use. I made the exprement, found that they became perfectly soft by boiling, but had a very bitter taste, which was naucious to my pallate, and I transfered them to the Indians who had eat them heartily."

Today, the bitterroot is the floral emblem of Montana as well as the source of several of Montana's place names: Bitterroot Mountains, Bitterroot Valley, and Bitterroot River.

Bitterroot *Lewisia rediviva*

Thin-Leaved Owlclover

Orthocarpus tenuifolius (Pursh) Benth.
FIGWORT FAMILY (Scrophulariaceae)

Plants: Annual herbs, 4 to 12 inches tall, covered with fine hairs. Leaves alternate, narrow, and often have slender lobes. **Flowers:** Pink-tipped, leaflike bracts are attached at the base of the yellow flowers, partially concealing them. The lower margin of these bracts is lined with cilia-like hair. The lower floral lip is slightly shorter than the upper lip; hook occurs at the tip of upper lip. **Fruits:** Capsules with numerous seeds. **Flowering Season:** May to August. **Habitat/Range:** Open, dry, often disturbed places in the valleys, plains, and mountains from interior British Columbia to Oregon, and east to Montana.

Worm-Leaved Stonecrop

Sedum stenopetalum Pursh
STONECROP FAMILY (Crassulaceae)

Plants: Perennial, succulent herbs, less than 12 inches tall. Leaves alternate, linear, keeled on the lower surface (at least when dry), and have tiny plantlets (for asexual reproduction) in the axils of the upper leaves. **Flowers:** Yellow, starlike, arranged in tight cymes. **Fruits:** Follicles with widely divergent, horizontal limbs at maturity. **Flowering Season:** May to July. **Habitat/Range:** Dry, gravelly or rocky soils of grasslands and ponderosa pine forests from British Columbia to California and east to Alberta and Wyoming.

Small-Headed Clover

Trifolium microcephalum Pursh
BEAN FAMILY (Fabaceae)

Plants: Annual herbs with stems 4 to 28 inches long. Leaves compound with three leaflets; leaflike stipules at the base of the leafstalk about half as long as the leaves. **Flowers:** Small, white to pinkish, arranged in congested, headlike clusters of ten to sixty flowers. Leafy bracts form a cuplike structure (involucre) that surrounds and partially encloses the base of the flower arrangement. The involucre has about ten bristle-tipped lobes. **Fruits:** Legume pods with one or two seeds. **Flowering Season:** April to July. **Habitat/Range:** Moist meadows, sandy riverbanks, and dry hillsides from British Columbia to Baja, California, and east to Montana and Arizona.

FROM THE JOURNALS: Lewis collected several new plants on July 1, 1806, while camped at "Travellers rest," including thin-leaved owlclover, worm-leaved stonecrop, and small-headed clover. The worm-leaved stonecrop specimen appears on the same herbarium sheet as lance-leaved stonecrop.

In his journal for July 2, 1806, Lewis wrote: "I found two speceis of native clover here, the one with a very narrow small leaf and a pale red flower [small-headed clover], the other nearly as luxouriant as our red clover with a white flower the leaf and blume of the latter are proportionably large. I found several other uncommon plants specemines of which I preserved." The larger clover was probably long-stalked clover *(Trifolium longipes)*.

Top left: Thin-Leaved Owlclover
Orthocarpus tenuifolius

Top right: Small-Headed Clover
Trifolium microcephalum

Bottom: Worm-Leaved Stonecrop
Sedum stenopetalum

Yellow Monkey-Flower

Mimulus guttatus DC.
FIGWORT FAMILY (Scrophulariaceae)

Plants: Annual or perennial herbs, 3 inches to 3 feet tall. Leaves opposite, simple, palmately veined, and coarsely toothed on the margin. **Flowers:** Yellow with maroon spots on the flared and hairy throat of the lower lip. Arranged in racemes, or singly, from the leaf axils. **Fruits:** Capsules. **Flowering Season:** March to September. **Habitat/Range:** Along streams and wet, seepy areas from Alaska to Mexico and east to the Great Plains.

FROM THE JOURNALS: On July 3, 1806, while at "Travellers rest," the Captains parted, each of them leading a separate group of men in different directions. They had agreed to join again at the confluence of the Yellowstone and Missouri Rivers. Lewis described this parting in his journal that day: "I took leave of my worthy friend and companion Capt. Clark and the party that accompanyed him. I could not avoid feeling much concern on this occasion although I hoped this seperation was only momentary." The next day Lewis described parting with his Nez Perce guides: "I now ordered the horses saddled smoked a pipe with these friendly people and at noon bid them adieu. . . . these affectionate people our guides betrayed every emmotion of unfeigned regret at seperating from us; they said that they were confidint that the Pahkees [their enemies] . . . would cut us off."

Lewis collected a specimen of yellow monkey-flower on July 4. He and his party of nine men traveled that day from their camp on Grant Creek, west of present-day Missoula, Montana, to a campsite along "a river they called Cokahlarishkit, or the *river of the road to buffaloe*." The evening of July 4 they camped about 8 miles above the confluence of the Blackfoot River and the "East branch of Clark's [Clark Fork] river."

Missouri Iris

Iris missouriensis Nutt.
IRIS FAMILY (Iridaceae)

Plants: Perennial herbs, 8 to 24 inches tall. Long leaves about ¼ inch wide with parallel veins; taper to a sharp point. **Flowers:** Pale blue with yellow patches and purple veins. Each large, showy flower has three showy sepals, three petals, and three petal-like styles that give the flower the appearance of nine petals. Flowers arranged in groups of two to four on the stem ends. **Fruits:** Dry capsules with three cells and numerous seeds. **Flowering Season:** May to July. **Habitat/Range:** Meadows and marshy areas that are wet in the spring, from Alaska to Baja, California, and east to Minnesota and Mexico.

FROM THE JOURNALS: On the label with the Missouri iris specimen, Frederick Pursh wrote, "A pale blue Species of Flag. Prairi of the Knobs Jul. 5th 1806." On July 5, Lewis wrote in his course-and-distance journal: "the road passing through an extensive high prarie rendered very uneven by a vast number of little hillucks and sinkholes. at the heads of these two creeks [Cottonwood and Monture Creeks]

Top left: Missouri Iris
Iris missouriensis

Top right: River of the Road to Buffalo (Blackfoot River)

Bottom:
Yellow Monkey-Flower
Mimulus guttatus

high broken mountains stand at the distance of 10 m. forming a kind of Cove." In his journal the next day he mentioned Missouri iris growing near this "prarie of knobs," which is near present-day Ovando, Montana: "the bois rague [red osier dogwood] in blume.—saw the common small blue flag [Missouri iris]."

Bitterbrush

Purshia tridentata (Pursh) DC.
ROSE FAMILY (Rosaceae)

Plants: Shrubs usually 3 to 6 feet tall. Leaves alternate, wedge shaped, and have three lobes on the tip, like big sagebrush *(Artemisia tridentata)*, but lack the sagebrush aroma. Upper leaf-surface green while the lower surface is a paler, grayish green. **Flowers:** Yellow, fragrant, arranged singly or in small clusters on short, leafy branch-spurs. **Fruits:** Achenes. **Flowering Season:** April to June. **Habitat/Range:** Grasslands, sagebrush plains, or ponderosa pine forests from interior British Columbia to California and east to Montana and New Mexico.

Silverberry

Elaeagnus commutata Bernh. ex Rydb.
OLEASTER FAMILY (Elaeagnaceae)

Plants: Shrubs 3 to 12 feet tall that often form dense colonies of flexible, willow-like branches. Leaves alternate, silvery, about 2 inches long and ¾ inch wide. The surface of the leaves and fruit covered with tiny, star-shaped scales. **Flowers:** Yellow, with a strong, lemony fragrance; arranged in pairs that hang down from the leaf axils. **Fruits:** Dry, mealy, silver colored, and drupelike. **Flowering Season:** May to July. **Habitat/Range:** Along streams and on moist slopes from Alaska to Quebec and south to Utah and Minnesota.

Shrubby Cinquefoil

Dasiphora fruticosa (L.) Rydb.
Also *Pentaphylloides floribunda* (Pursh) A. Love
Potentilla fruticosa L.
ROSE FAMILY (Rosaceae)

Plants: Shrubs 1 to 3 feet tall. Leaves bluish green, compound, with five pinnately arranged leaflets. Reddish brown bark, shredding, hangs loosely from the stems. **Flowers:** Yellow, solitary from the leaf axils, grouped three to seven on the stem ends. **Fruits:** Densely hairy achenes. **Flowering Season:** June to August. **Habitat/Range:** Moist, mountain meadows and open woods from Alaska to California and east to New Mexico, South Dakota, and North Carolina.

FROM THE JOURNALS: The explorers collected bitterbrush, silverberry, and shrubby cinquefoil on July 6, 1806, at the "prairi of the knobs" near present-day Ovando, Montana. On the label with the silverberry specimen Frederick Pursh wrote, "Silver tree of the Missouri From the prairi of the knobs." This label indicates that Lewis told Pursh that he had seen silverberry on both sides of the Continental Divide—east near the Missouri River and west near Ovando. On July 6, 1806, Lewis may have been referring to bitterbrush, silverberry, and shrubby cinquefoil when he wrote: "the southern wood and two other speceis of shrub are common in the prarie of knobs. preserved specemines of them." However, by "southern wood" Lewis may have been referring to big sagebrush *(Artemisia tridentata)*, which also occurs in the area and looks somewhat like bitterbrush. (*Purshia tridentata* was named in honor of Frederick Pursh.) The "knobs" Lewis referred to are the numerous small, steep hills of the kettle-knob glacial moraine topography of this area.

Bitterbrush *Purshia tridentata*

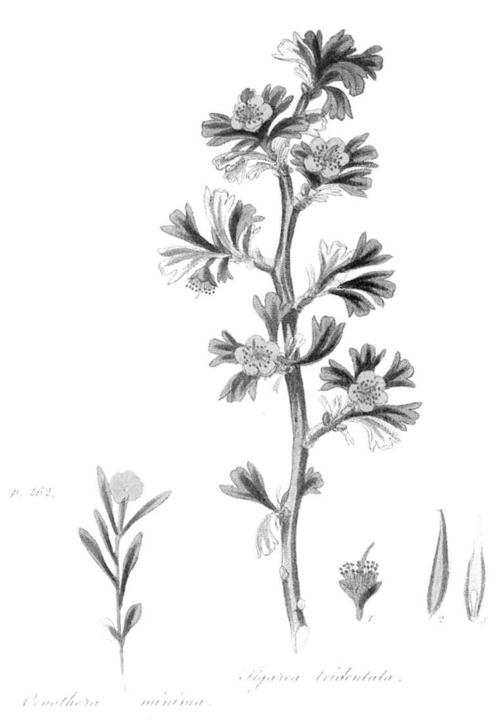

Bitterbrush illustration from Frederick Pursh's 1814 *Flora Americae Septentrionalis*

ilverberry *Elaeagnus commutata*

Shrubby Cinquefoil *Dasiphora fruticosa*

Elephant's Head

Pedicularis groenlandica Retz.
FIGWORT FAMILY (Scrophulariaceae)

Plants: Perennial herbs with clusters of several stems 6 to 28 inches tall. Both basal and stem leaves are compound and fernlike; each leaf has many pinnately arranged, toothed leaflets. **Flowers:** Pink to red, or purple, arranged in tight racemes. Each flower has two lips; the lower lip has three lobes, the upper lip drawn out into a long, upturned beak. Flowers resemble an elephant's head with droopy ears (lobes of lower lip) and a long, arching trunk (the beak). **Fruits:** Smooth capsules. **Flowering Season:** June to August. **Habitat/Range:** Cold, wet meadows from Alaska to California and east to New Mexico, Montana, and Quebec.

Fern-Leaved Lousewort

Pedicularis cystopteridifolia Rydb.
FIGWORT FAMILY (Scrophulariaceae)

Plants: Perennial herbs 4 to 18 inches tall. Basal and stem leaves compound, fernlike, with numerous pinnately arranged leaflets. Each leaflet sharply incised and toothed. **Flowers:** Purple, arranged in racemes. Each flower has two lips; the lower lip has three lobes, the upper lip is helmet shaped and has two small teeth but no beak. **Fruits:** Smooth capsules. **Flowering Season:** June to August. **Habitat/Range:** Open slopes in the mountains of Wyoming and Montana.

Bessey's Crazyweed

Oxytropis besseyi (Rydb.) Blank.
BEAN FAMILY (Fabaceae)

Plants: Perennial herbs with compound basal leaves that have seven to twenty-one pinnately arranged leaflets. Foliage covered with silvery, flat-lying hairs. **Flowers:** Reddish purple when fresh, fading to blue; arranged in congested racemes of five to thirty flowers. Keel petal has a short beak. **Fruits:** Hard, legume pods with sharp beaks and enlarged, persistent sepals. **Flowering Season:** June to July. **Habitat/Range:** Prairies, foothills, and along streams from Alberta and Saskatchewan south to Nevada and Colorado.

FROM THE JOURNALS: The specimens of elephant's head and fern-leaved lousewort have similar labels on which Frederick Pursh wrote: "On the low plains on the heath [shrubland] of Clarks R. Jul. 6th 1806." On July 6, 1806, the explorers traversed the Cokahlarishkit (Blackfoot) River valley from their camp near the mouth of Seamans' (Monture) Creek, just west of present-day Ovando, Montana, and camped near present-day Lincoln. Lewis often collected plants with similar features, enabling him to compare and separate them as new species. Notice that all three of these species have purple flowers arranged in congested racemes and pinnately compound leaves. To the untrained eye they are the same, but with closer inspection and comparison their differences become apparent.

The warning of their Nez Perce guides—that they faced danger from enemy tribes on this route—was still on their minds on July 6 when Lewis wrote: "the trail which we take to be a returning war-party of the Minnetares of Fort de prarie {Atsinas of Saskatchewan, allies of the Blackfeet} becomes much fresher. . . . these

Top left: Elephant's Head
Pedicularis groenlandica

Top right: Fern-Leaved Lousewort
Pedicularis cystopteridifolia

Bottom right: Bessey's Crazyweed
Oxytropis besseyi

plains continue their course S 75 E. and are wide where the river leaves them. up this valley and creek a road passes to Dearbourn's river and thence to the Missouri. . . . we expect to meet with the Minnetares and are therefore much on our guard both day and night."

Bearberry Honeysuckle

Lonicera involucrata (Rich) Banks ex Spreng.
HONEYSUCKLE FAMILY (Caprifoliaceae)

Plants: Shrubs, 2 to 6 feet tall, with opposite, entire leaves. **Flowers:** Yellow, arranged in pairs from the leaf axils. Just below the pair of flowers are four broad, leafy bracts; at first they are green and red and tinged purple but enlarge and turn purple as the fruit develops. **Fruits:** A pair of round, black berries surrounded by the purple bracts. **Flowering Season:** April to August. **Habitat/Range:** Along streams and in moist to wet woods from Alaska to California, east to Quebec and Michigan, and in Montana south to Mexico.

Blanketflower

Gaillardia aristata Pursh
ASTER FAMILY (Asteraceae)

Plants: Perennial herbs 8 to 28 inches tall. Leaves alternate; they can be entire, toothed, or deeply cut and lobed. Foliage covered with long, loose hairs. **Flowers:** Arranged in heads on the ends of the stems; head consists of yellow ray-flowers, purplish at the base, that surround the hairy, reddish purple, disk flowers. The tips of the ray petals have three obvious lobes. **Fruits:** Angular achenes with a tuft of basal hair and six to ten scales on the tip. **Flowering Season:** May to September. **Habitat/Range:** Prairies, dry meadows, and open woods from British Columbia to California and east to Quebec and New Mexico.

FROM THE JOURNALS: Lewis collected bearberry honeysuckle and blanketflower on July 7, 1806. On this day Lewis and his small party left their camp on Beaver Creek near present-day Lincoln, Montana, and headed up the Blackfoot River towards the Continental Divide. In his journal on July 6, Lewis described the area around their camp on Beaver Creek: "above it's mouth through a beatifull plain on the border of which we passed the remains of 32 old lodges. they appear to be those of the Minnetares [Atsinas] as are all those we have seen today. killed five deer and a beaver today. encamped on the creek *much sign* of beaver in this extensive bottom." Then on July 7 he wrote about their journey up the Blackfoot River: "with the road through a level beatifull plain on the North side of the [Blackfoot] river much timber in the bottoms hills also timbered with pitch [lodgepole] pine. no longleafed [ponderosa] pine since we left the praries of the knobs [near Ovando, Montana]. . . . passed the main creek [Landers Fork] . . . and kept up it on the wright hand side through handsom plain bottoms to the foot of a ridge which we ascended[.] the main stream [Landers Fork] boar N W & W. as far as I could see it."

Bearberry Honeysuckle
Lonicera involucrata

Blanketflower *Gaillardia aristata*

Silvery Lupine

Lupinus argenteus Pursh
BEAN FAMILY (Fabaceae)

Plants: Perennial herbs, 6 to 24 inches tall, that have foliage covered with silky hair. Leaves alternate, palmately compound, with six to nine leaflets that join at a common point. **Flowers:** Light to dark blue, sometimes bluish white; arranged in many-flowered racemes on the ends of the stems. The banner is slightly angled from the wings and keel forming a narrow V of about 45 degrees or less. The banner normally doesn't have hair on its back surface. **Fruits:** Pods with two to five seeds. **Flowering Season:** May to July. **Habitat/Range:** Grasslands and open woods from British Columbia to California and east to Manitoba and Oklahoma.

Showy Death Camas

Zigadenus elegans Pursh
LILY FAMILY (Liliaceae)

Plants: Perennial herbs, 6 to 28 inches tall, with several linear basal leaves that have parallel veins and only a few, much smaller leaves on the stems. **Flowers:** Greenish white, arranged in racemes. The petals have a dark green, heart-shaped gland near the base. Each flower has six stamens and three distinctly separate styles. **Fruits:** Capsules with three beaks. **Flowering Season:** June to August. **Habitat/Range:** Moist meadows and open woods from Alaska to Arizona and east to Quebec and Virginia.

FROM THE JOURNALS: The explorers collected specimens of silvery lupine and showy death camas on July 7, 1806. That day Lewis and his small party crossed the Continental Divide at present-day Lewis and Clark Pass in Montana. According to the labels, they collected the specimens on the west side of the pass in the Cokahlarishkit (Blackfoot) River drainage.

In his journal on July 7, Lewis described the trail from the Landers Fork of the Blackfoot River, up Alice Creek, and over the Continental Divide: "over two ridges and again striking the wrigthand fork [Alice Creek] at 4 ms. then continued up it on the left hand side much appearance of beaver many dams. bottoms not wide and covered with low willow and grass. halted to dine at a large beaver dam the hunters killed 3 deer and a fawn. deer are remarkably plenty and in good order. Reubin Fields wounded a moos deer this morning near our camp. my dog much worried . . . 3 m. up the same creek on the east side through a handsome narrow plain . . . 2 m. passing the dividing ridge betwen the waters of the Columbia and Missouri rivers at ¼ of a mile. from this gap which is low and an easy ascent on the W. side the fort mountain [Square Butte] bears North Eaast, and appears to be distant about 20 Miles. the road for one and ¾ miles desends the hill and continues down a branch . . . 7 ms. over several hills and hollows along the foot of the mountain hights passing five small rivulets running to the wright. saw some sighn of buffaloe early this morning in the valley where we encamped last evening from which it appears that the buffaloe do sometimes penetrate these mountains a few miles."

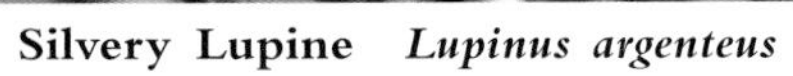

Silvery Lupine *Lupinus argenteus*

Showy Death Camas *Zigadenus elegans*

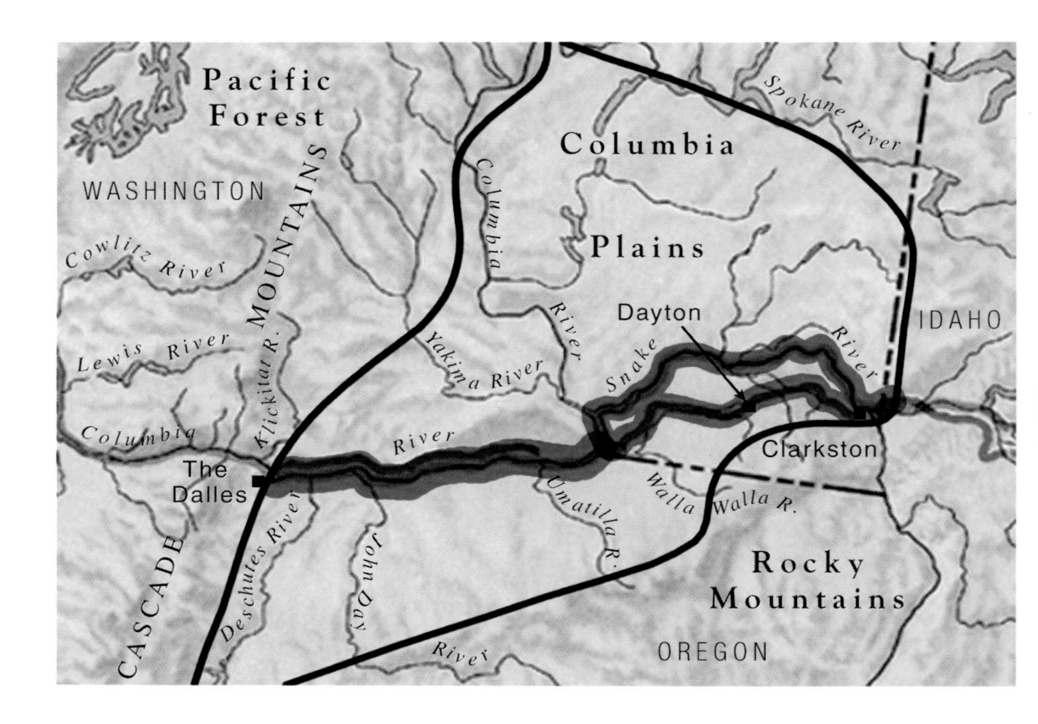

Lomatium species[1]
Rubus parviflorus
Lomatium nudicaule
Amelanchier alnifolia
Dodecatheon poeticum
Artemisia ludoviciana[2]
Claytonia perfoliata[3]
Ribes aureum[4]
Collomia linearis
Uropappus lindleyi
Collinsia parviflora
Plagiobothyrs tenellus

Amsinckia menziesii
Phacelia linearis
Trifolium macrocephalum
Triteleia grandiflora
Cerastium arvense
Osmorhiza occidentalis
Crataegus douglasii
Machaeranthera canescens
Lomatium cous
Coreopsis tinctoria
Aster eatonii

1. See Lomatium grayi.
2. See Tallgrass Prairie.
3. See Pacific Forest.
4. See Rocky Mountains.

The Columbia Plains

The Columbia Plains region of Washington and Oregon is a semidesert area between the Cascade and Rocky Mountains. The bedrock is basalt formed from ancient lava flows. This basalt is exposed in many places, especially along the Columbia River. The terrain is generally flat to gently sloping with steep canyon-walls along the rivers and streams. Rolling hills of windblown silt are common in the eastern quarter of this region known as the Palouse Prairie. The climate is dry, with only 7 to 18 inches of annual precipitation, and low humidity year-round.

Big sagebrush dominates the vegetation in most of the region, while bunchgrasses are more pervasive in the eastern rolling-hills. Bluebunch wheatgrass, Idaho fescue, bitterbrush, lupine, arrow-leaved balsamroot, and pink carpets of phlox are common.

Lewis and Clark first passed through the Columbia Plains from October 10 to October 28, 1805, as they were swept down the Snake and Columbia Rivers in their freshly made canoes on their way to the Pacific Ocean. In the spring of 1806, they again traveled through the region from April 15 to May 5. Faced with pulling the canoes up the spring-swollen waters of the Columbia River, they obtained horses (with some difficulty) and traveled by land. They rode along the north

The Columbia Plains

(Washington) side of the Columbia, then crossed it near the mouth of the Walla Walla River, and followed a more direct, overland route through present-day Dayton, Washington, to the confluence of the Snake and Clearwater Rivers.

On April 17, 1806, while the explorers were at "rockfort camp" near present-day The Dalles, Oregon, Lewis described the difference between the Columbia Plains and the adjacent Pacific Forest: "even at this place which is merely on the border of the plains of Columbia the climate seems to have changed the air feels dryer and more pure. the earth is dry and seems as if there had been no rain for a week or ten days. the plain is covered with a rich virdure of grass and herbs from four to nine inches high and exhibits a beautifull seen [scene] particularly pleasing after having been so long imprisoned in mountains and those almost impenetrably thick forrests of the seacoast." Then on May 1, 1806, near present-day Waitsburg, Washington, Clark compared the Columbia Plains with the High Plains: "I See Very little difference between the apparant face of the Country here and that of the plains of the Missouri. only that those [Columbia Plains] are not enlivened by the vast herds of Buffalow, elk &c. [etc.] which animated those of the Missouri."

The twenty-three species of plants that the explorers collected in the Columbia Plains are still intact in the Lewis and Clark Herbarium in Philadelphia. Three of these species are duplicates of plants discussed elsewhere in this book: *prairie sagewort* in the *Tallgrass Prairie, miner's lettuce* in the *Pacific Forest,* and *golden currant* in the *Rocky Mountains.* A fourth specimen consists of plant parts that cannot be identified, but botanists believe the fragments belong to a desert-parsley *(Lomatium)* species that I discuss in the *Pacific Forest.* The remaining nineteen species are discussed below, arranged geographically from west to east.

The Columbia Plains and Mount Hood in Oregon
seen from Dallesport, Washington

Thimbleberry

Rubus parviflorus Nutt.
ROSE FAMILY (Rosaceae)

Plants: Erect shrubs, 1½ to 7 feet tall, with gray, flaking, peeling bark. Leaves simple, palmately five-lobed with a toothed margin, 4 to 8 inches long and about as wide. **Flowers:** White, arranged in corymbs of about three to seven flowers. **Fruits:** Thimble-shaped aggregate of edible druplets. **Flowering Season:** May to July. **Habitat/Range:** Moist woods from Alaska to California, east to the Great Lakes region, and south in the Rocky Mountains to northern Mexico.

FROM THE JOURNALS: Lewis and Clark collected a specimen of thimbleberry either near present-day Lyle, Washington, or The Dalles, Oregon. Frederick Pursh wrote on its label: "A Shrub of which the natives eat the young Sprout without kooking. On the Columbia Aprl. 15th 1806." In the Pacific Forest near the coast Lewis had confused thimbleberry with salmonberry *(Rubus spectabilis),* which also has an erect stem with peeling bark; he called them both "larged leafed thorn." Lewis corrected himself on April 8, 1806, near present-day Shepperds Dell State Park in Oregon when he described salmonberry and then stated, "the shrub [thimbleberry] which I have heretofore confounded with this [salmonberry] grows in similar situations, has a stem precisely like it except the thorn and bears a large three loabed leaf."

Bare-Stemmed Desert-Parsley

Lomatium nudicaule (Pursh) Coult. and Rose
PARSLEY FAMILY (Apiaceae)

Plants: Perennial herbs 8 to 32 inches tall. Leaves compound with three to thirty large, bluish green leaflets. Each leaflet about 1 to 3 inches long and ½ to 2½ inches wide. **Flowers:** Yellow, arranged in many-flowered, compound umbels, with rays of unequal lengths. **Fruits:** Dry schizocarp with wings about half as wide as the body. **Flowering Season:** April to June. **Habitat/Range:** Dry, open shrublands or woods from British Columbia to California and east to Alberta, Idaho, and Utah.

FROM THE JOURNALS: Lewis and Clark collected bare-stemmed desert-parsley either near present-day Lyle, Washington, or The Dalles, Oregon. Frederick Pursh wrote on its label: "Supposed to be a Smyrnium the natives eat the tops & boil it Sometimes with their Soup. On the Columbia Aprl. 15th 1806." Pursh named this new species *Smyrnium nudicaule* in his 1814 *Flora Americae Septentrionalis,* in which he repeated the statement above about its use by Native Americans and added, "the same as we use celery." On April 15, 1806, the expedition stopped at "sepulchre rock" (Lower Memaloose Island) where Native Americans had placed their dead in canoes, which Lewis described: "we halted a few minutes at the sepulchre rock, and examined the deposits of the ded at that place . . . some of them were more than half filled with dead bodies. there were thirteen sepulchres [burial canoes] on this rock which stands near the center of the river and has a surface of about 2 acres above high-water mark." The explorers camped that evening at their "rockfort camp," where they remained until April 18.

Thimbleberry *Rubus parviflorus*

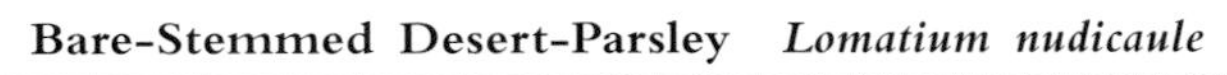

Bare-Stemmed Desert-Parsley *Lomatium nudicaule*

Western Serviceberry

Amelanchier alnifolia (Nutt.) Nutt. ex Roem.
ROSE FAMILY (Rosaceae)

Plants: Shrubs 3 to 16 feet tall. Leaves simple, toothed along the upper half of the margin, with soft, silvery hair (at least on the lower surface). **Flowers:** White, arranged in short racemes of three to twenty flowers. **Fruits:** Purple, edible berries. **Flowering Season:** April to July. **Habitat/Range:** Open woods from sea level to high elevations in the mountains from Alaska to California and east to Quebec and New Mexico.

FROM THE JOURNALS: Lewis and Clark collected three western-serviceberry specimens in 1806. They collected one on April 15 near "rockfort camp," another on May 7 along the Clearwater River either near present-day Lenore or Peck, Idaho, and the final one on June 27 along the Lolo Trail beyond Lolo Creek in Idaho. On the first specimen's label Frederick Pursh wrote, "Service berry A Small bush the Narrows of the Columbia R. Aprl. 15th 1806." In his April 8, 1806, weather notes, Lewis remarked, "the serviceburries, chokecherries, the growth which resembles the beach [red alder], the small birch and grey willow have put fourth their leaves." On April 11, near the present-day Bonneville Dam on the Columbia River, Clark stated: "vegitation is rapidly progressing. Sarvis berry, Sackacommis [kinnikinnick] and the large leafed ash [big-leaved maple] is in blume." While at their rockfort camp on April 15, Lewis described the dress of the Indians that visited: "their men have generally leging mockersons and large robes, many of them wear shirts . . . highly ornamented with the quills of the porcupine as are also their mockersons and legings."

Poet's Shooting Star

Dodecatheon poeticum L. F. Hend.
PRIMROSE FAMILY (Primulaceae)

Plants: Perennial herbs with leafless stems up to 12 inches tall, covered with fine gland-bearing hairs. Leaves basal, simple, widest above the middle and tapering gradually towards the winged petioles. Margin of leaf often lined with fine, sharp teeth. **Flowers:** Bright pink and showy, the petals swept back away from the sharp-pointed tips. **Fruits:** One-celled capsules opening by valves on the tip. **Flowering Season:** March to May. **Habitat/Range:** Wet soil on the east side of the Cascade Mountains from Yakima County, Washington, to Wasco and Hood River Counties, Oregon.

FROM THE JOURNALS: Frederick Pursh wrote on the label with the poet's shooting star specimen, "Near the narrows of Columbia R. Aprl. 16th 1806." Pursh evidently failed to recognize the specimen as a new species, and it wasn't until 1930 that this species was described in the botanical journal *Rhodora*. The specimen has been misidentified as *Dodecatheon media,* which doesn't occur in the area, and *Dodecatheon jeffreyi,* which usually occurs at higher elevations and blooms later than poet's shooting star. Lewis stated in his journal on April 16, 1806: "I was visited today by several of the natives, and amused myself in making a collection of the

Western Serviceberry flowers
Amelanchier alnifolia

Western Serviceberry fruit

esculent [edible] plants in the neighbourhood such as the Indians use, a specemine of which I preserved. I also met with sundry other plants which were strangers to me which I also preserved, among others there is a currant which is now in blume and has yellow blossom [golden currant, *Ribes aureum*]."

Poet's Shooting Star
Dodecatheon poeticum

Narrow-Leaved Collomia

Collomia linearis Nutt.
PHLOX FAMILY (Polemoniaceae)

Plants: Small, annual herbs, 4 to 24 inches tall. Leaves simple, lance shaped, 2½ inches long or less. **Flowers:** Pink, arranged in dense clusters on the ends of the stems and in the leaf axils. **Fruits:** Capsules open at the tip. **Flowering Season:** May to August. **Habitat/Range:** Dry, open, often disturbed places from British Columbia to California and east to Ontario and New Mexico.

FROM THE JOURNALS: Narrow-leaved collomia was one of seven small, annual species that Lewis collected on April 17, 1806, while at "rockfort camp." Lewis often collected plants in a series like this—plants with similar botanical characteristics and/or habitat—for comparative botanical study, a technique he may have learned from Dr. Benjamin Barton in Philadelphia. Clark had described their "rockfort camp" in his journal of October 25, 1805, as they descended the Columbia River: "we Came too, under a high point of rocks on the Lard. Side below a creek [Mill Creek] of 20 yards wide . . . our Camp on the top of a high point of rocks, which forms a kind of fortification . . . this Situation we Concieve well Calculated for defence, and Conveniant to hunt under the foots of the mountain . . . and appears to be handsom Coverts for the Deer, in oke [Oregon oak, *Quercus garryana*] woods."

Lindley's Microseris

Uropappus lindleyi (DC.) Nutt.
Also *Microseris lindleyi* (DC.) A. Gray
ASTER FAMILY (Asteraceae)

Plants: Tender, annual herbs with milky juice, 4 to 24 inches tall. Leaves narrow, 6 to 8 inches long, gradually taper to a sharp point, and often have a few widely spaced teeth on the margin. **Flowers:** Yellow, arranged in heads of a few ray flowers on the ends of the stems. **Fruits:** Thin, black achenes with five long, narrow scales on the tip. Each scale has a two-pronged end with a thin bristle in the notch between the prongs. **Flowering Season:** March to June. **Habitat/Range:** Dry openings in the valleys, foothills, and plains east of the Cascade Mountains from Washington to California and east to Idaho and New Mexico.

FROM THE JOURNALS: Lewis collected a specimen of Lindley's microseris on April 17, 1806, near "rockfort camp." Lewis's party was busy that day constructing packsaddles to carry the expedition's gear on horseback while Clark and his party were attempting to buy horses across the river. That day Lewis described the eggs of a magpie that he examined: "Joseph Feilds brought me today three eggs of the party [pretty] coloured corvus [magpie], they are about the size and shape of those of the pigeon. they are bluish white much freckled with dark redish brown irregular spots, in short it is reather a mixture of those colours in which the redish brown predominates, particularly towards the larger end."

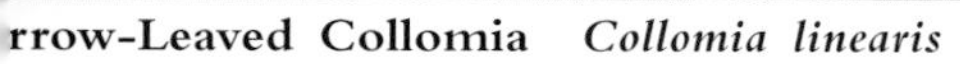

rrow-Leaved Collomia *Collomia linearis*

Lindley's Microseris *Uropappus lindleyi*

Small Blue-Eyed Mary

Collinsia parviflora Lindl.
FIGWORT FAMILY (Scrophulariaceae)

Plants: Annual herbs 2 to 16 inches tall. Leaves in opposite pairs, or the upper ones whorled. The lowest pair of leaves rounded or elliptical while the rest are narrow to oblong; up to 2 inches long. **Flowers:** Blue with a white upper-lip, the tube bent abruptly at its base; on long, thin stalks. The upper flowers clustered in the leaf axils while the lower ones occur singly. **Fruits:** Capsules that split open along four sutures. **Flowering Season:** March to July. **Habitat/Range:** Seasonally moist places, often in disturbed soil from Alaska to California and east to Ontario and New Mexico.

FROM THE JOURNALS: Lewis collected a specimen of small blue-eyed Mary on April 17, 1806, while at "rockfort camp." Clark was across the Columbia River in present-day Washington attempting to obtain horses for overland travel. On April 16, Clark wrote in his journal: "we Set out and arrived at the Village at Sunset. after Some Serimony I entered the house of the Chief. I then informed them that I would trade with them for their horses in the morning . . . The Chief Set before me a large platter of Onions which had been Sweeted [sweated, or steamed]. I gave a part of those onions to all my party and we all eate of them, in this State the root is very Sweet and the tops tender. the nativs requested the party to dance which they very readily consented and Peter Cruzat played on the Violin and the men danced Several dances & retired to rest in the houses of the 1st and Second Cheif."

Slender Popcorn Flower

Plagiobothrys tenellus (Nutt.) Gray
BORAGE FAMILY (Boraginaceae)

Plants: Annual herbs, 2 to 10 inches tall, covered with stiff, bristly hairs. Leaves on the stem alternate, widely spaced, and smaller than the numerous basal leaves. **Flowers:** White, arranged in cymes that are spiraled like a snail shell prior to opening. **Fruits:** Four nutlets, each with four limbs, like a cross. **Flowering Season:** April to June. **Habitat/Range:** Dry, open, often disturbed places from British Columbia to Baja, California, and east to Idaho, Utah, and Nevada.

FROM THE JOURNALS: Lewis collected a specimen of slender popcorn flower on April 17, 1806, at "rockfort camp." Clark described his morning that day in his journal: "I rose early and took a position near to the village and exposed the artiles [articles] I had for Sale Great numbers of Indians Came from different derections, Some from below Some above and others across the Countrey from the Tapteet [Yakima] river . . . I obtained a Sketch of the Columbia as also Clarks river." The sketch was a detailed map of the Columbia River and its tributaries, the Lolo Trail over the Bitterroot Mountains, the Clark Fork River, and the trail up the Blackfoot River in present-day Montana. This map was the first of several that Clark obtained from various Native American advisors as the expedition ascended the Columbia, Snake, and Clearwater Rivers on their homeward journey.

Small Blue-Eyed Mary
Collinsia parviflora

Slender Popcorn Flower
Plagiobothrys tenellus

Small-Flowered Fiddleneck

Amsinckia menziesii (Lehm.) Nels. and Macbr.
Also *Amsinckia retrorsa* Suksd.
BORAGE FAMILY (Boraginaceae)

Plants: Annual herbs 4 to 28 inches tall. Stems and leaves have stiff, bristly hairs, and often shorter, softer, downward-directed hairs on the stems below the flower arrangement. Leaves alternate, narrow to oblong, up to 5 inches long and ⅘ inch wide. **Flowers:** Light yellow to orange, sometimes red on the throat. Flowers arranged in coiled spikes spiraled like a snail shell that open and elongate as the flowers open. Petal tubes rarely extend beyond the five sepals. **Fruits:** Nutlets, oval in outline. **Flowering Season:** April to July. **Habitat/Range:** Dry, open places from Alaska to California and east to Idaho, Manitoba, and Texas.

FROM THE JOURNALS: Lewis collected a specimen of small-flowered fiddleneck on April 17, 1806, at "rockfort camp." Clark was on the Washington side of the Columbia River having difficulty bartering for horses. He wrote in his journal: "I made a bargin with the Chief for 2 horses, about an hour after he canseled the bargin and we again bargained for 3 horses which were brought foward, only one of the 3 could be possibly used the other two had Such intolerable backs as to render them entirely unfit for Service. I refused to take two of them which displeased him and he refused to part with the 3rd. I then packed up the articles and was about Setting out for the Village above when a man Came in and Sold me two horses, and another man Sold me one horse."

Thread-Leaved Phacelia

Phacelia linearis (Pursh) Holtz.
WATERLEAF FAMILY (Hydrophyllaceae)

Plants: Annual herbs, 4 to 20 inches tall, with dense, fine hair on the stems and foliage. Leaves alternate, narrow, entire, or with one to four lobes below the middle. **Flowers:** Blue to lavender, arranged in crowded clusters on the ends of the stems and in the leaf axils. **Fruits:** Capsules that split open on the back and expel coarsely pitted seeds. **Flowering Season:** April to June. **Habitat/Range:** Dry, open, often disturbed places of the foothills and plains from British Columbia to California and east to Alberta, South Dakota, Wyoming, and Utah.

FROM THE JOURNALS: Lewis collected a specimen of thread-leaved phacelia on April 17, 1806, at "rockfort camp." Clark was attempting to purchase horses in an Indian village on the Washington side of the Columbia River when he wrote: "Maney of the nativs from different villages on the Columbia above offered to trade, but asked Such things as we had not and double as much of the articles which I had as we could afford to give. . . . I purchased 3 dogs for the party with me to eate and Some Chap-pa-lell *[Lomatium cous]* for my Self." Clark had purchased cous bisquit-root, an often-mentioned food and trade item of the Native Americans of the upper Columbia River drainage.

Small-Flowered Fiddleneck
Amsinckia menziesii

Thread-Leaved Phacelia
Phacelia linearis

Big-Head Clover

Trifolium macrocephalum (Pursh) Poiret
BEAN FAMILY (Fabaceae)

Plants: Perennial herbs 4 to 12 inches tall with compound leaves and hairy foliage. Each leaf has five to nine leaflets radiating from a common point. **Flowers:** Pink to rose colored; arranged in large, solitary, headlike racemes on the ends of the stems. The large flower heads are oval to round in outline, about 2 inches long and 1½ inches wide. **Fruits:** One-seeded legume pods. **Flowering Season:** April to June. **Habitat/Range:** Sagebrush plains and dry woods east of the Cascade Mountains from Washington to California and east to Idaho and Nevada.

FROM THE JOURNALS: There are two sheets of big-head clover in the herbarium. The explorers collected both on April 17, 1806, near "rockfort camp." Clark's party was busy bartering for horses on the north side of the Columbia River when he wrote: "industously employd. our Selves with the great multitude of indians of differant Nations about us trying to purchase horses. Shabono purchased a verry fine Mare for which he gave Hurmen [ermine pelts], Elks Teeth, a belt and Some other articles of no great value. no other purchase was made in the Course of this day. . . . I was envited into the house of the 2nd Chief where Concluded to Sleep. this man was pore nothing to eat but dried fish, and no wood to burn. altho' the night was Cold they Could not rase as much wood as would make a fire."

Douglas's Wild Hyacinth

Triteleia grandiflora Lindl.
Also *Brodiaea douglasii* Wats.
LILY FAMILY (Liliaceae)

Plants: Perennial herbs with leafless stems 8 to 28 inches tall. One or two basal leaves, narrow and grasslike, 10 to 20 inches long. **Flowers:** Pale blue to purplish, arranged in simple umbels. The three petal-like sepals and three petals join together for half their length or more, forming a basal tube. **Fruits:** Capsules. **Flowering Season:** April to July. **Habitat/Range:** Grasslands, sagebrush plains, and juniper woodlands on the east side of the Cascade Mountains from British Columbia to California and east to Montana and Utah.

FROM THE JOURNALS: Two specimens of Douglas's wild hyacinth still exist, both with labels that state the explorers collected them on April 20, 1806, when they were near present-day Horsethief State Park in Washington. Lewis described this species in his journal on April 17, 1806, while at "rockfort camp": "there is a species of hiasinth in these plains the bulb of which the natives eat either boiled baked or dryed in the sun. this bulb is white, not entirely solid, and of a flat form; the bulb of the present year overlays, or crowns that of the last, and seems to be pressed close to it, the old bulb is withered much thiner equally wide with that of the present year and sends fourth from it's sides a number of small radicles [roots].—this hiasinth is of a pale blue colour and is a very pretty flower. I preserved a specemine of it."

Top left: Big-Head Clover
Trifolium macrocephalum

Top right: Big-Head Clover illustration from Frederick Pursh's 1814
Flora Americae Septentrionalis

Bottom right: Douglas's Wild Hyacinth *Triteleia grandiflora*

Field Chickweed

Cerastium arvense L.
PINK FAMILY (Caryophyllaceae)

Plants: Perennial herbs 12 to 14 inches tall or, more often, trailing on the ground forming low mats. Leaves opposite, narrow, and lance shaped, usually with clusters of secondary leaves in their axils. **Flowers:** White, arranged in cymes. Petals have two deep lobes. **Fruits:** Capsules with golden seeds. **Flowering Season:** April to August. **Habitat/Range:** Grasslands and meadows from sea level to alpine elevations, occurring throughout most of Canada and south to California, New Mexico, and Georgia.

FROM THE JOURNALS: Lewis and Clark collected a specimen of field chickweed on April 22, 1806, northeast of present-day Wishram, Washington. The party camped that night on the Washington side of the Columbia River near the present-day John Day Dam. Clark wrote: "we find the horses very troublesom perticularly the Stud which Compose 10⁄13 of our number of horses. the air I find extreemly Cold which blows Continularly from Mt. Hoods Snowey regions. those Indians reside in Small Lodges built of the mats of Grass [bulrush?], flags [cattails] &c. [etc.] and Crouded with inhabitents . . . we made 14 miles to day with the greatest exirtion. Serjt. Gass & R. Fields joined us with one Canoe this evening. the other Canoe with Colter & pots is a head."

Western Sweet-Cicely

Osmorhiza occidentalis (Nutt.) Torr.
PARSLEY FAMILY (Apiaceae)

Plants: Perennial herbs 16 to 48 inches tall with a strong licorice-like aroma. Leaves one- to three-times compound. The ultimate leaflets are usually divided into three segments; up to 4 inches long and 2 inches wide, lance shaped, with a toothed margin. **Flowers:** Yellow or greenish, arranged in compound umbels on the ends of the stems. **Fruits:** Smooth, narrow, almost cylindrical in shape, up to ¾ inch long. **Flowering Season:** April to July. **Habitat/Range:** Moist, rich soil of streams, meadows, and forests from British Columbia to California and east to Alberta and Colorado.

FROM THE JOURNALS: There is one herbarium sheet in the Lewis and Clark Herbarium that does not contain any plant material but does have a label on which Frederick Pursh wrote: "A Species of Fennel root eaten by the Indians of an Annis [anise] Seed taste. Flowers white. Columbia R. Aprl. 25th 1806." Some botanists believe the specimen is western sweet-cicely because Pursh's label indicates that the specimen had a strong anise-seed taste, which sweet-cecily does. Botanists have also suggested Yampah *(Perideridia montana),* but it lacks the anise flavor and tastes more like domestic parsnip.

On April 25, 1806, the expedition camped near Alder Creek near present-day Alderdale, Washington. They had traveled roughly 20 miles up the Columbia River. They don't mention western sweet-cicely in the journals for April 25, but on May 16, while camped at Camp Chopunnish near present-day Kamiah, Idaho,

Field Chickweed *Cerastium arvense*

Western Sweet-Cicely
Osmorhiza occidentalis

Lewis wrote, "Sahcargarmeah geathered a quantity of the roots of a speceis of fennel which we found very agreeable food, the flavor of this root is not unlike annis seed, and they dispell the wind which the roots called Cows *[Lomatium cous]* and quamash *[Camassia quamash]* are apt to create particularly the latter."

Black Hawthorn

Crataegus douglasii Lindl.
ROSE FAMILY (Rosaceae)

Plants: Large shrubs 3 to 13 feet tall, or taller, with stout thorns ⅜ to ¾ inch long. Leaves alternate and simple with a toothed, sometimes shallowly lobed margin. **Flowers:** White, arranged in clusters (corymbs) of a few flowers from the leaf axils. **Fruits:** Dark purple to black, smooth, berrylike pomes. **Flowering Season:** April to June. **Habitat/Range:** Streams and valleys from Alaska to California and east to Ontario and Utah.

FROM THE JOURNALS: Frederick Pursh wrote on the black-hawthorn specimen's label, "Deep purple Haw. Columbia R. Aprl. 29th 1806." On April 28–29, 1806, the expedition was crossing the Columbia River—assisted by the Walla Walla Indians—heading to the mouth of the Walla Walla River in present-day Washington. Clark wrote in his journal for April 28: "This morning early the Great Chief *Yel lip pet* brought a very eligant white horse to our Camp and presented him to me. . . . he insisted on our remaining with him this day at least . . . that he had Sent for the *Chim-na-pums* [Yakima Indians] his neighbours to come down and join his people this evening and dance for us. . . . a little before Sun Set the Chim nah poms arrived. . . . and formed a half Circle arround our camp where they waited verry patiently to See our party dance. the fiddle was played and the men amused themselves with danceing about an hour. we then requested the Indians to dance which they very Chearfully Complyed with; they Continued their dance untill 10 at night . . . about 350 men women and Children Sung and danced at the Same time."

Hoary Aster

Machaeranthera canescens (Pursh) A. Gray
Also *Aster canescens* Pursh
ASTER FAMILY (Asteraceae)

Plants: Biennial or perennial herbs 4 to 20 inches tall. Leaves alternate, usually covered with fine, gray hair and often bearing spine-tipped teeth on the margin (especially the lower leaves). Fluid-filled glandular hair is usually present on the herbage. **Flowers:** Bluish purple rays with a yellow disk; arranged in heads on the stem ends and in the leaf axils. **Fruits:** Achenes with numerous pappus bristles. **Flowering Season:** July to October. **Habitat/Range:** Dry places in the plains and foothills from British Columbia to California and east to Saskatchewan and Texas.

FROM THE JOURNALS: Frederick Pursh wrote on the hoary aster's label, "On the Columbia. Octbr. 1805." The explorers arrived at the confluence of the Snake and Columbia Rivers on October 16, 1805, on their outbound trip, and they traveled down the Columbia River through the Columbia Plains from October 18 to 24. Clark wrote in his journal on October 18: "Took our leave of the Chiefs and all those about us and proceeded on down the great Columbia river. . . . Saw a mountain [Mount Adams] bearing S. W. Conocal form Covered with Snow . . . Soon after we landed, our old Chiefs informed us that the large camp above 'was the Camp

Black Hawthorn *Crataegus douglasii*

Hoary Aster
Machaeranthera canescens

of the 1st Chief of all the *tribes* in this quarter' . . . the Chief came down accompanied by 20 men, and formed a Camp a Short distance above, the chief brought with him a large basket of mashed berries which he left at our Lodge as a present . . . we made 21 miles today."

Cous Bisquit-Root

Lomatium cous (S. Wats.) Coult. and Rose
PARSLEY FAMILY (Apiaceae)

Plants: Perennial herbs 4 to 14 inches tall. Leaves compound, smooth, dissected into many small segments. **Flowers:** Yellow, arranged in compound umbels on the ends of the stems. A whorl of small, green bractlets surround the point where the flower stalks join together. These bractlets are broadly egg shaped or spatula shaped. **Fruits:** Smooth, or rough from granules, and have lateral wings almost as wide as the fruit body. **Flowering Season:** April to July. **Habitat/Range:** Dry, open, rocky slopes—sagebrush plains to alpine slopes—from Washington to Nevada and east to North Dakota and Utah.

FROM THE JOURNALS: The specimen of cous bisquit-root still has a large, intact root. Frederick Pursh wrote on its label: "An umbelliferous plant of the root of which the Wallowallows [Walla Walla Indians] make a kind of bread. The natives calld it Shappalell. Aprl. 29th 1806." The Chopunnish (Nez Perce) Indians called this plant "cous" or "cows." It was one of the most important food plants and trade items for the Native Americans of the upper Columbia River drainage, and Lewis and Clark mentioned it often in the journals.

On April 29, 1806, across the Columbia from the mouth of the Walla Walla River, Lewis wrote in his journal, "This morning Yellept [Chief of the Walla Walla Indians] furnished us with two canoes and we began to transport our baggage over the [Columbia] river . . . we purchased some dogs and shappellell this morning." On May 9, north of present-day Nezperce, Idaho, Lewis wrote: "among other roots those called by them the Quawmash [camas] and Cows [cous] are esteemed the most agreeable and valuable as they are also the most abundant. the cows is a knobbed root of an irregularly rounded form not unlike the Gensang [American ginseng, *Panax quinquefolius*] in form and consistence. this root they collect, rub of a thin black rhind which covers it and pounding it expose it in cakes to the sun. these [cous] cakes ate [at] about an inch and ¼ thick and 6 by 18 in width, when dryed they either eat this bread alone without any further preperation, or boil it and make a thick muselage; the latter is most common and much the most agreeable. the flavor of this root is not very unlike the gensang.— this [cous] root they collect as early as the snows disappear in the spring and continue to collect it untill the quawmash supplys it's place which happens about the latter end of June."

The next day Lewis wrote, "we decended the hills to Commearp Creek [Lawyer Creek near present-day Kamiah, Idaho] arrived at the Village of Tunnachemootoolt [Broken Arm] . . . the Cheif spoke to his people and they produced us about 2 bushels of the Quawmas roots dryed, four cakes of the bread of *cows* [cous] and a dryed salmon trout." That same day Clark stated: "The Village of the *broken Arm* consists of one house or Lodge only which is 150 feet in length . . . it contains 24 fires and about double that number of families . . . I prosume they could raise 100 fighting men. the noise of their women pounding the cows roots remind me of a nail factory."

Top: Cous Bisquit-Root showing the roots

Bottom: Cous Bisquit-Root
Lomatium cous

On June 6, 1806, still near Kamiah, Lewis related this: "The broken arm gave Capt. C, a few dryed Quawmas roots as a great present, but in our estimation those of cows are much better, I am confident they are much more healthy. The men . . . obtained a good store of roots and bread . . . on examination we find that our whole party have an ample store of bread and roots for our [Lolo Trail] voyage."

Columbia Tickseed

Coreopsis tinctoria Nutt.
Also *Coreopsis atkinsoniana* Dougl. Ex Lindl.
ASTER FAMILY (Asteraceae)

Plants: Annual or biennial herbs, 1 to 4 feet tall, with pinnately compound leaves that have numerous long, narrow leaflets. **Flowers:** Numerous heads with orange to yellow rays, reddish brown at the base, with brown disk flowers. Bracts surround the heads in two series: the outer narrow and short, the inner much wider and longer. **Fruits:** Black achenes with narrow wings, sometimes with two small teeth or no pappus at all. **Flowering Season:** June to September. **Habitat/Range:** Streambanks along the Columbia River and its tributaries in Washington, Oregon, Idaho, and Montana.

FROM THE JOURNALS: Frederick Pursh wrote on the Columbia tickseed's label, "On Lewis's R. [Snake River] Octbr: 1805." From October 11 to 16, 1805, the expedition plied their newly constructed canoes through the rapids of the Snake River aided by Nez Perce Indians. Clark described an event on October 12 while near present-day Riparia, Washington: "we passed to day rapids Several of them very bad and came to at the head of one (at 30 miles) on the Stard. Side to view it before we attemptd. to dsend through it. The Indians had told us was verry bad—we found long and dangerous about 2 miles in length, and maney turns necessary to Stear Clare of the rocks, which appeared to be in every direction. The Indians went through & our Small Canoe followed them, as it was late we deturmined to camp above untill the morning." The next day he continued, "we passed over this bad rapid Safe."

Eaton's Aster

Aster eatonii (Gray) Howell
ASTER FAMILY (Asteraceae)

Plants: Perennial herbs, 16 to 40 inches tall, with fine hair on the upper stems. Leaves alternate, entire, narrow, up to 6 inches long and ¾ inch wide, but usually smaller. **Flowers:** White or pink, arranged in heads on the ends of short, leafy stems from the leaf axils. Leafy bracts surround the head and barely overlap each other. Flower arrangement long, narrow, leafy, and panicle-like, consisting of many flower heads. **Fruits:** Hairy achenes with numerous capillary bristles. **Flowering Season:** July to September. **Habitat/Range:** Streambanks and other wet places from British Columbia to California and east to Saskatchewan and New Mexico.

FROM THE JOURNALS: Lewis and Clark collected a specimen of Eaton's aster along the Snake River sometime between October 10 and 18, 1805. On October 10 Clark wrote: "The Countrey about the forks is an open Plain on either Side. . . . I think Lewis's [Snake] River is about 250 yards wide, the *Koos koos ke* [Clearwater] River about 150 yards wide and the river below the forks about 300 yards wide . . . The *Cho-pun-nish* [Nez Perce] or Pierced nose Indians are Stout likeley men, handsom women, and verry dressey in their way, the dress of the men are a white Buffalow robe or Elk Skin dressed with Beeds which are generally white, Sea Shells. . . . with a plat of twisted grass [sweetgrass] about their necks."

Columbia Tickseed *Coreopsis tinctoria*

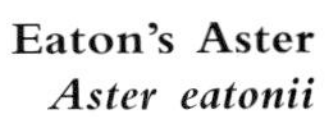

Eaton's Aster
Aster eatonii

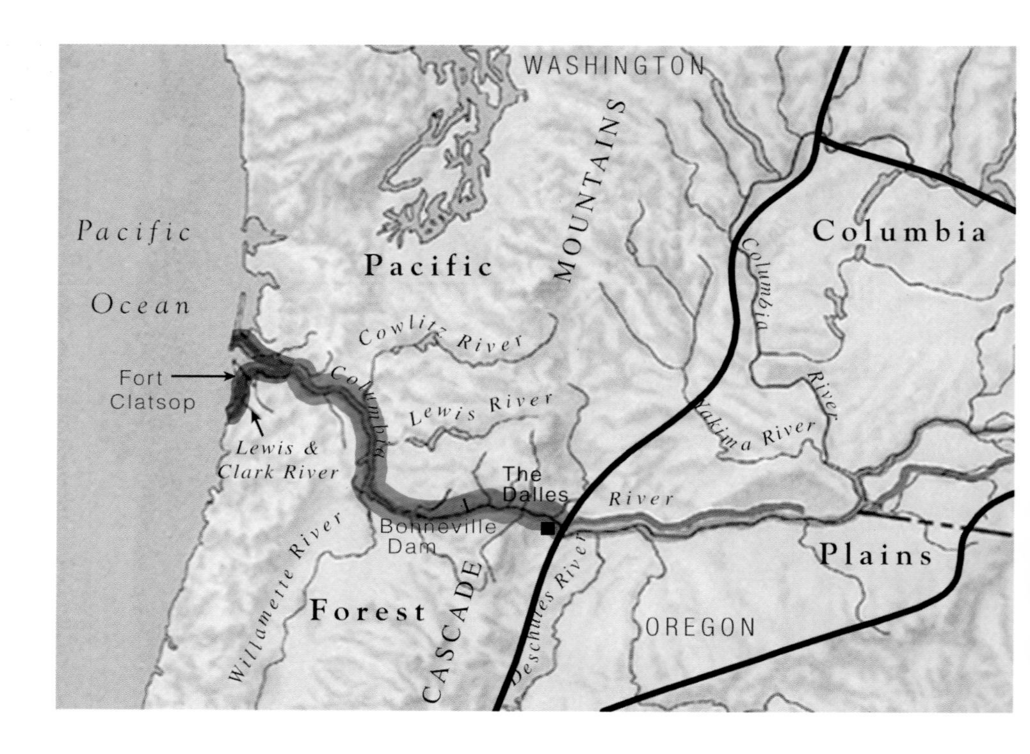

Paxistima myrsinites
Physocarpus capitatus
Leymus mollis
Lupinus littoralis
Egregia menziesii
Gaultheria shallon
Eurhynchium oreganum
Blechnum spicant
Dryopteris carthusiana
Vaccinium parvifolium
Vaccinium ovatum
Pseudotsuga menziesii
Sambucus cerulea
Cirsium edule
Hordeum jubatum[1]
Argentina anserina

Claytonia parviflora
Quercus garryana
Alnus rubra
Ribes sanguineum
Rubus spectabilis
Cardamine nuttallii
Cornus nuttallii
Ribes divaricatum
Claytonia sibirica
Arbutus menziesii
Acer macrophyllum
Acer circinatum
Trillium ovatum
Fritillaria affinis
Berberis aquifolium
Berberis nervosa
Balsamorhiza sagittata
Delphinium menziesii
Lomatium grayi
Lomatium species

1. See High Plains.

The Pacific Forest

The Pacific Forest runs from southeastern Alaska to northern California. While in this region, Lewis and Clark traveled through present-day Oregon and Washington via the Columbia River Gorge, through the Cascade Mountains, past the mouth of the Willamette River, through the Coast Ranges, finally reaching their winter home on the Pacific Coast. Elevation relief in this region is extreme, ranging from sea level to the summits of glacier-clad volcanoes: 11,240-foot Mount Hood and 14,410-foot Mount Rainier.

The Pacific Ocean and westerly oceanic winds control the Pacific Forest climate. Temperatures are mild throughout the year. High humidity, fog, and heavy rainfall—from 30 to 150 inches a year—are the dominant climatic features. The amount of rainfall peaks in the winter and is at its minimum during the short, dry summer. At higher elevations annual snowfall can exceed 50 feet in some areas.

Dense coniferous forests of red cedar, hemlock, Douglas-fir, grand fir, silver fir, and Sitka spruce clothe the western mountain slopes. East of the Cascade summits, Douglas-fir, ponderosa pine, and Oregon oak dominate the forests. Deciduous forests of red alder and black cottonwood occur along the streams. Numerous ferns, Oregon grape, and tall shrubs like salal, huckleberry, and the beautiful Pacific flowering dogwood are common in the forest understory.

The expedition entered the Pacific Forest at the Columbia Gorge just west of present-day The Dalles, Oregon, on October 29, 1805. They arrived "in full view of the ocien" at "Haleys" (Baker) Bay near the present-day Fort Columbia State Park in Washington on November 15, 1805, and camped there until November 25. They built Fort Clatsop up the Lewis and Clark River a few miles from the ocean near present-day Astoria, Oregon. The party remained there from December 7, 1805, to March 23, 1806. It was a damp, uncomfortable winter at Fort Clatsop. Even though it rained 106 out of the 128 days, Clark remarked as they left, "we . . . have lived as well as we had any right to expect." When the huckleberries began to bloom with the promise of spring, the group gladly left the coast and plied their boats up the flooding Columbia River, through the rapids, and exited the Pacific Forest onto the drier Columbia Plains on April 15, 1806.

The explorers found many new and interesting plant species while in the Pacific Forest, and they preserved specimens of a marine algae, a moss, ferns, flowering shrubs, and majestic forest trees. Today, the Lewis and Clark Herbarium includes thirty-one plant species that they collected in this region. In addition, we know they collected Pacific ninebark and Douglas-fir specimens—which have been lost—because Frederick Pursh credited the explorers' collection when he described these species in his 1814 *Flora Americae Septentrionalis.*

In this book I included all thirty-three species the explorers collected in the Pacific Forest. However, I discussed foxtail barley, which they collected in both the High Plains and the Pacific Forest, in the *High Plains.* I also included Chinook licorice, bull kelp, blue elderberry, and Pacific flowering dogwood; we aren't sure the explorers actually collected these species, but they mentioned them in the journals. I arranged the plants geographically from west to east according to where the expedition collected or discussed them.

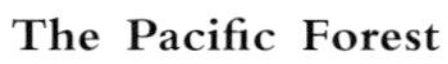

The Pacific Forest

Western Red Cedar *Thuja plicata*

Mountain Lover

Paxistima myrsinites (Pursh) Raf.
STAFF TREE FAMILY (Celastraceae)

Plants: Low shrubs, less than 4 feet tall, with glossy, opposite, evergreen leaves that have toothed margins. **Flowers:** Small, with four maroon petals and four yellow stamens. **Fruits:** One- or two-seeded capsules about ⅛ inch long. **Flowering Season:** April to June. **Habitat/Range:** Forest undergrowth from British Columbia to California and east in the Rocky Mountains from Montana to New Mexico.

FROM THE JOURNALS: Three sheets of mountain lover still exist. Lewis and Clark collected two specimens near the mouth of the Columbia River on November 16, 1805, and the other one in the Rocky Mountains near Hungery Creek along the Lolo Trail in present-day Idaho on June 16, 1806. On November 16, 1805, the expedition camped with a view of the Pacific Ocean for the first time, which by Clark's calculation was 4,142 miles from the mouth of the Missouri River. The expedition had traveled an arduous year and a half. Clark described their November 16 "Haleys Bay" campsite: "this morning Clear and butifull; I had all our articles of every discription examined and put out to Dry . . . The Waves high & look dismal indeed breaking with great fury on our beech . . . The Countrey on the Stard Side above Haley Bay is high broken and thickley timbered[;] on the Lard Side from Point Adams the Contrey appears low for 15 or 20 miles back to the mountains, a pinical of which now is Covered with Snow or hail . . . our hunters and fowlers killed 2 Deer 1 Crain & 2 Ducks, and my man York killed 2 geese and 8 Brant."

Pacific Ninebark

Physocarpus capitatus (Pursh) Kuntze
ROSE FAMILY (Rosaceae)

Plants: Shrubs, usually 6 to 12 feet tall, with bark that exfoliates in long, stringy layers. Leaves 2 to 3 inches long and about as wide with three to five lobes and a toothed margin. **Flowers:** White, arranged in closely spaced, umbel-like racemes, rounded in outline. **Fruits:** A cluster of three to five follicles. **Flowering Season:** May to June. **Habitat/Range:** Margins of streams and moist woods west of the crest of the Cascade and Sierra Nevada Mountains from Alaska to California; discontinuous in northern Idaho.

FROM THE JOURNALS: Frederick Pursh named this new species *Spiraea capitata* in his book and stated, "An imperfect specimen of this species I observed in the Lewisian Herbarium, gathered on the Columbia." That specimen has since been lost or destroyed. Near the mouth of the Columbia River on December 1, 1805, Lewis described Pacific ninebark, "the broad leave shrub which grows something like the quill wood but has no joints, the leaf broad and deeply indented the bark pals [peels] hangs on the stem and is of a yelowish brown colour." On the same day Clark wrote, "The Sea which is imedeately in front roars like a repeeted roling thunder and have rored in that way ever Since our arrival in its borders which is now 24 Days Since we arrived in Sight of the Great Western Ocian, I cant Say Pasific as Since I have Seen it, it has been the reverse."

Mountain Lover
Paxistima myrsinites

Pacific Ninebark *Physocarpus capitatus*
—Kathleen Sayce photo

Dune Wildrye

Leymus mollis (Trin.) Pilger
Also *Elymus mollis* Trin.
GRASS FAMILY (Poaceae)

Plants: Perennial grasses that grow in large clumps, up to 5 feet tall, with flat leaves up to ½ inch wide. **Flowers:** Arranged in closely spaced, paired spikelets that have soft hair on the lemmas, which are sharp-pointed but don't have long bristles on the tips. **Fruits:** Grains. **Flowering Season:** June to August. **Habitat/Range:** Coastal dunes from Alaska to California, Greenland to New York, and around Lakes Michigan and Superior.

FROM THE JOURNALS: A specimen of dune wildrye still exists, but it doesn't have a label to establish the date or place of collection. Lewis may have collected it at their "Haleys Bay" camp, which Clark described as having a "butifull Sand beech." He might have collected it somewhere along the Oregon and Washington Coast, from the Expedition's "salt works" near present-day Seaside, Oregon, to Long Beach, Washington. On November 18, 1805, Clark described arriving at the shore of the Pacific Ocean at Cape Disappointment: "I crossed the neck of Land low and ½ of a mile wide to the main Ocian, at the foot of a high open hill . . . I assended this hill which is covered with high corse grass [probably dune wildrye]."

Chinook Licorice or Seaside Lupine

Lupinus littoralis Dougl.
BEAN FAMILY (Fabaceae)

Plants: Perennial herbs that grow flat on the ground and form low mats. Leaves palmately compound with five to seven leaflets attached at a common point. **Flowers:** Blue to purple. Arranged in racemes on the ends of branches with several flowers attached in whorls around the branches. **Fruits:** Pods with five to eight seeds. **Flowering Season:** May to August. **Habitat/Range:** Sand dunes along the Pacific Coast from British Columbia to California.

FROM THE JOURNALS: While the explorers were in the Pacific Forest, they wrote many journal entries referring to the Northwest Indians' use of a root—possibly Chinook licorice—that tasted like licorice. On November 17, 1805, while at "Haleys Bay," Clark wrote, "those Chinnooks made us a present of a rute boiled much resembling the common liquorice *[Glycyrrhiza lepidota]* in taste and Size." Chinook licorice is named for its licorice-like taste and its use as food by the Chinook people. Both wild licorice *(Glycyrrhiza lepidota)* and Chinook licorice occur near Fort Clatsop, and both are documented food sources of Northwest Indians. We have no evidence that Lewis and Clark ever collected specimens of either species.

Dune Wildrye *Leymus mollis*
—Kathleen Sayce photo

Seaside Lupine or Chinook Licorice
Lupinus littoralis —Kathleen Sayce photo

The Pacific Ocean near Cape Disappointment, Ilwaco, Washington

Feather Boa Kelp

Egregia menziesii (Turner) J. E. Areschoug
(Alariaceae)

Plants: Large marine brown algae or kelp seaweed, as much as 15 to 50 feet long, that clings to rocks with sturdy holdfasts. Flattened stalks (stipes), about ⅜ to 1½ inches wide, branch repeatedly within 3 feet of the base. These flattened branches have a rough surface densely covered with blunt projections. A number of small floats and leaflike blades, up to ¾ inch wide, are attached along the edge of the upper stalks, which are brown to olive green. **Flowers/ Fruits:** No flowers; reproduction occurs both asexually (via zoospores) and sexually (via antheridia and oogonia). **Flowering Season:** May be fertile year-round, especially from April to November. **Habitat/Range:** Attached to rocks in the lower-intertidal and subtidal zones of the Pacific Coast from Alaska to California.

FROM THE JOURNALS: The explorers collected a specimen of feather boa kelp at the mouth of the Columbia River on November 17, 1805. On that day they were camped at "Haleys Bay" where they remained until November 25. Clark described the site as being "in full view of the *Ocian* from *Point Adams* to Cape Disapointment." Although Lewis and Clark don't mention seaweed in the journals at the time they collected this specimen, on March 17, 1806, Lewis described two seaweed species "which we also find thrown up by the waves," even though he thought he was only describing one: "at one extremity [this seaweed] consists of a large vesicle or hollow vessell which would contain from one to two gallons, of a conic form, the base of which forms the extrem end and is convex and globelar bearing on it's center some short broad and irregular fibers. the substance is about the consistence of the rind of a citron mellon and ¾ of an inch thick. the rihind is smooth. from the small extremity of the cone a long, hollow, celindrick, and regularly tapering tube extends to 20 or thirty feet." This first species was bull kelp *(Nereocystis leutkeana).*

Lewis continued by describing feather boa kelp, apparently thinking that because the two species were attached they were one organism: " . . . [this seaweed] is then terminated with a number of branches which are flat ½ an inch in width rough particular on the edges where they are furnished with a number of little ovate vesicles or bags of the size of a pigeon's egg. this plant seems to be calculated to float at each extremity while the little end of the tube from whence the branches proceed, lies deepest in the water."

Clark described another species of what he and Lewis thought was seaweed—"Seawreck"—on March 18: "it resembles a large pumpkin, it is Solid and it's Specific Gravity reather greater than the water, tho' it is Sometimes thrown out by the waves. it is of a pale yellowish brown colour. the rhind Smooth and consistency harder than that of the pumpkin, tho' easily cut with a knife. there are Some fibers of a lighter colour and much harder than any other part which pass Longitudinally through the pulp or fleshey Substance which forms the interior of this marine production." Marine biologists who have studied Clark's description believe that this "large pumpkin" was more likely a marine animal than another type of seaweed.

Feather Boa Kelp *Egregia menziesii*

Bull Kelp *Nereocystis leutkeana*

The author with Bull Kelp

Salal

Gaultheria shallon Pursh
HEATH FAMILY (Ericaceae)

Plants: Low, evergreen shrubs up to 4 feet tall with hairy stems. Leaves alternate, egg shaped, pointed at the tip, and lined with fine teeth on the margin. **Flowers:** Pink, urn shaped, and covered with glandular hairs on the back. **Fruits:** Edible, purplish pseudoberries. **Flowering Season:** May to July. **Habitat/Range:** Under dense, forest cover along the coast to the west slope of the Cascade Mountains from British Columbia to California; discontinuous in Idaho.

FROM THE JOURNALS: Salal is one of the most abundant ground-cover plants in the Pacific Forest. Lewis and Clark collected it near Fort Clatsop on January 20, 1806. The specimen still exists. On December 9 and December 27, 1805, Clark wrote about meals native people prepared for him in which salal was a major ingredient. Lewis described the species in careful detail in his journal of February 8, 1806: "The *Shallon* [salal] is the production of a shrub which I have heretofore taken to be a species of loral [laurel] and mentioned as abounding in this neighbourhood and that the Elk fed much on it's leaves. it generally rises to the hight of 3 feet . . . it grows very thick . . . the bark of the older or larger part of the stock is of a redish brown colour while that of the younger branches and succulent shoots are red where most exposed to the sun and green elsewhere . . . the leaf is oval four & ¾ inches in length and 2½ in width . . . the fruit is a deep perple berry about the size of a buck short or common black cherry . . . these to the number of ten or twelve issue from a common peduncle [main flower stalk] or footstalk which . . . forms the termination of the twig of the present years growth." Frederick Pursh described salal in his 1814 *Flora Americae Septentrionalis* and included an illustration of it.

Oregon Moss

Eurhynchium oreganum (Sull.) Jaeg.
Also *Kindbergia oregana* (Sull.) Ochyra
Hypnum oreganum Sull.
(Brachytheciaceae)

Plants: Large mosses with stems up to 12 inches long that are simple-pinnate (featherlike) and form beautiful green to yellowish green mats. **Flowers/Fruits:** None. Reproduction is by spores from brown or reddish brown, long-beaked capsules that hang down when dry. **Flowering Season:** Not applicable. Spore production mostly in the spring. **Habitat/Range:** Logs, rotten wood, and humus in the woods from sea level to about 4,000 feet along the Pacific Coast from Alaska to California; discontinuous in Idaho.

FROM THE JOURNALS: The explorers collected a specimen of Oregon moss at Fort Clatsop on January 20, 1806. Lewis and Clark did not mention moss (or this specimen) in their journals while in the Pacific Forest, but on May 8, 1806, while in the Rocky Mountains near Big Canyon Creek in present-day Idaho, Lewis wrote, "we are informed that the natives in this quarter were much distressed for food in the course of the last winter; they were compelled to collect the moss which

Salal ***Gaultheria shallon***

Salal illustration from Frederick Pursh's 1814 *Flora Americae Septentrionalis*

Oregon Moss
Eurhynchium oreganum

grows on the pine which they boiled and eat." Lewis's "moss" was probably a lichen, possibly the edible horsehair lichen *(Bryoria fremontii),* which hangs from pine trees and resembles horsehair.

Deer Fern

Blechnum spicant (L.) Roth
CHAIN FERN FAMILY (Blechnaceae)

Plants: Perennial ferns with sterile leaves (fronds) up to 3 feet long that taper towards both the tip and base. Fertile leaves longer (up to 4 feet) and more erect. Leaves once-pinnate, featherlike, with thirty-five to seventy pairs of leaflets on either side of the rachis. Fertile leaflets much narrower and appear more widely spaced than the wider, sterile leaflets. **Flowers/ Fruits:** No true flowers or fruits. Reproduction is by spores produced in the fruiting bodies (sori), which fill the underside of the fertile leaflets. **Flowering Season:** Spores produced in spring and summer. **Habitat/Range:** Moist or wet, dense woods from sea level to middle elevations in the mountains from coastal Alaska to coastal California and Idaho.

FROM THE JOURNALS: The explorers collected a specimen of deer fern while they were at Fort Clatsop on January 20, 1806. Lewis described deer fern in his journal on February 13, 1806: "The *small firn* also rises with a common footstalk from the radix [root] and are from four to eight in number. About 8 inches long; the central rib marked with a slight longitudinal groove throughout it's whole length. the leafets are oppositely pinnate about ⅓rd of the length of the common footstalk from the bottom and thence alternately pinnate; the footstalk terminating in a simple undivided nearly entire lanceolate leafet. the leafets are oblong, obtuse, convex absolutely entire, marked on the upper disk with a slight longitudinal groove in place of the central rib, smooth and of a deep green. near the upper extremity these leafets are decursively pinnate as are also those of the *large firn.*" The large fern is common Christmas or sword fern *(Polystichum munitum),* which Lewis described and sketched in his notes of February 13, 1806.

Mountain Wood Fern

Dryopteris carthusiana (Vill.) H. P. Fuchs
Also *Dryopteris austriaca* (Jacq.) Woynar
WOOD FERN FAMILY (Dryopteridaceae)

Plants: Large, perennial ferns up to 3 feet tall. Leaves (fronds) are broadly triangular in outline, and three times pinnately compound. The lower, secondary leaf segments (pinnules) are distinctly longer than those on the opposite (upper) side of the axis. **Flowers/ Fruits:** No flowers or fruit. Reproduction is by spores produced in roundish, fruiting dots (sori) located on veins of the underside of the leaflets. The outgrowths of the sori, called *indusia,* are horseshoe or kidney shaped. **Flowering Season:** No flowers. **Habitat/Range:** Moist or wet woods and streambanks from coastal Alaska to California and east to Newfoundland and South Carolina.

FROM THE JOURNALS: The explorers collected a specimen of mountain wood fern at Fort Clatsop on January 20, 1806. Although there isn't a description of mountain wood fern in the journals, Lewis described western bracken fern *(Pteridium aquilinum)* at Fort Clatsop on January 22, 1806: "There are three species of fern in this neighbourhood the root one of which the natves eat; this [western bracken fern] grows very abundant in the open uplands and praries . . . the center of the

Deer Fern ***Blechnum spicant***

Mountain Wood Fern
Dryopteris carthusiana

root is divided into two equal parts by a strong flat & white ligament like a piece of thin tape[.] on either side of this there is a white substance which when the root is roasted in the embers is much like wheat dough and not very unlike it in flavour, though it has also a pungency which becomes more visible after you have chewed it some little time; this pungency was disagreeable to me, but the natives eat it very voraciously and I have no doubt but it is a very nutricious food."

Red Huckleberry

Vaccinium parvifolium Smith
HEATH FAMILY (Ericaceae)

Plants: Tall shrubs, 3 to 12 feet tall, with many closely spaced, noticeably angled, green branches. Leaves light green, rounded, usually don't have teeth on the margin except for the young growth, which has teeth. **Flowers:** Arranged singly in the leaf axils, urn shaped, pale, yellowish pink. **Fruits:** Bright-red berries; edible. **Flowering Season:** May to August. **Habitat/Range:** Forest floors west of the Cascade Mountains from southeast Alaska to central California.

FROM THE JOURNALS: A specimen of huckleberry, collected at Fort Clatsop on January 20, 1806, still exists, but there is some controversy as to its correct identification. Frederick Pursh wrote on the specimen's label: "New Species. With a purple Small berry eatable, an evergreen Fort Clatsop Jan. 20th 1806." Some botanists believe that the specimen is low huckleberry *(Vaccinium myrtillus),* because of its noticeably angled, green stems (a trait it shares with red huckleberry) and Pursh's indication that it had purple berries. Low huckleberry is what this specimen is identified as in the Lewis and Clark Herbarium in Philadelphia. However, low huckleberry only grows east of the Cascade Mountains and not in the Fort Clatsop area or the Columbia Gorge.

The specimen actually has no berries, and Pursh could have confused the berry color with various other huckleberry species the Native Americans dried. The plant biologists at Fort Clatsop, and other botanists that I contacted in Oregon, all agree that Lewis's specimen is red huckleberry. Red huckleberry is common at Fort Clatsop and its low, juvenile growth has evergreen clusters with finely toothed leaves that resemble those of the 1806 specimen.

The day before leaving Fort Clatsop, March 22, 1806, Lewis wrote, "the leafing of the hucklebury riminds us of spring."

Evergreen Huckleberry

Vaccinium ovatum Pursh
HEATH FAMILY (Ericaceae)

Plants: Evergreen shrubs 1½ to 13 feet tall. Leaves glossy green with minute teeth on the thickened margins; arranged alternately in horizontal rows. **Flowers:** Bright pink, narrowly bell shaped, arranged three to ten in clusters from the leaf axils. **Fruits:** Deep purple to black berries; edible. **Flowering Season:** March to August. **Habitat/Range:** Forests from the Pacific Coast to the west side of the Cascade Mountains from British Columbia to California.

FROM THE JOURNALS: The explorers collected a specimen of evergreen huckleberry on January 27, 1806, near Fort Clatsop. In his journal on the previous day, Lewis wrote a detailed botanical description of this species followed by these remarks: "this shrub retains it's virdure very perfectly during the winter and is a beautifull shrub.—the natives either eat these berrys when ripe immediately from the bushes or dryed in the sun or by means of their sw{e}ating kilns; very frequently they pound them and bake then in large loaves of 10 or fifteen pounds; this bread keeps very well during one season and retains the moist jeucies of the fruit much

Red Huckleberry *Vaccinium parvifolium*
—berry inset from a Kathleen Sayce photo

Evergreen Huckleberry *Vaccinium ovatum*

better than by any other method of preservation. this bread is broken and stired in could water until it be sufficiently thick and then eaten; in this way the natives most generally use it." On March 22, 1806, Lewis wrote in the margin of his weather notes: "the leaves and petals of the flowers of the green Huckleburry have appeared. some of the leaves have already obtained ¼ of their size."

Douglas-Fir

Pseudotsuga menziesii (Mirb.) Franco
PINE FAMILY (Pinaceae)

Plants: Large forest trees up to 300 feet or more tall and 15 feet in diameter. Leaves needlelike, about 1 inch long, flat and blunt. Dormant, sharp-pointed terminal buds. **Flowers:** Unisexual cones; male cones less than $\frac{3}{8}$ inch long; female cones up to 4 inches long, have three-pronged bracts attached to the back of the scales, and hang down from the branches. **Fruits:** A pair of naked, winged seeds produced on the inner surface of the scales. **Flowering Season:** April to May. **Habitat/Range:** Humid to subhumid forests from the Pacific Coast of British Columbia, south to California, and east in the Rocky Mountains to Alberta and Mexico.

FROM THE JOURNALS: Although the Douglas-fir specimen that Lewis collected has been lost, Frederick Pursh, in his 1814 book, wrote that he inspected a dried specimen of "Pinus taxifolia" (Douglas-fir) that Lewis had collected "On the banks of the Columbia." On February 4, 1806, while spending the winter at Fort Clatsop, Lewis wrote in his journal, "There are sveral species of fir in this neighbourhood which I shall discribe as well as my slender botanicall skil will enable me and for the convenience of comparison with each other shal number them." Over the next few days Lewis wrote detailed descriptions of six evergreen, coniferous tree species: Sitka spruce, western hemlock, grand fir, Pacific silver fir (possibly a second grand-fir specimen), Douglas-fir, and western white pine. Of his "No. 5" Douglas-fir specimen, he wrote: "it affords but little rosin and the wood is redish white $\frac{2}{3}$ ds of the diameter in the center, the ballance white, somewhat porus and tough . . . the leaves are acerose, $\frac{1}{20}$th of an inch in width, and an inch in length, sessile, inserted on all sides of the bough . . . and more thickly placed than in either of the other species . . . the upper disk has a small longitudinal channel and is of a deep green tho' not so glossy as the balsam fir, the under disk is of a pale green."

On February 9, 1806, Lewis described the Douglas-fir cone: "the cone is $2\frac{1}{2}$ inches in length and $3\frac{3}{4}$ in it's greatest circumpherence, which is near it's base, and from which it tapers regularly to a point. it is formed of imbricated [overlapping] scales of a bluntly rounded form, thin not very firm and smoth. a thin leaf [bract] is inserted into the pith of the cone, which overlays the center of and extends $\frac{1}{2}$ an inch beyond the point of each scale. the form of this leaf [bract] is somewhat thus overlaying one of the imbricated scales." Lewis's description of Douglas-fir demonstrates his keen observational skills and his ability to communicate. Leaving nothing to chance, Lewis also drew a fine illustration of the characteristic Douglas-fir cone-scale bract in his notes for February 9.

Reconstructed Fort Clatsop near Astoria, Oregon

Left: Douglas-Fir ***Pseudotsuga menziesii***

Below: Douglas-Fir cones

Blue Elderberry

Sambucus cerulea Raf.
HONEYSUCKLE FAMILY (Caprifoliaceae)

Plants: Shrubs, 6 to 24 feet tall, that have smooth stems with a powdery, white surface, and pithy centers. Leaves compound with five to seven leaflets. **Flowers:** White to cream colored, arranged in flat-topped cymes. **Fruits:** Large clusters of pale, powdery blue, edible berries. **Flowering Season:** May to July. **Habitat/Range:** Moist open forests and stream bottoms from British Columbia to California and east to Montana and New Mexico.

FROM THE JOURNALS: We have no evidence that Lewis and Clark collected a specimen of blue elderberry, but they mentioned it several times in the journals. On December 1, 1805, near the mouth of the Columbia River, Lewis listed plants he saw that day, including "the large elder with skey blue buries." Lewis wrote in his journal of February 7, 1806: "This evening we had what I call an excellent supper it consisted of a marrowbone a piece and brisket of boiled Elk that had the appearance of a little fat on it. this for Fort Clatsop is living in high stile . . . The Elder also common to our country grows in great abundance in the rich woodlands on this side of the rocky Mountains; tho' it differs Here in the colour of it's berry, this being of a pale sky blue while that of the U' States is a deep perple." In the weather records for March 25, 1806, Lewis remarked, "the Elder, Gooseberry, & honeysuckle are now putting fourth their leaves."

Edible Thistle

Cirsium edule Nutt.
ASTER FAMILY (Asteraceae)

Plants: Biennial or short-lived perennial herbs with thick, succulent stems 1 to 6 feet tall. Leaves green with spines on the margin and sparse, cobweblike hair on the surface. **Flowers:** Bright pinkish purple, in heads arranged in small clusters or singly on the ends of the stems. Bracts of the heads are slender and gradually taper. **Fruits:** Achenes with featherlike bristles. **Flowering Season:** July to September. **Habitat/Range:** Wet meadows and moist woods from the Cascade Mountains to the Pacific Coast from Alaska to Oregon and Idaho.

FROM THE JOURNALS: The explorers collected a specimen of edible thistle near Fort Clatsop on March 13, 1806. Lewis and Clark mentioned the edible thistle in the journals several times during the winter of 1805–6. On January 20, 1806, Lewis wrote, "The native roots which furnish a considerable proportion of the subsistence of the indians in our neighbourhood are those of a species of Thistle, fern and rush." The next day Lewis wrote a detailed botanical description of edible thistle and remarked: "The root of the thistle, called by the natives *shan-ne-tah-que* . . . the consistence when first taken from the earth is white and nearly as crisp as a carrot; when prepared for uce . . . it becomes black, and is more shugary than any fuit [fruit] or root that I have met with in uce among the natives; the sweet is precisely that of the sugar in flavor."

Above: Blue Elderberry fruit

Right: Blue Elderberry
Sambucus cerulea

Edible Thistle
Cirsium edule
—Kathleen Sayce photo

Silverweed

Argentina anserina (L.) Rydb.
Also *Potentilla anserina* L.
ROSE FAMILY (Rosaceae)

Plants: Low, perennial herbs that spread by long, red runners that root at the nodes like strawberry plants. Leaves compound and have fifteen to twenty-five leaflets pinnately arranged in opposite pairs. White, silky hair covers the underside of the leaflets. **Flowers:** Yellow, occurring singly at the nodes of the runners. **Fruits:** Achenes; each has a persistent style attached midway on its length. **Flowering Season:** May to August. **Habitat/Range:** Wetlands from Alaska to California and east to the Atlantic Coast.

FROM THE JOURNALS: The explorers collected a specimen of silverweed on March 13, 1806, near Fort Clatsop. Most likely from information Lewis provided, Frederick Pursh wrote on this specimen's label, "The roots are eat by the natives, & taste like Sweet Potatoes, grows in marshy ground." On this day the explorers were preparing for their return voyage. Drouillard, one of the expedition's interpreters, was sent to the Clatsop village to purchase a couple of canoes. In Clark's notes for March 12 he stated, "Our party are now furnished with 358 par of Mockersons exclusive of a good portion of Dressed leather, they are also previded with Shirts Overalls Capoes [capotes; long, hooded coats] of dressed Elk Skins for the homeward journey."

COLUMBIA RIVER GORGE

Miner's Lettuce

Claytonia perfoliata Donn ex Willd.
Also *Montia perfoliata* (Donn) Howell
PURSLANE FAMILY (Portulacaceae)

Plants: Annual herbs less than 16 inches tall with many long, narrow, gradually tapering basal leaves. The stem has a single pair of leaves joined at their margins forming a disk around the stem below the flower arrangement. **Flowers:** White to pinkish, arranged in a raceme on the ends of the stems. Each flower has two sepals, five petals, and five stamens. **Fruits:** Capsules with three shiny, black seeds. **Flowering Season:** March to July. **Habitat/Range:** Seasonally moist, sandy openings and shady woods from British Columbia to California and east to Montana and New Mexico.

FROM THE JOURNALS: Various investigators have identified an incomplete specimen in the Lewis and Clark Herbarium as either miner's lettuce or little-leaf montia *(Claytonia parviflora)*. The specimen doesn't have basal leaves, the main feature used to tell them apart, so I believe there isn't enough evidence to identify it as little-leaf montia. In addition, C. L. Hitchcock and A. Cronquist, in *Flora of the Northwest* (1973), list these two plant taxons as one species *(Montia perfoliata)*. The explorers collected this specimen while ascending the Columbia River on March 26, 1806, on their way back to St. Louis. Lewis estimated that they had traveled 18 miles that day and 65 miles in the four days since leaving Fort Clatsop. They passed an island

Silverweed *Argentina anserina*

Miner's Lettuce
Claytonia perfoliata

that they named "Fanny's Island" (Crims Island) west of present-day Longview, Washington. The land opposite Fanny's Island they called "fanny's bottom," which Clark described as an "extensive and an open leavel plain except near the river bank which is high dry rich oak land." He was describing the open, flat land along the Columbia River near present-day Clatskanie, Oregon.

Oregon Oak

Quercus garryana Dougl. ex Hook.
BEECH FAMILY (Fagaceae)

Plants: Deciduous trees up to 90 feet tall with trunks 3 feet or more in diameter. Leaves shiny, dark green on the upper surface and lighter underneath; three to seven lobes per side indented ½ to ¾ of the way to the midrib. **Flowers:** Unisexual; male and female flowers occur on the same tree. Male flowers in hanging catkins; female flowers occur singly, or in small clusters. **Fruits:** Acorns maturing in one season. Cup shallow, less than half the length of the acorn. **Flowering Season:** April to June. **Habitat/Range:** Dry foothills on the west side of the Cascade Mountains from Vancouver Island to California, through the Columbia Gorge to The Dalles, Oregon, and north to Yakima, Washington.

FROM THE JOURNALS: The explorers collected two specimens of Oregon oak on March 26, 1806, along the Columbia River near present-day Clatskanie, Oregon. Lewis remarked in his journal on that day: "after dinner we proceeded on and passed an Elegant and extensive bottom on the South side . . . the greater part of the bottom is a high dry prarie. near the river towards the upper point we saw a fine grove of whiteoak trees." The previous fall (November 4, 1805) Clark had described a similar landscape just north of present-day Portland, Oregon, and across the river from Vancouver Lake: "here I landed and walked on Shore, about 3 miles a fine open Prarie for about 1 mile, back of which the countrey rises gradually and wood land comencies Such as white oake, pine of different kinds, wild crabs with the taste and flavour of the common crab and Several Species of undergroth . . . a few Cottonwood trees & the Ash of this countrey grow Scattered on the riverbank."

Red Alder

Alnus rubra Bong.
BIRCH FAMILY (Betulaceae)

Plants: Deciduous trees, up to 80 feet tall and 32 inches in diameter, with thin, gray, smooth bark, and red wood. Leaves egg shaped, pointed on both ends, with toothed margins that are rolled towards the lower side. **Flowers:** Unisexual; male and female flowers on the same plant, blooming before the leaves have fully developed. Male flowers in long, pendulous catkins. Female flowers in woody, conelike clusters. **Fruits:** Winged nutlets. **Flowering Season:** March to April. **Habitat/Range:** Moist woods west of the crest of the Cascade Mountains from Alaska to California; discontinuous in Idaho.

FROM THE JOURNALS: The explorers collected a specimen of red alder on March 26, 1806, along the Columbia River near present-day Clatskanie, Oregon. The specimen's label, in Frederick Pursh's hand, states, "Black alder of the Pacific Ocean, grows to a large Size." Lewis described "black" (red) alder on February 9, 1806, while at Fort Clatsop, and mentioned it many times in the journals. In his weather observations for March 24, 1806, he wrote, "the black Alder is in blume." On March 27 he described the vegetation near their camp below Deer Island near present-day Goble, Oregon: "saw the Cottonwood, sweet willow, oak, ash and the broad leafed ash . . . the growth of the bottom lands while the hills are covered

Oregon Oak ***Quercus garryana***
Inset: Oregon Oak catkins

Red Alder ***Alnus rubra***

The leaves and catkins of Sitka Alder *(Alnus viridis)*, which are similar to Red Alder's

almost exclusively with the various speceis of fir heretofore discribed. the black Alder appears as well on some parts of the hills as the bottoms." On March 30, above present-day Ridgefield, Washington, Lewis wrote, "the black alder common on the coast has now disappeared."

Red Currant

Ribes sanguineum Pursh
CURRANT FAMILY (Grossulariaceae)

Plants: Deciduous shrubs, 3 to 9 feet tall, without prickles. Leaves have five lobes and teeth on the margin. **Flowers:** Red, arranged in upright racemes of ten to twenty flowers. On the flower tube and ovary there are glands with stalks. **Fruits:** Round, black berries with glands and a white dust; unpalatable. **Flowering Season:** March to June. **Habitat/Range:** Open slopes and woods from the Pacific Coast to the Coast Ranges and Cascade Mountains, from British Columbia to California.

FROM THE JOURNALS: The explorers collected a specimen of red currant near the mouth of the Cowlitz River in Washington or across the Columbia River in Oregon on March 27, 1806. On that day Lewis wrote the following notes in the margin of his weather records: "the red flowering currant are in blume, this I take to be the same speceis I first saw in the [Columbia-watershed side of the] Rocky Mountains; the fruit is a deep purple berry covered with a gummy substance and not agreeably flavoured. there is another speceis uncovered with gum which I first found on the waters [watershed] of the Columbia about the 12th of August last." Since red currant doesn't occur in the Rocky Mountains, Lewis likely confused red currant with sticky currant *(Ribes viscosissimum),* which also has red berries with glands on the surface that render them unpalatable. Lewis described another currant (probably *Ribes hudsonianum*) on August 12, 1805, growing along Horseshoe Bend Creek below Lemhi Pass in present-day Idaho, and commented, "here I first tasted the water of the great Columbia river."

Red Currant *Ribes sanguineum*

Columbia Gorge at Crown Point in Oregon

Salmonberry

Rubus spectabilis Pursh
ROSE FAMILY (Rosaceae)

Plants: Erect to arching shrubs, up to 15 feet tall, which often form thickets. Bark is brownish, shredding. Lower stems very prickly while the upper ones are less prickly. Leaves compound, usually with three leaflets that have a doubly toothed margin. **Flowers:** Showy, red to reddish purple, arranged one or two on short, leafy branchlets. **Fruits:** Yellow to reddish orange, raspberrylike aggregate of druplets. **Flowering Season:** March to June. **Habitat/Range:** Moist woods and streambanks from the Pacific Coast to the Cascade Mountains from Alaska to California.

FROM THE JOURNALS: The explorers collected a specimen of salmonberry on March 27, 1806, near the mouth of the Cowlitz River in present-day Washington or Oregon. Lewis first described salmonberry near the mouth of the Columbia River on December 1, 1805: "the brier with a brown bark and three laves which put forth at the extremety of the twigs like the leaves of the blackbury brier, tho' is a kind of shrub and rises sometimes to the hight of 10 fe{et}." On February 13, 1806, near Fort Clatsop, Lewis mentioned salmonberry as "the briary bush with a wide leaf," and from then on he referred to salmonberry as "the larged leafed thorn." Lewis corrected himself and provided a detailed botanical description of salmonberry on April 8, 1806, near present-day Shepperds Dell State Park in Oregon: "with rispect to the shrub I have hithertoo called the large leafed thorn. the leaf of this thorn is small, being only about 2½ inches long, is petiolate, conjugate; the leafets are petiolate acutely pointed, having their margins cut with unequal angular insissures. the corolla consists of five accute pale scarlet petals." Lewis further corrected his error with the statement, "The shrub [thimbleberry, *Rubus parviflorus*] which I have heretofore confounded with this [salmonberry] grows in similar situations, has a stem precisely like it except the thorn and bears a large three loabed leaf."

Salmonberry flowers *Rubus spectabilis*

Salmonberry fruit

Slender Toothwort

Cardamine nuttallii Greene
Also *Cardamine pulcherrima* Greene
Dentaria tenella Pursh
MUSTARD FAMILY (Brassicaceae)

Plants: Perennial herbs with erect stems less than 1 foot tall. Basal leaves generally simple with long petioles; one to three compound stem leaves with short petioles and three to five narrow leaflets. **Flowers:** Pink to reddish or purplish, arranged in few-flowered racemes. **Fruits:** Narrow, pointed, erect pods (siliques). **Flowering Season:** March to May. **Habitat/Range:** Moist woods, mostly west of the crest of the Cascade Mountains, from British Columbia to California.

FROM THE JOURNALS: The explorers collected two specimens of slender toothwort on April 1, 1806, near the mouth of the "quicksand" (Sandy) River near present-day Troutdale, Oregon. On that day Lewis and Clark sent three men on an exploratory trip up the Sandy River. Their report, along with information from local Native Americans, confirmed that this was not the river that drained the great Willamette Valley to the south. Lewis stated in his journal of the day, "we are now convinced that there must be some other considerable river which flowed into the columbia on it's south side below us which we have not seen . . . which we had heretofore supposed was the quicksand river." The next day Clark hired an Indian to guide him to the mouth of the "Mult no mah" (Willamette) River and noted: "three Small Islands are situated in it's mouth which hides the river from view from the Columbia. from the enterance of this river, I can plainly See Mt. Jefferson . . . Mt. Hood East, Mt St. Helians . . . I also Saw the Mt. Raneer Nearly North."

Pacific Flowering Dogwood

Cornus nuttallii Aud.
DOGWOOD FAMILY (Cornaceae)

Plants: Tall shrubs or trees up to 60 feet tall. Leaves are opposite, oval, sharp pointed, and have veins that run parallel to the leaf margin. **Flowers:** A round cluster of tiny, greenish white, purple-tinged flowers is flanked by large, white, petal-like bracts, giving the impression of a single flower. **Fruits:** A cluster of bright red drupes. **Flowering Season:** April to June. **Habitat/Range:** Moist woods from the Pacific Coast to the Cascade Mountains from British Columbia to California; discontinuous in Idaho.

FROM THE JOURNALS: On April 5, 1806, while camped near the mouth of the "quicksand" (Sandy) River near present-day Troutdale, Oregon, Clark mentioned Pacific flowering dogwood in his description of the vegetation: "among the plants of this prarie in which we are encamped I observe the pashequo, Shannetahque, and Compound firn, the root of which the nativs eate; also the water cress, Straw berry flowering pea not yet in blume, narrow dock, and *rush* which are luxuriant and abundent in the river bottoms . . . The red flowering Current is found here in considerable quantities on the upland, and the Common Dog wood is found on either Side of the river in this neighbourhood and above Multnomah [Willamette] river." Lewis's journal of the same day compared the Pacific flowering dogwood

Top: Slender Toothwort
Cardamine nuttallii

Bottom: Pacific Flowering Dogwood ***Cornus nuttallii***

with flowering dogwood *(Cornus florida)* found in the Atlantic states: "The dogwood grows abundantly on the uplands in this neighbourhood. it differs from that of the United States in the appearance of it's bark which is much smoother, it also arrives here to much greater size than I ever observed it elsewhere sometimes the stem is nearly 2 feet in diameter." We have no evidence that the expedition ever collected a specimen of Pacific flowering dogwood.

Straggly Gooseberry

Ribes divaricatum Dougl.
CURRANT FAMILY (Grossulariaceae)

Plants: Erect shrubs with arching branches 4 to 9 feet tall and stout spines at the nodes. Leaves have three to five lobes and a toothed margin. **Flowers:** Red to purplish sepals, the lobes recurved and two to three times longer than the tube. White to red petals. Stamens and pistil extend well beyond the sepals and petals. **Fruits:** Round, smooth, purplish black berries; edible. **Flowering Season:** March to May. **Habitat/Range:** Open woods from the Pacific Coast to the Cascade Mountains from British Columbia to California.

FROM THE JOURNALS: The explorers collected a specimen of straggly gooseberry on April 8, 1806, near present-day Shepperds Dell State Park in Oregon. It is likely that Lewis was referring to straggly gooseberry in his March 25, 1806, weather notes: "the Elder, Gooseberry, & honeysuckle are now putting fourth their leaves. the nettle and a variety of other plants are now springing up. the flower of the broad leafed thorn [salmonberry] is nearly blown. several small plants in blume." Then on April 12 Lewis described the vegetation in the Columbia Gorge near the present-day Bridge of the Gods: "near the river we find the Cottonwood, sweet willow, broad leafed ash, a species of maple, the purple haw, a small speceis of cherry; purple currant, gooseberry, red willow, vining and white burry honeysuckle, huckkle burry, sacacommis [kinnikinnick], two speceis of mountain holley, & common ash."

Candy Flower

Claytonia sibirica L.
Also *Montia sibirica* (L.) Howell
PURSLANE FAMILY (Portulacaceae)

Plants: Annual herbs with several stems up to 2 feet tall. Many lance-shaped to egg-shaped basal leaves with long petioles. A single pair of opposite leaves on the stem. **Flowers:** White to pink, arranged in two or three racemes with many flowers. **Fruits:** Capsules, usually with a single black seed. **Flowering Season:** March to September. **Habitat/Range:** Moist, shady places from low to middle elevations from Alaska to California and east to Montana and Utah.

FROM THE JOURNALS: The explorers collected a specimen of candy flower on April 8, 1806, near present-day Shepperds Dell State Park in Oregon. The next day the party stopped at an Indian village where the apartment-like houses were built with boards and were covered with cedar bark. Lewis wrote: "on our way to this village we passed several beautifull cascades which fell from a great hight over the stupendious rocks which cloles [clothes?] the river on both sides nearly . . . the most remarkable of these casscades falls about 300 feet perpendicularly over a solid rock into a narrow bottom of the river on the south side . . . several small streams fall from a much greater hight, and in their decent become a perfect mist which collecting on the rocks below again become visible and decend in the second time in the same manner." Lewis was describing Multnomah Falls, Oregon, and the other waterfalls of the present-day Columbia River Gorge National Scenic Area.

Straggly Gooseberry *Ribes divaricatum*

Candy Flower *Claytonia sibirica*

Pacific Madrone

Arbutus menziesii Pursh
HEATH FAMILY (Ericaceae)

Plants: Beautiful shrubs or trees up to 100 feet tall with smooth, red, exfoliating bark. The leathery, evergreen leaves are oval and rounded on both ends. **Flowers:** White to yellowish, or pinkish, urn shaped, arranged in large, compound racemes on the ends of the stems. **Fruits:** Many-seeded, orangish red berries. **Flowering Season:** April to May. **Habitat/Range:** Drier areas west of the Cascade and Sierra Nevada Mountains from British Columbia to Baja, California.

FROM THE JOURNALS: The expedition collected a specimen of Pacific madrone on November 1, 1805. Frederick Pursh wrote on this specimen's label, "A middle size tree with a remarkable smooth bark which Scales off in the manner of the birch; & red berries in clusters." On this day the expedition traveled 7 miles passing the last of the "Great Rapids" of the Columbia River at and below the present-day Bonneville Dam. Clark wrote in his course-and-distance notes: "passed the Grand Shoote which is ¼ of a mile long the water confined with in 150 yds. passing over imince Stones with tremendious force & low mountain Slipping in on the Stard Side high on the Lard Side[;] great numbers of Sea otters." A month later, on December 1, near the mouth of the Columbia River, Lewis described madrone: "the leaf like that of the small magnolia, and brark smoth and of a brickdust red coulour[;] it appears to be of the evergreen kind."

Big-Leaved Maple

Acer macrophyllum Pursh
MAPLE FAMILY (Aceraceae)

Plants: Large, widely spreading trees, typically 50 feet tall and 20 inches in diameter. The leaves have three to five lobes and are often about 12 inches wide, although sometimes as much as 24 inches. **Flowers:** Greenish white, arranged on long, many-flowered racemes or panicles from the leaf axils. Some flowers have both pistils and stamens, and some only have stamens. **Fruits:** Winged samaras diverge at less than a 90-degree angle. **Flowering Season:** March to June. **Habitat/Range:** Moist woods from Alaska to California, mostly west of the Cascade and Sierra Nevada Mountains.

FROM THE JOURNALS: Lewis and Clark collected two specimens of big-leaved maple on April 10, 1806, at the "Grand Rapids" of the Columbia River, the site of present-day Bonneville Dam. Lewis usually referred to big-leaved maple as the "large leafed ash." On December 1, 1805, near the mouth of the Columbia River, Lewis noted "the ash with a remarkable large leaf." On April 11, 1806, Clark observed: "vegitation is rapidly progressing. Sarvis berry, Sackacommis [kinnikinnick] and the large leafed ash is in blume." On March 30, on "Wappetoe Island" (Sauvie Island just below Portland, Oregon), Lewis noted, "there is a heavy growth of Cottonwood, ash, the large leafed ash and sweet willow on most parts of this island." Before that, on February 10, 1806, Lewis entered a detailed botanical description of big-leaved maple in his journal: "the leaf is . . . palmate lobate, divided

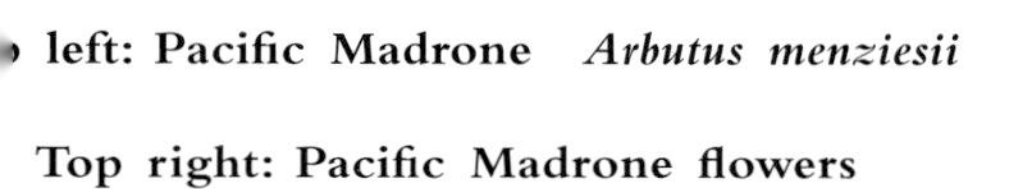

left: Pacific Madrone *Arbutus menziesii*

Top right: Pacific Madrone flowers

ttom right: Big-Leaved Maple flowers
Acer macrophyllum

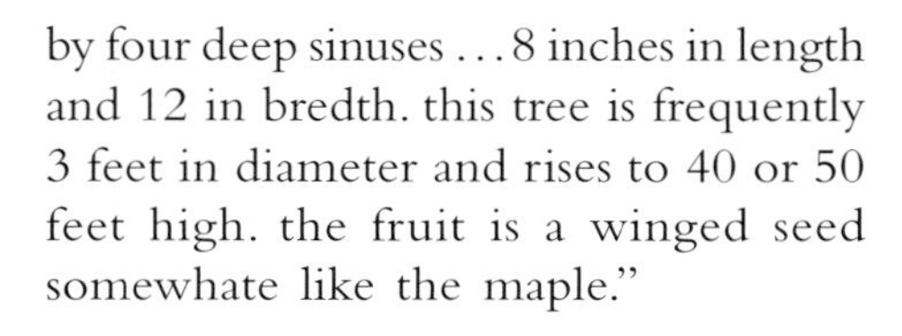

by four deep sinuses . . . 8 inches in length and 12 in bredth. this tree is frequently 3 feet in diameter and rises to 40 or 50 feet high. the fruit is a winged seed somewhate like the maple."

Vine Maple

Acer circinatum Pursh
MAPLE FAMILY (Aceraceae)

Plants: Shrubs or small trees up to 26 feet tall, often forming thickets. Leaves have seven to nine shallow lobes. **Flowers:** Few, clustered in the leaf axils; sepals purplish; petals white and shorter than the sepals; eight stamens. **Fruits:** Samaras with widely spread wings that almost form a 180-degree angle. **Flowering Season:** March to June. **Habitat/Range:** Moist woods from the east side of Cascade Mountains to the Pacific Coast, from Alaska to California.

FROM THE JOURNALS: Two herbarium sheets of vine maple still exist. Frederick Pursh wrote on this specimen's label: "A very handsome Species of Maple. On the great rapids of Columbia. Octbr: 1805." While at Fort Clatsop on February 10, 1806, Lewis wrote a botanical description of vine maple and inserted a sketch of its leaf in his notes: "in the same part of the country there is also another growth which resembles the white maple [big-leaved maple?] in its appearance, only that it is by no means so large; seldom being more than from 6 to 9 inches in diamater, and from 15 to 20 feet high; they frequently grow in clusters as if from the same bed of roots spreading and leaning outwards . . . the leaf is petiolate, plane, scattered nearly circular, with it's margin cut with accute angular incissures of an inch in length and from six to 8 in number . . . it is 3 inches in length, and 4 in width. the petiole celindric smooth and one and a ¼ inches long. the fruit or flower not known."

White Trillium or Wakerobin

Trillium ovatum Pursh
LILY FAMILY (Liliaceae)

Plants: Perennial herbs with erect stems, up to 16 inches long, and three broad leaves (4 inches long and 4 inches wide) that join the stem at a common point. **Flowers:** Arranged singly on the ends of the stems. Flowers have three green sepals and three petals, white when first blooming, but turning pink to purple as they age. Flower stalks about 2 inches long. **Fruits:** Fleshy capsules that are noticeably triangular in cross section. **Flowering Season:** March to June. **Habitat/Range:** Moist woods from British Columbia to California, east to Alberta and south to Colorado.

FROM THE JOURNALS: The explorers collected a specimen of white trillium on April 10, 1806, near the "Grand Rapids" of the Columbia River near the present-day Bonneville Dam. On that day the expedition was struggling to get their canoes through the rapids. Lewis wrote in his journal: "we drew them up the rapid by a cord about a quarter of a mile . . . in passing [crossing] the river which is here about 400 yds. wide the rapidity of the currant was such that it boar us down a considerable distance notwithstanding we employed five oars." On April 11, Lewis continued, "these rapids are much worse than they were fall when we passed them . . . the water appears to be upwards of 20 feet higher than when we descended the river."

Vine Maple fruit
Acer circinatum

White Trillium or Wakerobin
Trillium ovatum

Checker Lily

Fritillaria affinis (Schultes) Sealy
Also *Fritillaria lanceolata* Pursh
LILY FAMILY (Liliaceae)

Plants: Perennial herbs with stems 4 to 48 inches tall. Lower leaves arranged in one to four whorls of two to eight leaves; upper leaves alternate. **Flowers:** Single, or two to five, nodding, purple, mottled green or yellow. The six tepals are ¾ to 1½ inches long. **Fruits:** Winged capsules about ¾ inch long. **Flowering Season:** April to June. **Habitat/Range:** Grasslands and open woods up to 5,000 feet in elevation from British Columbia to California and east to northern Idaho.

FROM THE JOURNALS: The expedition collected checker lily on April 10, 1806, near the "Great Rapids" of the Columbia River near the present-day Bonneville Dam. Lewis wrote on the label: "Specemin of lilliacious plant obtained on Brant Island 10th of apl 1806. the root of this plant is a squawmus [scaly] bulb and is eaten by the natives. The Clah-clel-lar [Indians] opposite this Island call it tel-lak-thil-pah." The Clah-clel-lar Indians were part of the Sha-ha-la Nation, which Clark estimated at 2,800 people occupying sixty-two houses or lodges. The Sha-ha-la people were part of a larger group of Indians now referred to as Watlala Chinookans. Clark estimated that there were 80,000 Indians in the ninety named tribes that they encountered west of the Rocky Mountains. Unlike the imagined vacant wilderness, the expedition had been traveling through the homelands and villages of diverse and long-established native people.

Shiny Oregon Grape

Berberis aquifolium Pursh
Also *Mahonia aquifolium* (Pursh) Nuttall
BARBERRY FAMILY (Berberidaceae)

Plants: Evergreen shrubs 1 to 14 feet tall. Leaves smooth and glossy, compound, with five to nine leaflets. Each leaflet is pinnately nerved from the central vein and has five to twenty-one teeth tipped with spines. **Flowers:** Dense racemes of thirty to sixty bright yellow flowers. **Fruits:** Blue berries with white, powdery surface. **Flowering Season:** March to June. **Habitat/Range:** Open woods on both sides of the Cascade Mountains from British Columbia to California and east to northern Idaho and northwestern Montana.

FROM THE JOURNALS: The Captains mentioned shiny Oregon grape many times in their journals. Clark referred to it as "red holley" on November 6, 1805. While at Fort Clatsop, Lewis wrote a detailed botanical description on February 12, 1806, comparing it with dull Oregon grape and illustrating both in his journal: "There are two species of ever green shrubs which I first met with at the grand rappids of the Columbia and which I have since found in this neighbourhood also . . . the stem of the 1st [shiny Oregon grape] is from a foot to 18 inches high . . . and erect. it's leaves are cauline [attached to the stem], compound and spreading. the leafets are jointed and oppositely pinnate, 3 pare & terminating in one . . . each point of the their crenate margins armed with a subulate thorn or spine . . . they are also veined, glossy, carinated [keeled] and wrinkled . . . resembles the plant common

Top left: Checker Lily ***Fritillaria affinis***

Top right: Shiny Oregon Grape illustration from Frederick Pursh's 1814 ***Flora Americae Septentrionalis***

Bottom right: Shiny Oregon Grape ***Berberis aquifolium***

to many parts of the U' States called the mountain holley." On April 9, 1806, near the present-day Bonneville Dam on the Columbia River, Lewis remarked in his weather records, "the dogtoothed violet is in blume as is also both the speceis of the mountain holley." Two days later, in the same location, he collected a specimen of shiny Oregon grape. Shiny Oregon grape is now the floral emblem of the state of Oregon.

Dull Oregon Grape

Berberis nervosa Pursh
Also *Mahonia nervosa* (Pursh) Nuttall
BARBERRY FAMILY (Berberidaceae)

Plants: Evergreen shrubs 4 to 32 inches tall. Leaves dull green to somewhat glossy, often whitish underneath, compound with nine to twenty-one leaflets. Each leaflet is palmately nerved with three to eight nerves from the leaf base. The leaf margin has six to thirteen teeth tipped with spines. **Flowers:** Dense racemes of thirty to seventy bright yellow flowers. **Fruits:** Blue berries with white powdery surface. **Flowering Season:** March to June. **Habitat/Range:** Open or dense woods west of the Cascade Mountains from British Columbia to California; discontinuous in northern Idaho.

FROM THE JOURNALS: The explorers collected a specimen of dull Oregon grape near the "Great Rapids" of the Columbia River near the present-day Bonneville Dam. The label, in Frederick Pursh's hand, gives the date "Octbr: 1805." The explorers were near the Great Rapids from October 30 to November 2. While at Fort Clatsop, Lewis distinguished dull Oregon grape from shiny Oregon grape in his journal for February 12, 1806: "There are two species of ever green shrubs which I first met with at the grand rappids of the Columbia . . . The stem of the 2nd [dull Oregon grape] is procumbent . . . jointed and unbranched. it's leaves are cauline [attached to the stem], compound . . . the leafets 2½ inches long and 1 inch wide. greatest width ½ inch from their base . . . they are jointed and oppositely pinnate, consisting of 6 pare and terminating in one, sessile serrate, or like the teeth of a whipsaw, each point terminating in a small subulate spine, being from 25 to 27 in number; veined, smooth, plane and of a deep green." Lewis's remarkable observational skills helped him recognize the difference between these two similar species.

Arrow-Leaved Balsamroot

Balsamorhiza sagittata (Pursh) Nuttall
ASTER FAMILY (Asteraceae)

Plants: Perennial herbs with stems 1 to 3 feet tall. Large basal leaves, up to 12 inches long and 6 inches wide, shaped like arrowheads; they have long stalks. Leaves on the stems are small and narrow. Dense, woolly hair covers the leaves and stems. **Flowers:** Arranged in large, solitary heads on the ends of the stems. Each head has eight to twenty-five yellow rays around a yellow to brownish disk. **Fruits:** Smooth achenes. **Flowering Season:** April to July. **Habitat/Range:** Dry valleys and forest openings from British Columbia to California and east to Alberta, South Dakota, and Colorado.

FROM THE JOURNALS: A single sheet of arrow-leaved balsamroot includes leaves and flowers of two different specimens. Clark likely collected one specimen on April 14, 1806, above the mouth of "Canoe Creek" (White Salmon River) in Washington. Frederick Pursh wrote on this specimen's label, "The stem is eaten by the natives, without any preparation." The second specimen was collected on July 7, 1806, near present-day Lewis and Clark Pass in the Rocky Mountains of Montana. On April 14, 1806, Clark wrote: "after dinner we proceeded on our voyage.

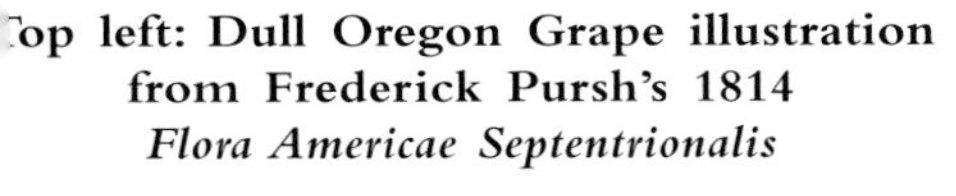

Top left: Dull Oregon Grape illustration from Frederick Pursh's 1814 ***Flora Americae Septentrionalis***

Top right: Dull Oregon Grape ***Berberis nervosa***

Bottom right: Arrow-Leaved Balsamroot ***Balsamorhiza sagittata***

I walked on Shore with Shabono on the N. Side through a handsom bottom. met Several parties of women and boys in Serch of herbs & roots to Subsist on maney of them had parcels of the Stems of the Sun flower [arrow-leaved balsamroot]. I joined Capt Lewis and the party at 6 miles, at which place the river washed the bottom of high Clifts on the N. side."

Cliff Larkspur

Delphinium menziesii DC.
BUTTERCUP FAMILY (Ranunculaceae)

Plants: Perennial herbs covered with fine hair that have single stems 4 to 20 inches tall. Leaves round in outline and deeply dissected into many lobes. **Flowers:** Blue to purple, arranged in racemes of three to fifteen showy flowers. Spurs ½ inch long. **Fruits:** Follicles with wings around the margins of the seeds. **Flowering Season:** April to July. **Habitat/Range:** Bluffs and meadows west of the Cascade Mountains from British Columbia to Oregon and in the Columbia River Gorge.

FROM THE JOURNALS: The expedition collected a specimen of cliff larkspur on April 14, 1806, near present-day White Salmon, Washington. Clark described the Columbia Gorge in his journal that day: "the river from the rapids to the Commencement of the narrows is from ½ to ¾ of a Mile in wedth, and possesses but little Current . . . the Mountains through which the river passes nearly to Cataract [Klickitat] River are high broken rocky, particularly Covered with fir and white Cedar, and in maney places very romantic scenes. Some handsom Cascades are Seen on either Side tumbling from the Stupendious rocks of the mountains into the river. I observe near the river the long leafed [ponderosa] Pine which increas as we assend and Superseeds the fir altogether about the Sepulchre rock." "Sepulchre rock" is now known as Lower Memaloose Island below present-day Lyle, Washington.

Gray's Desert-Parsley

Lomatium grayi Coult. and Rose
PARSLEY FAMILY (Apiaceae)

Plants: Perennial herbs branching at the base into several stems 6 to 20 inches tall. Leaves finely divided into many small segments. **Flowers:** Yellow, arranged in compound umbels with rays of unequal lengths. **Fruits:** Schizocarp with wings about ⅓ to ⅔ as wide as the body. **Flowering Season:** April to May. **Habitat/Range:** Dry, rocky places east of the Cascade Mountains from Washington to Oregon, east to Idaho, and southeast to Colorado.

FROM THE JOURNALS: Three specimens of desert parsley, collected April 14–15, 1806, still exist. On April 15, the explorers traveled from the Pacific Forest to the Columbia Plains; therefore they may have collected the third specimen in the Columbia Plains region. Two of the specimens have little or no plant material left on their herbarium sheets, which makes it difficult to properly identify their species. There is controversy among botanists over the identification of the third specimen, but I believe it is *Lomatium grayi,* which is common today on both sides of the Columbia River near Lower Memaloose Island between present-day Mosier, Oregon, and Lyle, Washington. Frederick Pursh wrote on the labels of all three specimens. On the first unknown specimen's label he wrote: "An umbelliferous plant of which the native don't eat the root. On the Columbia. Aprl. 14th 1806." On the second one he wrote, "An umbelliferous plant with a large fusiform root, which the natives bake & eat On the Columbia. Aprl. 15th 1806." On the label accompanying the specimen identified as Gray's desert-parsley, he wrote: "A large fusiform root, which the natives prepare by baking; Near the Sepulchre rock [Lower

Top: Gray's Desert-Parsley
Lomatium grayi

Bottom: Cliff Larkspur
Delphinium menziesii

Memaloose Island] On the Columbia R. Aprl. 14th 1806." In his journal for April 7, 1806, Clark stated: "about 4 oClock P M all the Indians left us, and returned to their Village. they had brought with them Wappato, & pasequa roots Chapellel cakes, and a Species of Raspberry for Sale, none of which they disposed of as they asked Such enormous prices for those articles that we were not able to purchase any." "Chapellel" are the dried, pounded cakes of cous bisquit-root *(Lomatium cous),* another species of desert parsley that was a major food source and trade item of the Native Americans of the Columbia River drainage.

Glossary

achene. A small, dry, one-seeded fruit that does not split open upon maturity.

alternate. Placed singly along a stem or axis, one after another, usually each successive item is on a different side from the previous one; often used in reference to the arrangement of leaves on a stem.

angular. Having angles or sharp corners; generally used in reference to stems, in contrast to round stems.

annual. A plant completing its life cycle, from seed germination to production of new seeds, within a year and then dying.

anther. The pollen-producing tip of the stamen.

antheridium. The male sexual organ of bryophytes and thallophytes (including algae).

appressed. Lying flat against a structure.

archegonium. The female sexual organ of bryophytes.

awn. A slender, stiff bristle or fiber attached at its base to another part, such as a leaf tip.

axil. The upper angle formed between the main stem and any organ that arises from it, like a leaf.

banner. The upper petal of a typical flower of the bean family (Fabaceae).

basal. At the base or bottom of; generally used in reference to leaves.

biennial. A plant that completes its life cycle in two years; it normally doesn't produce flowers during the first year.

bract. A reduced or modified leaf that is often associated with flowers.

bristle. A stiff hair, usually erect or curving away from its attachment point.

bulb. An underground plant part derived from a short, usually rounded shoot that is covered with scales or leaves.

calyx. The outer set of flower parts, composed of the sepals, which may be separate or joined together; usually green.

capsule. A dry fruit that releases seeds through splits or holes.

circumboreal. Found around the world at high latitudes or elevations.

clasping. Surrounding or partially wrapping around a stem or branch.

cluster. Any grouping or close arrangement of individual flowers that is not dense or continuous.

compound leaf. A leaf that is divided into two to many leaflets, each of which may look like a complete leaf but lacks buds. Compound leaves may have leaflets arranged along an axis like the pinnae of a feather or radiating from a common point like the fingers on a hand.

corolla. The petals, collectively, which may be free or united; often brightly colored.

corymb. A broad, flat-topped flower arrangement in which the outer flowers open first.

cyme. A broad, flat-topped flower arrangement in which the inner, central flowers open first.

dioecious. Having unisexual flowers, with male and female flowers borne on separate plants.

disk flower. Any of the small, tubular flowers in the central portion of the flower head of many plants in the aster family (Asteraceae).

disturbed. Referring to habitats that have been impacted by actions or processes associated with European settlement such as ditching, grading, or long intervals of intense grazing.

draw. A small, elongate depression with gentle side slopes in an upland landscape; resembles a miniature valley or ravine.

druplets. Small, fleshy, one-seeded fruits arranged in aggregates, as in raspberries.

ecosystem. A complex interacting system of organisms and their environment.

entire. A leaf with an even margin, without teeth or divisions.

epithet. The second portion of a scientific name that identifies a particular species; for instance, in silky lupine *(Lupinus sericeus),* the specific epithet is *sericeus.*

erect. Upright; standing vertically or perpendicular from a surface.

escape. A plant that has been cultivated in an area and has spread from there into the wild.

family. A group of plants having biologically similar features such as flower anatomy, fruit type, etc.

fellfield. An area within the alpine zone made up primarily of broken rock, possibly interspersed with accumulations of soils and plant life.

filament. The part of the stamen that supports the anther; also can refer to any threadlike structure.

flower head. As used in this guide, a dense and continuous group of flowers without obvious branches or space between them; used especially in reference to the aster family (Asteraceae).

follicle. A dry fruit that splits open along one suture at maturity.

generic name. A name applied to a group of closely related species; for example, the generic name *Viola* is applied to all the violet species.

genus. A group of closely related species, for example; the genus *Viola,* which encompasses the violets.

gland. A bump, projection, or round protuberance, usually a different color than the object on which it occurs, and it is often sticky or produces sticky or oily secretions.

glumes. A pair of bracts at the base of a grass spikelet.

herbaceous. Having a fleshy stem; not woody.

holdfast. A structure that anchors seaweed to rocks or other supporting material.

hood. A curving or folded, petal-like structure interior to the petals and exterior to the stamens in certain flowers.

hooded. Arching over and partially concealing or shielding.

incomplete flower. A flower that lacks sepals, petals, stamens, pistils, or one or more other parts.

inflorescence. The way the flowers are arranged on an individual plant.

involucel. Secondary bracts located below the junction of the flower stalks in the parsley family (Apiaceae).

keel. A sharp, lengthwise fold or ridge, referring particularly to the two fused petals that form the lower lip in a typical flower of the bean family (Fabaceae).

keeled. Ridged on the back of a structure, like the keel of a boat.

leaflet. A distinct, leaflike segment of a compound leaf.

lemma. The lower (outer) of the two bracts that enclose a grass flower.

lobe. A segment of an incompletely divided plant part, typically rounded; often used in reference to leaves.

margin. The edge of a leaf or petal.

mat. Densely interwoven or tangled, low plant growth.

node. The point on a stem where the leaf(s) attaches.

oogonium. The female reproductive organ in algae and other thallophytes.

opposite. Paired directly across from one another along a stem or axis.

ovary. The portion of the flower where the seeds develop, usually a swollen area below the style (if present) and stigma.

palea. The upper (inner) of the two bracts that enclose a grass flower.

palmate. Spreading like the fingers of a hand; usually used in reference to leaf shape.

panicle. A flower arrangement with a central axis with branches that are again branched before bearing a flower.

pappus. Thistledown; the scalelike or fine bristlelike sepals of flowers in the aster family (Asteraceae).

parallel. Side by side, approximately the same distance apart, for the entire length; often used in reference to veins or to the edges of a leaf.

pedicel. The fruit or flower stalk.

perennial. A plant that normally lives for three or more years.

perfect. A plant with functional male and female parts (stamen and pistil).

petal. A part of the corolla, the inner floral envelope; often the most brightly colored and visible part of the flower.

petiole. The stem of a leaf.

pinnate. Having leaflets, lobes, or other divisions along each side of a leafstalk, resembling a feather.

pistil. The seed-producing, or female, unit of a flower, consisting of the ovary, style (if present), and stigma; a flower may have one to several separate pistils.

pod. A dry fruit that splits open along the edges.

pollen. The tiny, often powdery, male reproductive microspores formed in the stamens and necessary for sexual reproduction in flowering plants.

pome. A fleshy fruit with seeds encased in a papery cell; for example, pears and apples.

prickle. A small, sharp, spinelike outgrowth from the outer surface.

raceme. A flower arrangement with a central axis along which simple pedicels of equal length bear flowers.

ray. The radiating branches of an umbel.

ray flower. A flower in the aster family (Asteraceae) with a single, strap-shaped corolla that resembles one flower petal; ray flowers may surround the disk flowers in a flower head, or, in some species, such as dandelions, the flower heads may be composed entirely of ray flowers.

resinous. Containing or covered with sticky to semisolid, clearish sap or gum.

rhizome. An underground stem that produces roots and shoots at the nodes.

rosette. A dense cluster of basal leaves from a common underground part, often in a flattened, circular arrangement.

runner. A long, trailing stem.

samara. A winged, single-seeded fruit, as in maple trees.

schizocarp. The fruit of the parsley family (Apiaceae), in which the wall of the ovary splits into one-seeded portions.

sepal. A component part of the calyx, the outer floral envelope typically green but sometimes enlarged and brightly colored.

serrate. Possessing sharp, forward-pointing teeth.

shrub. A multistemmed, woody plant.

simple leaf. A leaf that has a single leaflike blade, although this may be lobed or divided.

spike. An elongate, unbranched cluster of stalkless or nearly stalkless flowers.

spine. A thin, stiff, sharp-pointed projection.

spreading. Extending outward from; at right angles to; widely radiating.

spur. A hollow, tubular projection from the base of a petal or sepal; often produces nectar.

stalk. As used here, the stem supporting the leaf, flower, or flower cluster.

stalkless. Lacking a stalk. A stalkless leaf is attached directly to the stem at the leaf base.

stamen. The male unit of a flower, which produces pollen; typically consists of a long filament with a pollen-producing tip (the anther).

sterile. In flowers, refers to an inability to produce seeds; in habitats, refers to poor nutrient and mineral availability in the soil.

stigma. The portion of the pistil receptive to pollination; usually at the top of the style and often appears fuzzy or sticky.

stipule. A bract or leafy structure that occurs in pairs at the base of a leafstalk.

style. The portion of the pistil between the ovary and the stigma; typically a slender stalk.

subspecies. A group of plants within a species that has consistent, repeating, genetic and structural distinctions.

swale. A depression or shallow hollow in the land, typically moist.

taproot. A stout, main root extending downward.

tendril. A slender, coiled, or twisted filament with which climbing plants attach to their support.

tepals. Petals and sepals that cannot be distinguished from each other.

toothed. Bearing teeth or sharply angled projections along the edge.

tuber. A thick, creeping underground stem; sometimes also used for a thickened portion of a root.

tubular. Narrow, cylindrical, and tubelike.

umbel. A flower arrangement in which the flower stalks (pedicels) have a common point of attachment, like an umbrella.

variety. A group of plants within a species that has a distinct range, habitat, or structure.

vein. A small tube that carries water, minerals, and nutrients.

vestigial. Rudimentary or atrophied organ or part that isn't fully developed.

whorl. Three or more parts attached at the same point along a stem or axis and often surrounding the stem.

winged. Having thin bands of leaflike tissue attached edgewise along the length.

woody. Firm-stemmed or branched.

zoospores. Free moving (swimming) spores for asexual reproduction.

APPENDIX
The Plant Collections

Since many of Lewis and Clark's specimens were lost, botanists have had to use different sources to determine what species Lewis and Clark collected. Botanists identified some species using Lewis's Fort Mandan plant transmittal list (from Moulton, vol. 3, chap. 10, pt. 3). The numbers listed in the "Lewis" column are the numbers Lewis assigned to certain specimens. Botanists also used Frederick Pursh's *Flora Americae Septentrionalis* to identify species from Lewis's collection. The numbers listed in this column represent the page where the species can be located in Pursh's book.

Scientific Name	Common Name	Extant	Lost	Lewis	Pursh
	EASTERN DECIDUOUS FOREST				
Amorpha fruticosa	Indigo Bush		x	03	
Anemone caroliniana	Carolina Anemone		x		386
Asarum canadense	Eastern Wild Ginger		x	10	
Astragalus crassicarpus	Ground Plum		x	11	
Hydrastis canadensis	Golden Seal		x	08	
Maclura pomifera	Osage Orange	x			
Populus deltoides	Plains Cottonwood		x	04	
Thlaspi arvense	Field Pennycress		x	01	
	TALLGRASS PRAIRIE				
Ampelopsis cordata	Raccoon Grape	x			
Andropogon gerardii	Big Bluestem		x	23	
Anemone canadensis	Meadow Anemone	x			
Artemisia frigida	Fringed Sagewort	x		41	521
Artemisia ludoviciana	Prairie Sagewort		x	30	
Calystegia sepium	Hedge Bindweed		x	28	
Chamaecrista fasciculata	Showy Partridge Pea		x	29	
Cleome serrulata	Rocky Mtn. Bee Plant	x		43	441
Dalea candida	White Prairie Clover		x	16	461
Dalea purpurea	Purple Prairie Clover	x		53A	461
Desmanthus illinoensis	Illinois Bundleflower		x	18	
Elymus canadensis	Canada Wildrye		x	20	
Elymus virginicus	Virginia Wildrye		x	21	
Equisetum arvense	Field Horsetail	x		31	
Euphorbia marginata	Snow-on-the-Mountain		x	27	
Grindelia squarrosa	Curly-Cup Gumweed	x		40	559
Mentzelia decapetala	Evening Star		x		327
Mirabilis nyctaginea	Wild Four-O'Clock	x		44	97
Phalaris arundinacea	Reed Canarygrass		x	19, 61	
Polanisia dodecandra	Clammy-Weed	x			

Scientific Name	Common Name	Extant	Lost	Lewis	Pursh
Psoralidium lanceolatum	Lemon Scurfpea	x			475
Ribes americanum	Wild Black Currant		x	12	
Salix amygdaloides	Peach-leaved Willow		x	14	
Salix exigua	Sandbar Willow		x	13	
Symphoricarpos occidentalis	Western Snowberry		x	26	
	THE HIGH PLAINS				
Allium textile	Textile Onion		x		223
Amorpha fruticosa	Indigo Bush	x			
Amorpha nana	Dwarf Wild Indigo		x		466
Aquilegia canadensis	Canada Columbine		x	100	
Arctostaphylos uva-ursi	Kinnikinnick, Bearberry	x		33	
Artemisia campestris	Western Sagewort		x		521
Artemisia cana	Silver Sagebrush	x		55,56,60	521
Artemisia dracunculus	Silky Wormwood	x		52	521
Artemisia frigida	Fringed Sagebrush	x		51	521
Artemisia longifolia	Long-Leaved Sagewort	x		53	520
Artemisia ludoviciana	Prairie Sagewort	x			520
Aster oblongifolius	Aromatic Aster	x			
Astragalus canadensis	Canada Milkvetch	x		46	
Astragalus missouriensis	Missouri Milkvetch	x		36	
Astragalus tenellus	Pulse Milkvetch		x		473
Atriplex canescens	Four Wing Saltbush	x			370
Atriplex gardneri	Moundscale	x			
Chrysothamnus nauseosus	Rubber Rabbitbrush	x		54	517
Corispermum hyssopifolium	Hyssop-Leaved Tickseed		x		4
Dalea purpurea	Purple Prairie Clover	x			461
Echinacea angustifolia	Narrow-Leaved Purple Coneflower		x	101	
Euphorbia cyathophora	Fire-on-the-Mountain	x		38	
Euphorbia marginata	Snow-on-the-Mountain	x			
Gutierrezia sarothrae	Broom Snakeweed	x		32, 59	540
Hordeum jubatum	Foxtail Barley	x			89
Juniperus communis	Common Juniper	x		47	
Juniperus horizontalis	Creeping Juniper	x		49, 104	647
Juniperus scopulorum	Rocky Mountain Juniper	x		58	647
Krascheninnikovia lanata	Winterfat		x		602
Liatris aspera	Rough Blazing Star	x		58	
Liatris pycnostachya	Tall Blazing Star	x		35	
Lilium philadelphicum	Wood Lily		x		229
Linum lewisii	Lewis's Blue Flax	x			210
Lupinus pusillus	Rusty Lupine	x			468
Machaeranthera pinnatifida	Spiny Goldenweed	x			564

Scientific Name	Common Name	Extant	Lost	Lewis	Pursh
Nicotiana quadrivalvis	Indian Tobacco	x		45	141
Nicotiana rustica	Arikara tobacco		x	107	
Oenothera caespitosa	Gumbo Evening Primrose	x			263
Pediomelum argophyllum	Silver-Leaved Scurfpea	x		48, 103	475
Pediomelum esculentum	Indian Breadroot	x			475
Polygala alba	White Milkwort	x			750
Populus deltoides	Plains Cottonwood	x			
Potentilla pensylvanica	Pennsylvania Cinquefoil		x		356
Prunus virginiana	Chokecherry	x			
Psoralidium tenuiflorum	Slender Flowered Scurfpea	x			475
Quercus macrocarpa	Bur Oak	x		34	
Rhus aromatica	Fragrant Sumac	x		57	
Rosa arkansana	Prairie Wild Rose	x		50	
Salvia reflexa	Lance-Leaved Sage	x			19
Sarcobatus vermiculatus	Greasewood	x			
Senecio canus	Wooly Groundsel		x		528
Shepherdia argentea	Silver Buffaloberry	x		39A	115
Solidago rigida	Rigid Goldenrod	x			
Sphaeralcea coccinea	Scarlet Globemallow	x			453
Stipa comata	Needle-and-Thread Grass	x			72
Symphoricarpos occidentalis	Western Snowberry		x		162
Zea mays	Indian Corn		x		46
Zizania aquatica	Wild Rice	x		59	
	THE ROCKY MOUNTAINS				
Achillea millefolium	Yarrow	x			563
Allium geyeri	Geyer's Onion	x			300
Amelanchier alnifolia	Western Serviceberry	x			
Anemone piperi	Piper's Anemone	x			
Angelica arguta	Angelica	x			
Balsamorhiza sagittata	Arrowleaved Balsamroot	x			564
Bazzania trilobata	Braided Liverwort	x			
Calochortus elegans	Cat's Ear Mariposa Lily	x			240
Calypso bulbosa	Fairy Slipper	x			593
Camassia quamash	Blue Camas	x			226
Camissonia subacaulis	Long-Leaved Evening Primrose	x			304
Ceanothus sanguineus	Redstem Ceanothus	x			167
Ceanothus velutinus	Buckbrush Ceanothus	x			
Chrysothamnus viscidiflorus	Green Rabbitbrush	x			
Clarkia pulchella	Elkhorns	x			260
Claytonia lanceolata	Western Spring Beauty	x			175
Clematis hirsutissima	Sugarbowls	x			385

Scientific Name	Common Name	Extant	Lost	Lewis	Pursh
Cornus canadensis	Bunchberry	x			
Dasiphora fruticosa	Shrubby Cinquefoil	x			355
Elaeagnus commutata	Silverberry	x			114
Erigeron compositus	Cut-Leaved Daisy	x			535
Eriophyllum lanatum	Oregon Sunshine	x			560
Erysimum capitatum	Rough Wallflower	x			
Erythronium grandiflorum	Glacier Lily	x			
Festuca idahoensis	Idaho Fescue	x			
Frasera fastigiata	Clustered Elkweed	x			
Fritillaria pudica	Yellow Bell	x			228
Gaillardia aristata	Blanketflower	x			573
Geum triflorum	Prairie Smoke	x			352
Holodiscus discolor	Creambush Oceanspray	x			342
Ipomopsis aggregata	Scarlet Gilia	x			
Iris missouriensis	Missouri Iris	x			30
Juniperus communis	Common Juniper	x			
Koeleria macrantha	Prairie Junegrass	x			85
Lewisia rediviva	Bitterroot	x			368
Lewisia triphylla	Three-Leaved Lewisia	x			
Lomatium dissectum	Fern-Leaved Desert-Parsley	x			195
Lomatium triternatum	Nine-Leaved Desert-Parsley	x			197
Lonicera ciliosa	Trumpet Honeysuckle	x			
Lonicera involucrata	Bearberry Honeysuckle	x			
Lonicera utahensis	Utah Honeysuckle	x			
Lupinus argenteus	Silvery Lupine	x			468
Lupinus sericeus	Silky Lupine	x			468
Matricaria matricarioides	Pineapple Weed	x			520
Menziesia ferruginea	Fool's Huckleberry		x		264
Mimulus guttatus	Yellow Monkey-Flower	x			426
Mimulus lewisii	Lewis's Red Monkey-Flower		x		427
Orthocarpus tenuifolius	Thin-Leaved Owlclover	x			429
Oxytropis besseyi	Bessey's Crazyweed	x			473
Paxistima myrsinites	Mountain-Lover	x			119
Pedicularis cystopteridifolia	Fern-Leaved Lousewort	x			425
Pedicularis groenlandica	Elephant's Head	x			426
Penstemon fruticosus	Shrubby Penstemon	x			423
Penstemon wilcoxii	Wilcox's Penstemon	x			
Phacelia heterophylla	Virgate Phacelia	x			140
Philadelphus lewisii	Mockorange	x			329
Phlox speciosa	Showy Phlox	x			149
Phyllodoce empetriformis	Red Mtn. Heather		x		264

Scientific Name	Common Name	Extant	Lost	Lewis	Pursh
Pinus ponderosa	Ponderosa Pine	x			
Poa secunda	Sandberg's Bluegrass	x			76
Polemonium pulcherrimum	Showy Jacob's Ladder	x			
Polygonum bistortoides	American Bistort	x			271
Populus trichocarpa	Black Cottonwood	x			
Prunus emarginata	Bittercherry	x			
Prunus virginiana	Chokecherry	x			
Pseudoroegneria spicata	Bluebunch Wheatgrass	x			83
Purshia tridentata	Bitterbrush	x			333
Rhamnus purshiana	Cascara Buckthorn	x			166
Ribes aureum	Golden Currant	x			164
Ribes viscosissimum	Sticky Currant	x			163
Scutellaria angustifolia	Narrow-Leaved Skullcap	x			412
Sedum lanceolatum	Lance-Leaved Stonecrop	x			
Sedum stenopetalum	Worm-Leaved Stonecrop	x			324
Sorbus scopulina	Cascade Mountain-Ash	x			
Symphoricarpos albus	Common Snowberry	x			161
Synthyris missurica	Mountain Kittentails	x			10
Trifolium microcephalum	Small-Headed Clover	x			24
Trillium petiolatum	Purple Trillium	x			244
Veratrum californicum	California False Hellebore	x			
Xerophyllum tenax	Beargrass	x			243
Zigadenus elegans	Showy Death Camas	x			241
	THE COLUMBIA PLAINS				
Amelanchier alnifolia	Western Serviceberry	x			
Amsinckia menziesii	Small-Flowered Fiddleneck	x			
Artemesia ludoviciana	Prairie Sagewort	x			520
Aster eatonii	Eaton's Aster	x			
Cerastium arvense	Field Chickweed	x			321
Claytonia perfoliata	Miner's Lettuce	x			
Collinsia parviflora	Small Blue-Eyed Mary	x			421
Collomia linearis	Narrow-Leaved Collomia	x			
Coreopsis tinctoria	Columbia Tickseed	x			
Crataegus douglasii	Black Hawthorn	x			337
Dodecatheon poeticum	Poet's Shooting Star	x			
Lomatium cous	Cous Bisquit-Root	x			
Lomatium nudicaule	Bare-Stemmed Desert-Parsley	x			196
Lomatium species	Desert-Parsley	x			
Machaeranthera canescens	Hoary Aster	x			547
Osmorhiza occidentalis	Western Sweet-Cicely	x			
Phacelia linearis	Thread-Leaved Phacelia	x			134

Scientific Name	Common Name	Extant	Lost	Lewis	Pursh
Plagiobothrys tenellus	Slender Popcorn Flower	x			
Ribes aureum	Golden Currant	x			164
Rubus parviflorus	Thimbleberry	x			
Trifolium macrocephalum	Big-Head Clover	x			24
Triteleia grandiflora	Douglas's Wild Hyacinth	x			223
Uropappus lindleyi	Lindley's Microseris	x			
	THE PACIFIC FOREST				
Acer circinatum	Vine Maple	x			267
Acer macrophyllum	Big-Leaved Maple	x			267
Alnus rubra	Red Alder	x			41
Arbutus menziesii	Pacific Madrone	x			282
Argentina anserina	Silverweed	x			
Balsamorhiza sagittata	Arrow-Leaved Balsamroot	x			564
Berberis aquifolium	Shiny Oregon Grape	x			219
Berberis nervosa	Dull Oregon Grape	x			219
Blechnum spicant	Deer Fern	x			669
Cardamine nuttallii	Slender Toothwort	x			439
Cirsium edule	Edible Thistle	x			
Claytonia perfoliata	Miner's Lettuce	x			
Claytonia sibirica	Candy Flower	x			175
Delphinium menziesii	Cliff Larkspur	x			
Dryopteris carthusiana	Mountain Wood Fern	x			
Egregia menziesii	Feather Boa Kelp	x			
Eurhynchium oreganum	Oregon Moss	x			
Fritillaria affinis	Checker Lily	x			230
Gaultheria shallon	Salal	x			283
Hordeum jubatum	Foxtail Barley	x			89
Leymus mollis	Dune Wildrye	x			
Lomatium grayi	Gray's Desert-Parsley	x			
Lomatium species	Desert-Parsley	x			
Paxistima myrsinites	Mountain-Lover	x			119
Physocarpus capitatus	Pacific Ninebark		x		342
Pseudotsuga menziesii	Douglas-Fir		x		640
Quercus garryana	Oregon Oak	x			
Ribes divaricatum	Straggly Gooseberry	x			
Ribes sanguineum	Red Currant	x			164
Rubus spectabilis	Salmonberry	x			348
Trillium ovatum	White Trillium	x			245
Vaccinium ovatum	Evergreen Huckleberry	x			290
Vaccinium parvifolium	Red Huckleberry	x			

BIBLIOGRAPHY

Abbott, I. A., and G. J. Hollenberg. 1976. *Marine Algae of California.* California : Stanford University Press.

Bailey, R. G. 1995. *Description of the Ecoregions of the United States*, 2nd ed. USDA Forest Service Intermountain Forest and Range Experiment Station, Research Paper INT-218.

Barkley, T. M., ed. 1986. *Flora of the Great Plains.* Great Plains Flora Association. Lawrence, Kans.: University Press of Kansas.

Criswell, E. H. 1940. *Lewis and Clark: Linguistic Pioneers.* Columbia, Mo.: University of Missouri.

Cronquist, A., A. H. Holmgren, N. H. Holmgren, J. L. Reveal, P. K. Holmgren, and R. C. Barneby. 1977–97. *Intermountain Flora, Vascular Plants of the Intermountain West, U.S.A.,* vols. 3–6. Bronx, N.Y.: The New York Botanical Garden.

Cutright, P. R. 1969. *Lewis and Clark: Pioneering Naturalists.* Lincoln, Nebr., and London: University of Nebraska Press.

Dorn, R. D. 1984. *Vascular Plants of Montana.* Cheyenne, Wyo.: Mountain West Publishing.

Hickman, J. C., ed. 1993. *The Jepson Manual, Higher Plants of California.* Berkeley, Los Angeles, and London: University of California Press.

Hitchcock, C. L., and A. Cronquist. 1973. *Flora of the Pacific Northwest.* Seattle and London: University of Washington Press.

Hitchcock, C. L., A. Cronquist, M. Ownbey, and J. W. Thompson. 1955–69. *Vascular Plants of the Pacific Northwest,* 5 vols. Seattle and London: University of Washington Press.

Jolley, R. 1988. *Wildflowers of the Columbia Gorge.* Portland: Oregon Historical Society.

Ladd, D., and F. Oberle. 1995. *Tallgrass Prairie Wildflowers.* Helena and Billings, Mont.: Falcon Press Publishing Co., Inc.

Lawton, E. 1971. *Moss Flora of the Pacific Northwest.* Nichinan and Miyazaki, Japan: The Hattori Botanical Laboratory.

Lesica, P., and D. Hanna. 1996. *Vascular Plants of Pine Butte Swamp Preserve, An Annotated Checklist.* The Nature Conservancy of Helena, Mont.

Mantas, M. 1999. *Vascular Plant Checklist for the Flathead National Forest.* Checklist from the USDA Forest Service, Kalispell, Mont.

Meehan, T. 1898. The Plants of the Lewis and Clark Expedition Across the Continent, 1804–1806. *Proceedings of the Academy of Natural Sciences of Philadelphia, 1898:* 12–49.

Moulton, G. E., ed. 1983–99. *The Journals of the Lewis and Clark Expedition,* 12 vols. Lincoln, Nebr., and London: University of Nebraska Press.

Pursh, F. 1814. *Flora Americae Septentrionalis,* 2 vols. Fleet Street, London: White, Cochrane, and Co.

Pursh, F. 1814. *Flora Americae Septentrionalis,* ed. Joseph Ewan. 1979 reprint. Braunschweig, Germany: J. Cramer.

Reveal, J. L., G. E. Moulton, and A. E. Schuyler. 1999. The Lewis and Clark Collections of Vascular Plants: Names, Types, and Comments. *Proceedings of the Academy of Natural Sciences of Philadelphia.* 149: 1-64.

Sisk, R. L., and J. Tysdal-Sisk. 2000. *Common Plants of Theodore Roosevelt National Park.* Medora, N. D.: Theodore Roosevelt Nature and History Association.

Vitt, D. H., J. E. Marsh, and R. B. Bovey. 1988. *Mosses, Lichens & Ferns of Northwest North America.* Edmonton, Alberta: Lone Pine Publishing.

Waaland, R. J. 1977. *Common Seaweeds of the Pacific Coast.* Seattle: Pacific Search Press.

INDEX

ABOUT THE AUTHOR

H. Wayne Phillips has a bachelor's degree in forestry from the University of Montana and has done graduate work in ecology and silviculture. He worked as a Forest Service ecologist and forester and now teaches field classes for the Yellowstone and Glacier Institutes. He is active in the Montana Native Plant Society and has authored two other field guides, *Northern Rocky Mountain Wildflowers* and *Central Rocky Mountain Wildflowers.*

In 1961 Wayne was introduced to the plants of the Lewis and Clark Expedition while working for the U.S. Forest Service in Idaho. He spent the summer in a tent in the Clearwater National Forest, where he became familiar with the local lore of Lewis and Clark while visiting the camas meadows near Weippe and the site of Camp Chopunnish near Kamiah. His interest in the subject continued to grow during a thirty-three-year career with the Forest Service, especially during assignments on the Helena, Beaverhead, and Lewis and Clark National Forests, living in country through which Lewis and Clark had passed on their journey. He decided to share his interest with others by writing this book. A native of Texas, Phillips now lives in Great Falls, Montana.